Statistics 2

Steve Dobbs and Jane Miller

Series editor Hugh Neill

CAMBRIDGE
UNIVERSITY PRESS

PUBLISHED BY THE PRESS SYNDICATE OF THE UNIVERSITY OF CAMBRIDGE
The Pitt Building, Trumpington Street, Cambridge, United Kingdom

CAMBRIDGE UNIVERSITY PRESS
The Edinburgh Building, Cambridge CB2 2RU, UK
40 West 20th Street, New York, NY 10011–4211, USA
477 Williamstown Road, Port Melbourne, VIC 3207, Australia
Ruiz de Alarcón 13, 28014 Madrid, Spain
Dock House, The Waterfront, Cape Town 8001, South Africa

http://www.cambridge.org

First published 2001
Second edition 2004

Printed in the United Kingdom at the University Press, Cambridge

Typefaces StoneSerif 9/13pt and Formata   *System* LATEX 2$_\varepsilon$ [TB]

A catalogue record for this book is available from the British Library

ISBN 0 521 54894 2 paperback

Cover image © Digital Vision

Contents

Introduction

Cambridge Advanced Mathematics has been written especially for the OCR modular examination. It consists of one book or half-book corresponding to each module. This book is the second Statistics module, S2.

The books are divided into chapters roughly corresponding to syllabus headings. Occasionally a section includes an important result that is difficult to prove or is outside the syllabus. These sections are marked with an asterisk (*) in the section heading, and there is usually a sentence early on explaining precisely what it is that the student needs to know.

Occasionally within the text paragraphs appear in a grey box. These paragraphs are usually outside the main stream of the mathematical argument, but may help to give insight, or suggest extra work or different approaches.

The authors have assumed that the students have access to calculators with built-in statistical functions.

Numerical work is presented in a form intended to discourage premature approximation. In ongoing calculations inexact numbers appear in decimal form like $3.456\ldots$, signifying that the number is held in a calculator to more places than are given. Numbers are not rounded at this stage; the full display could be, for example, $3.456\,123$ or $3.456\,789$. Final answers are then stated with some indication that they are approximate, for example '1.23 correct to 3 significant figures'.

Most chapters contain practical activities. These can be used either as an introduction to a topic, or, later on, to reinforce the theory. The Practical activities also present opportunities for working on Key Skills.

There are plenty of exercises, and each chapter contains a Miscellaneous exercise which includes some questions of examination standard. Questions which go beyond examination requirements are marked by an asterisk. At the end of the book there is a Revision exercise and two practice examination papers. The authors thank Chris Hockley, Norman Morris and Rex Stephens, the OCR examiners who contributed to these exercises, and also Peter Thomas and William Germain, who read the books very carefully and made many extremely useful comments.

The authors thank OCR and Cambridge University Press for their help in producing this book. However, the responsibility for the text, and for any errors, remains with the authors.

1 Continuous random variables

This chapter looks at the way in which continuous random variables are modelled mathematically. When you have completed it you should

- understand what a continuous random variable is
- know the properties of a probability density function and be able to use them
- be able to use a probability density function to solve problems involving probabilities
- be able to find the median of a distribution in simple cases
- be able to calculate the mean and variance of a distribution.

1.1 Comparing discrete and continuous random variables

In S1 Section 6.1, you met the idea of a random variable and its probability distribution. In order to refresh your memory, consider the random variable, H, which is the number of heads obtained when two coins are spun. This random variable can take the values 0, 1 and 2 with probabilities of $\frac{1}{4}$, $\frac{1}{2}$ and $\frac{1}{4}$ respectively.

Check that you know how these probabilities were obtained.

The notation used to express these results is $P(H = 0) = \frac{1}{4}$, $P(H = 1) = \frac{1}{2}$ and $P(H = 2) = \frac{1}{4}$. Alternatively, you can display these results in a table, as in Table 1.1.

Number of heads, h	0	1	2
$P(H = h)$	$\frac{1}{4}$	$\frac{1}{2}$	$\frac{1}{4}$

Table 1.1. Probability distribution of H, the number of heads when two coins are spun.

The random variables which you studied in S1 were all discrete random variables; that is, there were clear steps between the possible values which the variable could take. There are many variables, however, which are not discrete.

Consider the following example. The 'cars' on a ski-lift are attached at equal intervals along a cable which travels at a fixed speed. The speed of the cars is so low that people can step in and out of the cars at the station without the cars having to stop. The time interval between one car and the next arriving at the station is 5 minutes. You do not know the timetable for the cars and so you turn up at the station at a random time and wait for a car. Your waiting time, X (measured in minutes), is an example of a random variable because its value depends on chance. However, it is also a continuous variable because the waiting time can take any value in the interval 0 to 5 minutes, that is $0 \leqslant X < 5$.

In S1 in order to describe a discrete random variable completely, you obtained a probability for each possible value of the random variable. If you try the same approach with a continuous random variable you run into difficulties: because the waiting time, X, can take an infinite number of values in the interval 0 to 5 minutes, you cannot write out a table like Table 1.1. However, you do know that if you arrive at the station at a random time, all values of X are equally likely. Would it be possible to describe the distribution by stating that all values of X between 0 and 5 are equally likely and by assigning the same non-zero probability to each one? This gives rise to another problem. The sum of the probabilities will not be one, as it should be, but will be infinite since X takes an infinite number of values. Obviously a different approach is needed in order to describe the probability distribution of a continuous random variable. This will be considered in the next section.

1.2   Defining the probability distribution of a continuous random variable

Although it is not possible to give the probability that X (the waiting time in Section 1.1) takes a particular value, it does make sense to talk about X taking a value within a particular range. For example, you would expect that $P(0 \leqslant X \leqslant 2.5) = \frac{1}{2}$ since the interval from 0 to 2.5 accounts for half the values which X can take, and all values are equally likely. Extending this idea, you would expect $P(0 \leqslant X < 1) = \frac{1}{5}$ since this interval covers $\frac{1}{5}$ of the total interval. Similarly $P(1 \leqslant X < 2) = P(2 \leqslant X < 3) = P(3 \leqslant X < 4) = P(4 \leqslant X < 5) = 0.2$. These probabilities could be represented on a diagram similar to a histogram, as shown in Fig. 1.2. In this diagram the area of each block gives the probability that X lies in the corresponding interval. Since the width of each block is 1 its height must be 0.2 in order to make the area equal to 0.2. Notice that the total area under the curve must be one since the probabilities must sum to one.

The choice of the intervals 0 to 1, 1 to 2 and so on is arbitrary. In order to make the model more general you need to be able to find the probability that X lies within any given interval. Suppose that the divisions between the blocks in Fig. 1.2 are removed so as to give Fig. 1.3. In this diagram, probabilities still correspond to areas. For example, $P(0.5 < X \leqslant 1)$ is given by the area under the curve between 0.5 and 1. This is shown as the shaded area in Fig. 1.4: its value is 0.1 as you would expect.

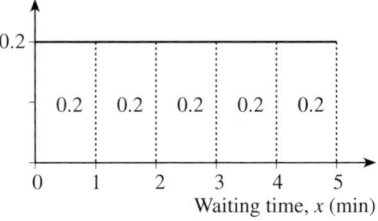

Fig. 1.2. Diagram to represent the probabilities of waiting times for a ski-lift.

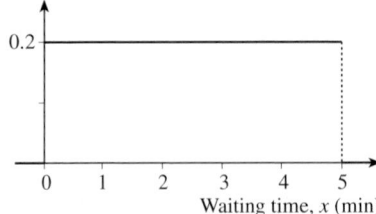

Fig. 1.3. Diagram to represent the distribution of waiting times for a ski-lift.

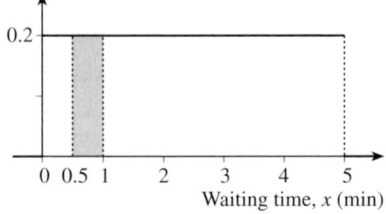

Fig. 1.4. Diagram to represent the probability of waiting between 0.5 and 1.0 minutes for the lift.

A distribution like this, with a constant height, is called a **uniform distribution**.

You should now be able to see that the probability distribution of the waiting times can be modelled by the continuous function f(x) which describes Fig. 1.3. The required function is

$$f(x) = \begin{cases} 0.2 & \text{for } 0 \leqslant x < 5, \\ 0 & \text{otherwise.} \end{cases}$$

> Note that it is usual to define f(x) for all real values of x.

Once f(x) has been defined, you can find probabilities by calculating areas below the curve $y = f(x)$. For example, $P(1.3 \leqslant X \leqslant 3.5) = 0.2 \times (3.5 - 1.3) = 0.44$.

Notice that, if you want the probability that $X = 1.3$ or the probability that $X = 3.5$, the answer is zero. These are just single instants of time, and although it is theoretically possible that a car may arrive at either of those instants, the probability is actually zero. This means that $P(1.3 < X < 3.5) = P(1.3 \leqslant X < 3.5) = P(1.3 < X \leqslant 3.5) = P(1.3 \leqslant X \leqslant 3.5)$. This situation is characteristic of continuous distributions.

The function f(x) is called a **probability density function**. It cannot take negative values because probabilities are never negative. It must also have the property that the total area under the curve $y = f(x)$ is equal to one. This is because this area represents the probability that X takes any real value and this probability must be one.

The suitability of this function as a model for actual waiting times could be tested by collecting some data and comparing a histogram of these experimental results with the shape of $y = f(x)$. Some results are given in Table 1.5.

Waiting time, x (min)	Frequency	Relative frequency	Class width	Relative frequency density
$0 \leqslant x < 1$	107	0.214	1	0.214
$1 \leqslant x < 2$	98	0.196	1	0.196
$2 \leqslant x < 3$	105	0.210	1	0.210
$3 \leqslant x < 5$	190	0.380	2	0.190

Table 1.5. Waiting times for the ski-lift for a sample of 500 people.

The third column gives the relative frequencies: these are found by dividing each frequency by the total frequency, in this case 500. The relative frequency gives the experimental probability that the waiting time lies in a given interval. The fifth column gives the relative frequency density: this is found by dividing the relative frequency by the class width. The data are illustrated by the histogram in Fig. 1.6.

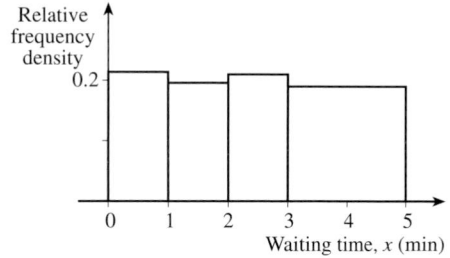

Fig. 1.6. Histogram of relative frequency for the data in Table 1.5.

Normally a histogram is plotted with frequency density rather than *relative* frequency density on the vertical axis. The reason for using relative frequency density in this case (and others in this section) is that area then represents *relative* frequency and hence experimental probability. As a result a direct comparison can be made between this diagram and Fig. 1.3, in which area represents theoretical probability. You can see that the diagrams are very similar. The experimental probabilities are not exactly equal to the theoretical ones. For example, the experimental probability of waiting between 1 and 2 minutes is 0.196 whereas theoretically it is 0.2. This is not surprising: you saw in S1 Section 4.1 that a probability model aims to describe what happens 'in the long run'.

The model for waiting times for a ski-lift was found by theoretical arguments and then confirmed experimentally. However, often it is not possible to predict the form of the probability density function. Instead, data are collected and the shape of the resulting histogram of the relative frequency density may suggest the form of the probability density function. Table 1.7 gives some more data; these relate to the time interval between one patient and the next going into the consulting room at a doctor's surgery. The doctor's receptionist always allows at least a 5-minute interval between the start of one consultation and the start of the next.

Time interval, x (min)	Frequency	Relative frequency	Class width	Relative frequency density
$5 \leqslant x < 6$	16	0.16	1	0.160
$6 \leqslant x < 7$	14	0.14	1	0.140
$7 \leqslant x < 8$	8	0.08	1	0.080
$8 \leqslant x < 9$	9	0.09	1	0.090
$9 \leqslant x < 10$	9	0.09	1	0.090
$10 \leqslant x < 11$	8	0.08	1	0.080
$11 \leqslant x < 13$	12	0.12	2	0.060
$13 \leqslant x < 15$	6	0.06	2	0.030
$15 \leqslant x < 20$	10	0.10	5	0.020
$20 \leqslant x < 25$	6	0.06	5	0.012

Table 1.7. Time intervals between patients entering the consulting room, for 100 patients.

Fig. 1.8 shows a histogram of the relative frequency densities. The shape of this histogram suggests that a very simple model to describe this situation might be the straight line segment shown in Fig. 1.9. This line has been drawn to cut the horizontal axis at 25 since all the time intervals were less than this value. You can find the equation of this line by remembering that the area under the graph of f(x) must be one, since the total probability must be one. Let f(5) equal c. Then, since the region under the graph of f(x) is a triangle of area 1,

$$\tfrac{1}{2} \times 20 \times c = 1, \quad \text{giving} \quad c = \tfrac{1}{10}.$$

Thus the gradient of the line is given by $\dfrac{0 - \frac{1}{10}}{25 - 5} = -\tfrac{1}{200}$ and the equation of the line is

$$y - \tfrac{1}{10} = -\tfrac{1}{200}(x - 5), \text{ or } y = -\tfrac{1}{200}x + \tfrac{1}{8}.$$

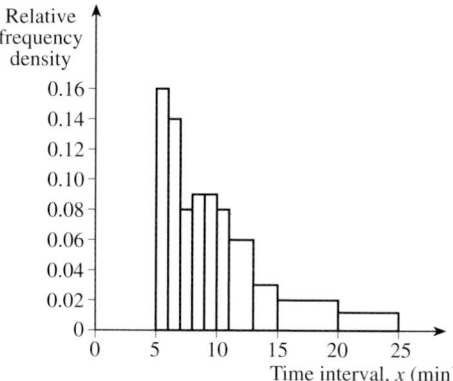

Fig. 1.8. Histogram of relative frequency for the data in Table 1.7.

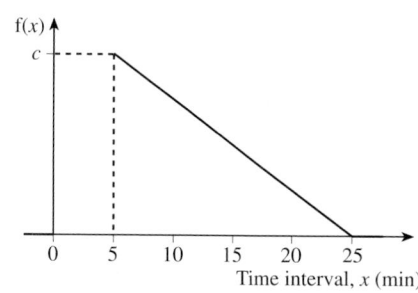

Fig. 1.9. Simple model for the time intervals between patients entering the consulting room.

The probability density function is therefore

$$f(x) = \begin{cases} -\frac{1}{200}x + \frac{1}{8} & \text{for } 5 \leqslant x \leqslant 25, \\ 0 & \text{otherwise.} \end{cases}$$

This model can then be used to find probabilities. For example the probability of a time interval of more than 17 minutes is given by the area of the shaded region in Fig. 1.10. This can be found by using simple geometry.

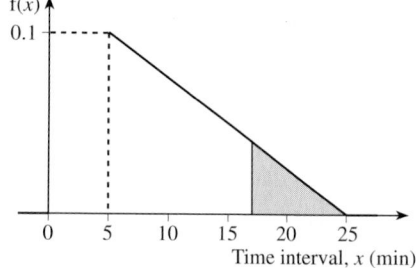

Fig. 1.10. Diagram to illustrate the theoretical probability of a time interval of more than 17 minutes.

When $x = 17$, $f(x) = -\frac{1}{200} \times 17 + \frac{1}{8} = \frac{1}{25}$.

So $P(X > 17) = \frac{1}{2} \times 8 \times \frac{1}{25} = \frac{4}{25}$.

Alternatively you can use integration to find the area:

$$P(X > 17) = \int_{17}^{25} \left(-\tfrac{1}{200}x + \tfrac{1}{8}\right) dx = \left[-\tfrac{1}{400}x^2 + \tfrac{1}{8}x\right]_{17}^{25}$$

$$= \left(-\tfrac{1}{400} \times 25^2 + \tfrac{1}{8} \times 25\right) - \left(-\tfrac{1}{400} \times 17^2 + \tfrac{1}{8} \times 17\right)$$

$$= \left(-\tfrac{625}{400} + \tfrac{25}{8}\right) - \left(-\tfrac{289}{400} + \tfrac{17}{8}\right)$$

$$= \left(-\tfrac{625}{400} + \tfrac{289}{400}\right) + \left(\tfrac{25}{8} - \tfrac{17}{8}\right) = -\tfrac{336}{400} + 1 = \tfrac{4}{25}, \text{ as before.}$$

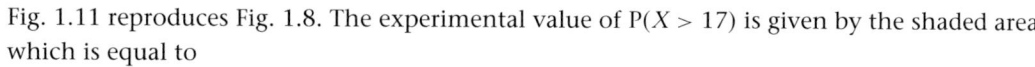

You should be able to deduce the value of $P(X \leqslant 17)$ without further detailed calculation.

Fig. 1.11 reproduces Fig. 1.8. The experimental value of $P(X > 17)$ is given by the shaded area which is equal to

$$(3 \times 0.02) + (5 \times 0.012) = 0.12 = \tfrac{3}{25}.$$

This agrees quite well with the theoretical value.

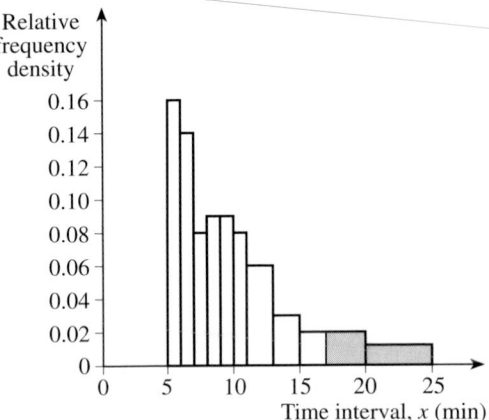

Fig. 1.11. Diagram to illustrate the experimental
probability of a time interval of more than 17 minutes.

Perhaps you can see a weakness in the model for time intervals in the doctor's surgery. The
model is based on a small data set in which no value is greater than 25 minutes. As a result the
model predicts that the time interval can *never* exceed 25 minutes. However, in the future it
might be longer. Fig. 1.12 is a histogram of the relative frequency density for results collected
from a larger sample of patients. You can see that quite a few values are greater than 25.

This histogram also shows another weakness in the original model: it looks as though a curve
would fit the data better than a straight line. For example, a function of the type $f(x) = \dfrac{k}{x^n}$
where n and k are positive constants might be more suitable.

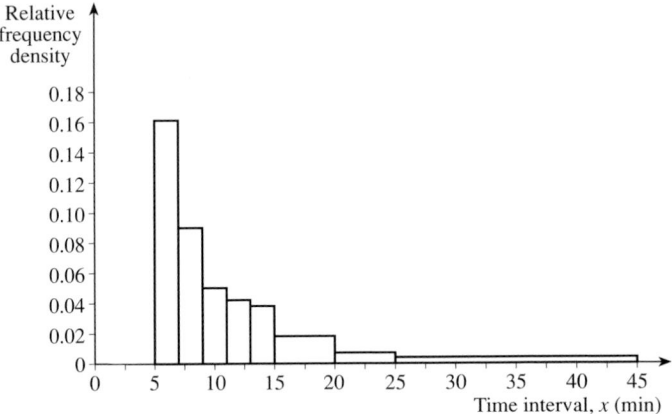

Fig. 1.12. Histogram of relative frequency for a larger sample of time
intervals.

It turns out that the function $f(x) = \dfrac{5}{x^2}$ for $x \geqslant 5$ fits the histogram quite well.

Fig. 1.13 shows the histogram with the graph of this function superimposed on it. You can see
that the curve and the histogram have similar shapes. This model has the advantage that it
sets no upper limit to the time interval.

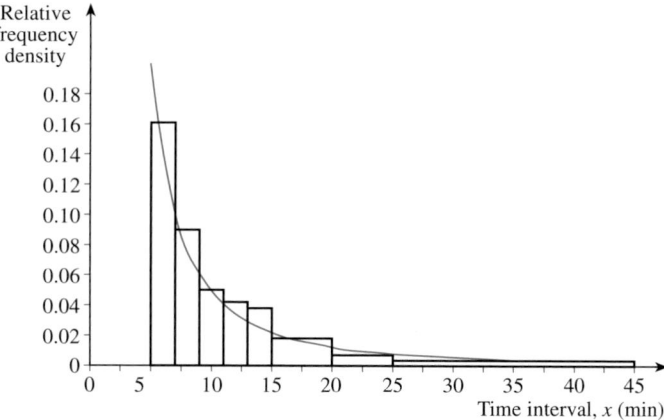

Fig. 1.13. Histogram in Fig. 1.12 with f(x) superimposed.

Since f(x) is always greater than zero it has one of the required properties of a probability density function. In order to accept this function as a probability density function, you also need to check that the area of the region underneath its graph is one. This can be done by integration as follows.

$$\text{Area} = \int_{-\infty}^{\infty} f(x)\,dx = \int_{-\infty}^{5} 0\,dx + \int_{5}^{\infty} \frac{5}{x^2}\,dx$$

$$= 0 + \left[-\frac{5}{x} \right]_{5}^{\infty} = -0 - (-1) = 1.$$

So the function

$$f(x) = \begin{cases} \dfrac{5}{x^2} & \text{for } x \geqslant 5, \\ 0 & \text{otherwise,} \end{cases}$$

has the properties required of a probability density function.

Here is a summary of the properties of a probability density function.

The **probability density function**, f(x), of a continuous random variable X is defined for all real values of x. It has the properties:

(a) $f(x) \geqslant 0$ for all x,

(b) $\displaystyle\int_{-\infty}^{\infty} f(x)\,dx = 1.$

The probability that X lies in the interval $a \leqslant x \leqslant b$ is given by the area under the graph of f(x) between a and b. This area can sometimes be found by using geometrical properties or it can be found from the integral

$$P(a \leqslant X \leqslant b) = \int_{a}^{b} f(x)\,dx.$$

Example 1.2.1

A continuous random variable X has the probability density function given by

$$f(x) = \begin{cases} \frac{2}{3}x & \text{for } 1 \leqslant x \leqslant 2 \\ 0 & \text{otherwise.} \end{cases}$$

(a) Show that $f(x)$ has the properties of a probability density function.

(b) Find $P(1.5 \leqslant X \leqslant 2)$.

(a) $f(x) \geqslant 0$ for all x since $\frac{2}{3}x > 0$ for $x > 0$.

$$\int_{-\infty}^{\infty} f(x)\,dx = \int_{1}^{2} \frac{2}{3}x\,dx$$

$$= \frac{2}{3} \times \left[\frac{1}{2}x^2\right]_1^2 = \frac{1}{3} \times (2^2 - 1^2) = \frac{1}{3} \times 3 = 1.$$

Therefore $f(x)$ has the properties of a probability density function.

(b) $P(1.5 \leqslant X \leqslant 2) = \int_{1.5}^{2} f(x)\,dx = \int_{1.5}^{2} \frac{2}{3}x\,dx$

$$= \frac{2}{3} \times \left[\frac{1}{2}x^2\right]_{1.5}^{2} = \frac{1}{3} \times (2^2 - 1.5^2)$$

$$= \frac{1}{3} \times 1.75 = 0.583, \text{ correct to 3 decimal places.}$$

Example 1.2.2

The continuous random variable X has the probability density function given by

$$f(x) = \begin{cases} k(1 + x^2) & \text{for } -1 \leqslant x \leqslant 1, \\ 0 & \text{otherwise,} \end{cases}$$

where k is a constant.

(a) Find the value of k.   (b) Find $P(0.3 \leqslant X \leqslant 0.6)$.   (c) Find $P(|X| < 0.2)$.

(a) Using the second property in the blue box,

$$\int_{-\infty}^{\infty} f(x)\,dx = \int_{-1}^{1} k(1 + x^2)\,dx$$

$$= k\left[x + \frac{1}{3}x^3\right]_{-1}^{1}$$

$$= k\left(1 + \frac{1}{3} \times 1^3\right) - k\left((-1) + \frac{1}{3} \times (-1)^3\right)$$

$$= k \times \frac{4}{3} - k \times \left(-\frac{4}{3}\right) = \frac{8}{3}k.$$

Since $\int_{-\infty}^{\infty} f(x)\,dx = 1$, $\frac{8}{3}k = 1$, giving $k = \frac{3}{8}$.

(b) $P(0.3 \leqslant X \leqslant 0.6) = \int_{0.3}^{0.6} \frac{3}{8}(1 + x^2)\,dx$

$$= \frac{3}{8}\left[x + \frac{1}{3}x^3\right]_{0.3}^{0.6}$$

$$= \frac{3}{8}(0.6 + \frac{1}{3} \times 0.6^3) - \frac{3}{8}(0.3 + \frac{1}{3} \times 0.3^3)$$

$$= 0.136, \text{ correct to 3 significant figures.}$$

(c) You will meet $|x|$, the modulus of x, in C3. The statement $|x| < 0.2$ is equivalent to $-0.2 < x < 0.2$.

$$P(|X| < 0.2) = P(-0.2 < X < 0.2) = \int_{-0.2}^{0.2} \tfrac{3}{8}(1 + x^2)\,dx = \tfrac{3}{8}\left[x + \tfrac{1}{3}x^3\right]_{-0.2}^{0.2}$$

$$= \tfrac{3}{8}\left(0.2 + \tfrac{1}{3} \times 0.2^3\right) - \tfrac{3}{8}\left((-0.2) + \tfrac{1}{3} \times (-0.2)^3\right) = 0.152.$$

Example 1.2.3

It is proposed to model the annual salary, X, measured in thousands of £, paid to sales persons in a large company by the probability density function

$$f(x) = \begin{cases} cx^{-\frac{7}{2}} & \text{for } x \geqslant 16, \\ 0 & \text{otherwise.} \end{cases}$$

(a) Find the value of c.

(b) Find the probability that a person in this profession chosen at random earns between £20,000 and £30,000 per year.

(a) $\displaystyle\int_{-\infty}^{\infty} f(x)\,dx = \int_{16}^{\infty} cx^{-\frac{7}{2}}\,dx = \left[-\tfrac{2}{5}cx^{-\frac{5}{2}}\right]_{16}^{\infty} = (-0) - \left(-\tfrac{2}{5}c \times 16^{-\frac{5}{2}}\right) = \tfrac{1}{2560}c.$

Since $\displaystyle\int_{-\infty}^{\infty} f(x)\,dx = 1$, $\tfrac{1}{2560}c = 1$, giving $c = 2560$.

(b) $\displaystyle P(20 \leqslant X \leqslant 30) = \int_{20}^{30} 2560x^{-\frac{7}{2}}\,dx = \left[2560 \times \left(-\tfrac{2}{5}\right)x^{-\frac{5}{2}}\right]_{20}^{30}$

$$= \left(2560 \times \left(-\tfrac{2}{5}\right) \times 30^{-\frac{5}{2}}\right) - \left(2560 \times \left(-\tfrac{2}{5}\right) \times 20^{-\frac{5}{2}}\right)$$

$$= 0.365, \text{ correct to 3 significant figures.}$$

Exercise 1A

In this and the following exercises, some questions involve the exponential function e^x. If you have not already met this function in C3, you should omit these questions.

In all the questions in this exercise, c and k are constants.

1 The probability density function $f(x) = \begin{cases} c\left(1 - \tfrac{1}{8}x\right) & 0 \leqslant x \leqslant 8, \\ 0 & \text{otherwise.} \end{cases}$

(a) Find the value of the constant c.   (b) Find $P(X \geqslant 6)$.

(c) Find $P(4 \leqslant X \leqslant 6)$.

2 The probability density function $f(x) = \begin{cases} kx^2 & 0 \leqslant x \leqslant 3, \\ 0 & \text{otherwise.} \end{cases}$

(a) Find the value of the constant k.   (b) Find $P(X \leqslant 2)$.   (c) Find $P(1.5 \leqslant X \leqslant 2.5)$.

(d) Given that the probability that X is less than h is 0.2, find the value of h, correct to 2 decimal places.

3 The probability density function $f(x) = \begin{cases} c(x^2 + 2) & 0 \leqslant x \leqslant 3, \\ 0 & \text{otherwise.} \end{cases}$

   (a) Find the value of the constant c.   (b) Find $P(X \leqslant 1.5)$.

4 The probability density function $f(x) = \begin{cases} c(4 - x^2) & -2 \leqslant x \leqslant 2, \\ 0 & \text{otherwise.} \end{cases}$

   (a) Find the value of the constant c.   (b) Find $P(X \geqslant 0)$.   (c) Find $P(X \geqslant 1)$.

   (d) Find $P(|X| \geqslant 1)$.   (e) Find $P(-0.5 \leqslant X \leqslant 0.5)$.

5 The life, X, of the StayBrite light bulb is modelled by the probability density function

$$f(x) = \begin{cases} ke^{-2x} & x \geqslant 0, \\ 0 & \text{otherwise,} \end{cases}$$

   where X is measured in thousands of hours.

   (a) Find k.

   (b) Find the probability that a StayBrite bulb lasts longer than 1000 hours.

   (c) Find the probability that a StayBrite bulb lasts less than 500 hours.

6 A computer ink cartridge has a life of X hours. The variable X is modelled by the probability density function $f(x) = \begin{cases} kx^{-2} & x \geqslant 400, \\ 0 & \text{otherwise.} \end{cases}$

   (a) Find k.

   (b) Find the probability that such a cartridge has a life of at least 500 hours.

   (c) Find the probability that a cartridge will have to be replaced before 600 hours of use.

   (d) Find the probability that two cartridges will have to be replaced before each has been used for 600 hours.

   (e) Find the probability that, out of four cartridges, two last for more than 600 hours and two last for less than 600 hours.

7 The probability density function

$$f(x) = \begin{cases} k(x - a)^2 & 0 \leqslant x \leqslant a, \\ 0 & \text{otherwise,} \end{cases}$$

   is shown in the sketch.

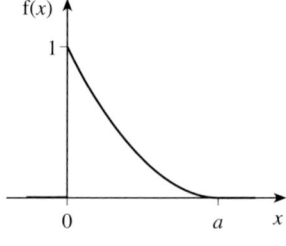

   (a) Use the information given in the sketch and the properties of probability density functions to find the values of a and k.

   (b) Find $P\left(X \geqslant \frac{1}{2}a\right)$.

1.3 The median of a continuous random variable

The median, M, of a continuous random variable is defined as the value which divides the area under the probability density function into two equal halves. Then the probability that X is above the median is equal to the probability that it is below. In mathematical terms the median is defined as follows.

> The median, M, of a continuous random variable is that value for which
> $$P(X \leqslant M) = \int_{-\infty}^{M} f(x)\,dx = \tfrac{1}{2}.$$

In simple cases the median can be found by considering symmetry. Fig. 1.14 reproduces Fig. 1.3 which showed the probability density function for the waiting times for the ski-lift.

The line $x = 2.5$, which is shown on the diagram, divides the area under $f(x)$ in half and so the median waiting time, M, is 2.5 minutes.

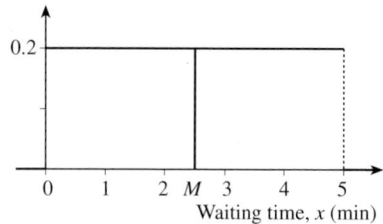

Fig. 1.14. Fig. 1.3 with the median shown.

Example 1.3.1

Two models are proposed for a garage's weekly sales, X, of petrol measured in units of 100 000 litres.

The first is $f(x) = \begin{cases} 2x & \text{for } 0 \leqslant x \leqslant 1, \\ 0 & \text{otherwise.} \end{cases}$

The second is $g(x) = \begin{cases} 12x^3(1 - x^2) & \text{for } 0 \leqslant x \leqslant 1, \\ 0 & \text{otherwise.} \end{cases}$

(a) Find the median for the first model.

(b) Show that median of the second model is the same as that of the first model.

(a) Fig. 1.15 shows the graph of $f(x)$. The median is denoted by M_1. The area of the shaded triangle is 0.5. When $x = M_1$, $f(x) = 2M_1$ so

$$\text{the area of shaded triangle} = \tfrac{1}{2} \times M_1 \times 2M_1$$
$$= 0.5,$$

giving $M_1 = \sqrt{\tfrac{1}{2}} = 0.707$, correct to 3 significant figures.

Alternatively, you could find the median by integration as follows.

The median, M_1, is given by

$$\int_{-\infty}^{M_1} f(x)\,dx = \tfrac{1}{2},$$

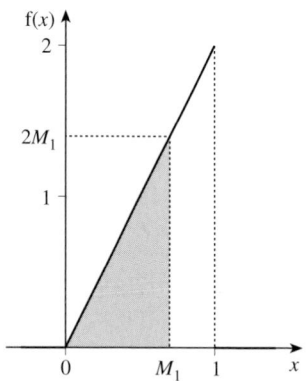

Fig. 1.15. Graph for part (a) of Example 1.3.1.

so $\displaystyle\int_{-\infty}^{M_1} 2x\,dx = \tfrac{1}{2},$

giving

$$[x^2]_0^{M_1} = \tfrac{1}{2}, \quad M_1^2 = \tfrac{1}{2}, \quad M_1 = \sqrt{\tfrac{1}{2}},$$

as before.

(b) Fig. 1.16 shows the graph of g(x), with the median, M_1, for the first model marked. If the shaded area in Fig. 1.16 is equal to 0.5 then M_1 is also the median for the second model.

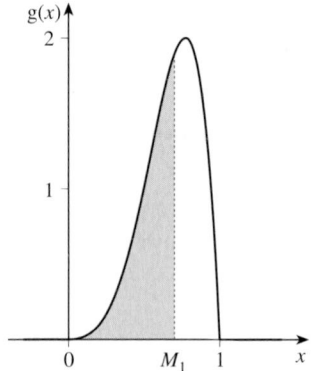

The area of the shaded region is

$$\int_0^{M_1} 12x^3(1-x^2)\,dx = \int_0^{M_1} (12x^3 - 12x^5)\,dx$$
$$= [3x^4 - 2x^6]_0^{M_1}$$
$$= 3M_1^4 - 2M_1^6$$
$$= M_1^2\left(3M_1^2 - 2M_1^4\right).$$

Recalling from part (a) that $M_1^2 = \tfrac{1}{2}$, the shaded area is

Fig. 1.16. Graph for part (b) of Example 1.3.1.

$$\tfrac{1}{2}\left(3 \times \tfrac{1}{2} - 2 \times \left(\tfrac{1}{2}\right)^2\right) = \tfrac{3}{4} - \tfrac{1}{4} = \tfrac{1}{2}.$$

Thus the median of the second model is the same as the median of the first model.

Example 1.3.2

Find the median salary (to the nearest £100) of the probability density function in Example 1.2.3.

Fig. 1.17 shows the graph of $f(x) = \begin{cases} 2560x^{-\frac{7}{2}} & \text{for } x \geqslant 16, \\ 0 & \text{otherwise.} \end{cases}$

The median is indicated by M and the shaded area is equal to 0.5.

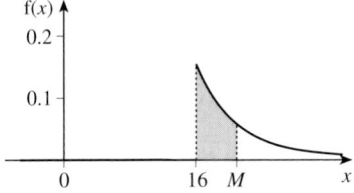

Fig. 1.17. Graph of the probability density function for Example 1.3.2.

Set the upper limit of the integral to M, form an equation and solve it for M as follows.

$$P(X \leqslant M) = \int_{-\infty}^{M} 2560x^{-\frac{7}{2}}\,\mathrm{d}x$$

$$= \int_{16}^{M} 2560x^{-\frac{7}{2}}\,\mathrm{d}x$$

$$= \left[2560 \times \left(-\tfrac{2}{5}\right) x^{-\frac{5}{2}} \right]_{16}^{M}$$

$$= \left(2560 \times \left(-\tfrac{2}{5}\right) \times M^{-\frac{5}{2}} \right) - \left(2560 \times \left(-\tfrac{2}{5}\right) \times 16^{-\frac{5}{2}} \right)$$

$$= -1024M^{-\frac{5}{2}} + 1.$$

This probability must equal 0.5, so $-1024M^{-\frac{5}{2}} + 1 = \tfrac{1}{2}$, giving $1024M^{-\frac{5}{2}} = \tfrac{1}{2}$.

Hence $M^{-\frac{5}{2}} = \frac{1}{2048}$, so $M^{\frac{5}{2}} = 2048$, giving $M = 21.1$, correct to 3 significant figures.

So the median salary is £21,100 to the nearest £100.

The method described above for finding the median can be extended to finding other percentiles. Suppose, for example, you wished to find the lower quartile, Q_1, of the distribution in Example 1.3.2. In this case

$$P(X \leqslant Q_1) = \int_{-\infty}^{Q_1} 2560x^{-\frac{7}{2}}\,\mathrm{d}x$$

$$= -1024Q_1^{-\frac{5}{2}} + 1 = \tfrac{1}{4}.$$

So $1024Q_1^{-\frac{5}{2}} = \tfrac{3}{4}$, giving $Q_1 = \left(\dfrac{4096}{3} \right)^{\frac{2}{5}} = 18.0$, correct to 3 significant figures.

You can check that the upper quartile is 27.9, correct to 3 significant figures.

Exercise 1B

1 The probability density function $f(x) = \begin{cases} \frac{1}{9}x^2 & 0 \leqslant x \leqslant 3, \\ 0 & \text{otherwise.} \end{cases}$

Find the median value of X, and the upper and lower quartiles of X.

2 A computer ink cartridge has a life of X hours. The variable X is modelled by the probability density function $f(x) = \begin{cases} 400x^{-2} & x \geqslant 400, \\ 0 & \text{otherwise.} \end{cases}$

Find the median lifetime of these cartridges.

3 The probability density function $f(x) = \begin{cases} 2x - 4 & 2 \leqslant x \leqslant 3, \\ 0 & \text{otherwise.} \end{cases}$

(a) Sketch the graph of $f(x)$.

(b) Find the median value of X.

(c) Find the interquartile range of X.

4 The life, X, of the StayBrite light bulb is modelled by the probability density function

$$f(x) = \begin{cases} 2e^{-2x} & x \geq 0, \\ 0 & \text{otherwise,} \end{cases}$$

where X is measured in thousands of hours.

(a) Sketch the graph of f(x).   (b) Find the median life of these StayBrite bulbs.

5 The probability density function $f(x) = \begin{cases} \frac{2}{5}\left(1 - \frac{1}{5}x\right) & 0 \leq x \leq 5, \\ 0 & \text{otherwise.} \end{cases}$

(a) Sketch the graph of f(x).   (b) Find the median value of X.

1.4 The expectation of a continuous random variable

> The expectation (or mean) of a continuous random variable, X, is defined by
>
> $$E(X) = \mu = \int_{-\infty}^{\infty} x f(x)\, dx. \qquad (1.1)$$

Note the correspondence between this equation and that for a discrete variable, which is $E(X) = \mu = \sum x P(X = x)$; the term $f(x)\, dx$ replaces $P(X = x)$ and the summation is replaced by an integral.

It is not possible to deduce this formula, but the following argument may help you to see why this definition makes sense. You may omit it if you wish, and go straight to Example 1.4.1

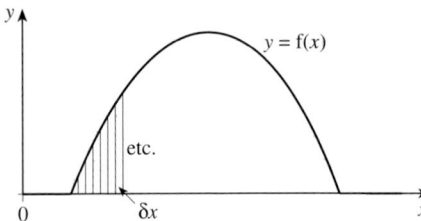

Fig. 1.18a. Generalised probability density function.

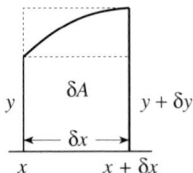

Fig. 1.18b. Enlarged version of one of the strips in Fig. 1.18a.

Look at Fig. 1.18a. This shows a probability density function, $f(x)$, for a continuous random variable, X. The region underneath $y = f(x)$ has been divided into narrow strips of width δx. Fig. 1.18b shows one of these strips, with some dotted lines added.

The probability that X takes a value between x and $x + \delta x$ is δA, the area of the strip.

Comparing with the equation $E(X) = \sum x P(X = x)$, this narrow strip makes a contribution to $E(X)$ which can be denoted by δE where

δE is between $x\, \delta A$ and $(x + \delta x) \times \delta A$.

You can say that δA lies between $y\delta x$ and $(y + \delta y)\delta x$ (this is shown in C2 Section 5.4), so

δE lies between $xy\delta x$ and $(x + \delta x)(y + \delta y)\delta x$.

Dividing through by δx gives

$\dfrac{\delta E}{\delta x}$ lies between xy and $(x + \delta x)(y + \delta y)$.

When δx tends to 0, $\dfrac{\delta E}{\delta x}$ tends to $\dfrac{\mathrm{d}E}{\mathrm{d}x}$. Also δy tends to 0, so $y + \delta y$ tends to y. It follows that

$$\frac{\mathrm{d}E}{\mathrm{d}x} = xy$$

Since $y = \mathrm{f}(x)$ this can also be written $\dfrac{\mathrm{d}E}{\mathrm{d}x} = x\mathrm{f}(x)$.

Integrating,

$$E = \int_{-\infty}^{\infty} x\mathrm{f}(x)\,\mathrm{d}x.$$

Example 1.4.1
At a garage, the weekly demand for petrol, X, in thousands of litres, can be modelled by the probability density function

$$\mathrm{f}(x) = \begin{cases} 120x^2(1 - x) & \text{for } 0 \leqslant x \leqslant 1, \\ 0 & \text{otherwise.} \end{cases}$$

Find the mean weekly demand for petrol.

From Equation 1.1

$$\begin{aligned}
\mathrm{E}(X) &= \int_{-\infty}^{\infty} x\mathrm{f}(x)\,\mathrm{d}x = \int_0^1 x \times 120x^2(1 - x)\,\mathrm{d}x \\
&= \int_0^1 (120x^3 - 120x^4)\,\mathrm{d}x \\
&= \left[30x^4 - 24x^5\right]_0^1 \\
&= (30 - 24) = 6.
\end{aligned}$$

Since X is measured in thousands of litres, the mean weekly demand is
$6 \times 1000 = 6000$ litres.

Example 1.4.2
Find the mean salary (to the nearest £100) of the probability density function defined in Example 1.2.3 and compare it with the median salary which was calculated in Example 1.3.2.

From Equation 1.1,

$$\begin{aligned}
\mu = \mathrm{E}(X) &= \int_{-\infty}^{\infty} x\mathrm{f}(x)\,\mathrm{d}x = \int_{16}^{\infty} x \times 2560x^{-\frac{7}{2}}\,\mathrm{d}x \\
&= \int_{16}^{\infty} 2560x^{-\frac{5}{2}}\,\mathrm{d}x = \left[2560 \times \left(-\tfrac{2}{3}\right)x^{-\frac{3}{2}}\right]_{16}^{\infty} \\
&= (0) - \left(2560 \times \left(-\tfrac{2}{3}\right) \times 16^{-\frac{3}{2}}\right) = 26\tfrac{2}{3}.
\end{aligned}$$

To the nearest £100, the mean salary is £26,700.

The mean is greater than the median (= £21,100) because the distribution is positively skewed.

1.5   The variance of a continuous random variable

The variance of a continuous random variable, X, is given by

$$\text{Var}(X) = \sigma^2 = \int_{-\infty}^{\infty} x^2 f(x)\, dx - \mu^2. \qquad (1.2)$$

$\int_{-\infty}^{\infty} x^2 f(x)\, dx$ is sometimes written as $\text{E}(X^2)$.

This formula shows the same parallel with the corresponding formula for a discrete random variable that was noted in the previous section. The variance of a discrete random variable is given by

$$\text{Var}(X) = \sum x^2 \text{P}(X = x) - \mu^2.$$

As in the expectation formula $f(x)\, dx$ replaces $\text{P}(X = x)$ and the summation is replaced by an integral.

Example 1.5.1
For the continuous random variable X with probability density function defined by

$$f(x) = \begin{cases} \frac{3}{4}x(2 - x) & \text{for } 0 \leqslant x \leqslant 2, \\ 0 & \text{otherwise,} \end{cases}$$

find

(a) the mean,   (b) the variance,   (c) $\text{P}(\mu - \sigma < X < \mu + \sigma)$.

(a) Using Equation 1.1

$$\mu = \text{E}(X) = \int_{-\infty}^{\infty} x\, f(x)\, dx = \int_{0}^{2} \frac{3}{4}x^2(2 - x)\, dx$$

$$= \int_{0}^{2} \left(\frac{3}{2}x^2 - \frac{3}{4}x^3\right) dx$$

$$= \left[\frac{3}{2} \times \frac{1}{3}x^3 - \frac{3}{4} \times \frac{1}{4}x^4\right]_{0}^{2}$$

$$= \left(\frac{1}{2} \times 2^3 - \frac{3}{16} \times 2^4\right)$$

$$= 4 - 3 = 1.$$

If you look at Fig. 1.19, which shows the graph of $y = f(x)$, you will see that there is a much quicker way of arriving at this result. Since this graph is symmetric about the line $x = 1$, the mean must be 1.

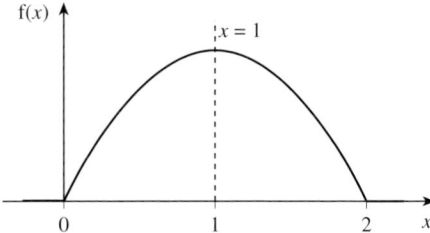

Fig. 1.19. Graph of the probability density function for Example 1.5.1.

For a symmetrical probability density function, the mean is most easily found by using symmetry.

(b) Using Equation 1.2

$$\sigma^2 = \text{Var}(X) = \int_{-\infty}^{\infty} x^2 f(x)\, dx - \mu^2$$

$$= \int_0^2 x^2 \times \tfrac{3}{4} x(2 - x)\, dx - 1^2$$

$$= \int_0^2 \left(\tfrac{3}{2} x^3 - \tfrac{3}{4} x^4\right) dx - 1$$

$$= \left[\tfrac{3}{2} \times \tfrac{1}{4} x^4 - \tfrac{3}{4} \times \tfrac{1}{5} x^5\right]_0^2 - 1$$

$$= \left(6 - \tfrac{24}{5}\right) - (0) - 1 = \tfrac{1}{5} = 0.2.$$

(c) $P(\mu - \sigma < X < \mu + \sigma) = P\left(1 - \sqrt{0.2} < X < 1 + \sqrt{0.2}\right)$

$$= \int_{1 - \sqrt{0.2}}^{1 + \sqrt{0.2}} \tfrac{3}{4} x(2 - x)\, dx$$

$$= \int_{1 - \sqrt{0.2}}^{1 + \sqrt{0.2}} \left(\tfrac{3}{2} x - \tfrac{3}{4} x^2\right) dx$$

$$= \left[\tfrac{3}{2} \times \tfrac{1}{2} x^2 - \tfrac{3}{4} \times \tfrac{1}{3} x^3\right]_{1 - \sqrt{0.2}}^{1 + \sqrt{0.2}}$$

$$= \left(\tfrac{3}{4}\left(1 + \sqrt{0.2}\right)^2 - \tfrac{1}{4}\left(1 + \sqrt{0.2}\right)^3\right)$$

$$\quad - \left(\tfrac{3}{4}\left(1 - \sqrt{0.2}\right)^2 - \tfrac{1}{4}\left(1 - \sqrt{0.2}\right)^3\right)$$

$$= \left(\tfrac{3}{4} \times 1.447\ldots^2 - \tfrac{1}{4} \times 1.447\ldots^3\right)$$

$$\quad - \left(\tfrac{3}{4} \times 0.552\ldots^2 - \tfrac{1}{4} \times 0.552\ldots^3\right)$$

$$= 0.626, \text{ correct to 3 significant figures.}$$

Exercise 1C

1 The probability density function $f(x) = \begin{cases} \frac{1}{9}x^2 & 0 \le x \le 3, \\ 0 & \text{otherwise.} \end{cases}$

   Find the mean and variance of X.

2 The probability density function $f(x) = \begin{cases} 2x - 4 & 2 \le x \le 3, \\ 0 & \text{otherwise.} \end{cases}$

   Find the mean and variance of X.

3 The probability density function $f(x) = \begin{cases} \frac{1}{4}(1 - \frac{1}{8}x) & 0 \le x \le 8, \\ 0 & \text{otherwise.} \end{cases}$

   (a) Sketch the graph of $f(x)$.   (b) Find the mean and variance of X.

4 The mass, X kg, of silicon produced in a manufacturing process is modelled by the

   probability density function $f(x) = \begin{cases} \frac{3}{32}(4x - x^2) & 0 \le x \le 4, \\ 0 & \text{otherwise.} \end{cases}$

   (a) Sketch the graph of $f(x)$.

   (b) Find the mean and variance of the mass of silicon produced.

5 The EverOn torch battery has a life of X hours. The variable X is modelled by the probability

   density function $f(x) = \begin{cases} 3000x^{-4} & x \ge 10, \\ 0 & \text{otherwise.} \end{cases}$

   (a) Sketch the graph of $f(x)$.

   (b) Find the mean and variance of the lives of these EverOn torch batteries.

6 A computer ink cartridge has a life of X hours. The variable X is modelled by the probability

   density function $f(x) = \begin{cases} kx^{-2} & 400 \le x \le 900, \\ 0 & \text{otherwise.} \end{cases}$

   (a) Sketch the graph of $f(x)$.   (b) Show that $k = 720$.

   (c) Find the mean and variance of the lives of these cartridges.

Miscellaneous exercise 1

1 A continuous random variable, X, has probability density function given by

   $$f(x) = \begin{cases} \frac{1}{8}x & 0 \le x \le 4, \\ 0 & \text{otherwise.} \end{cases}$$

   (a) Calculate $P(X < 2)$.   (b) Calculate the expected value of X.   (OCR, adapted)

2 A continuous random variable, X, has the probability density function

   $$f(x) = \begin{cases} \frac{1}{5} & 0 \le x \le 5, \\ 0 & \text{otherwise.} \end{cases}$$

   Find

   (a) the mean, $E(X)$,   (b) $\text{Var}(X)$.   (OCR, adapted)

3 The time, in minutes, between two consecutive calls to a telephone switchboard is modelled by a continuous random variable, X. The probability density function, f(x), for this random variable is given by

$$f(x) = \begin{cases} k(10 - x) & 0 \leqslant x \leqslant 10, \\ 0 & \text{otherwise.} \end{cases}$$

(a) Calculate the value of k.

(b) Find the mean time, E(X), between two consecutive calls.

(c) Find Var(X). (OCR)

4 A continuous random variable, X, has the probability density function, f(x), given by

$$f(x) = \begin{cases} k(4 - x) & 0 \leqslant x \leqslant 4, \\ 0 & \text{otherwise.} \end{cases}$$

(a) Sketch the probability density function.

(b) Determine the value of k.

(c) Calculate the probability that $X > 2.5$.

(d) Find E(X). (OCR)

5 A continuous random variable, X, has the probability density function

$$f(x) = \begin{cases} \frac{1}{2}x & 0 \leqslant x \leqslant 2, \\ 0 & \text{otherwise.} \end{cases}$$

(a) Find the median and lower and upper quartiles of X.

(b) Find E(X).

(c) Find Var(X). (OCR, adapted)

6 A continuous random variable, U, is uniformly distributed on $0.5 \leqslant u \leqslant 2.5$, as shown in the diagram.

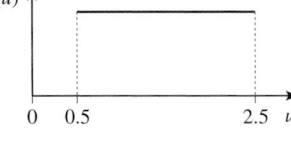

(a) Find the probability density function f(u).

(b) State the mean of U.

(c) Use integration to calculate the variance of U. (OCR)

7 The length, in metres, of 'offcuts' of wood found in a timber yard can be modelled by a continuous uniform distribution with density function, f(x), defined as

$$f(x) = \begin{cases} \dfrac{1}{k} & 0.2 \leqslant x \leqslant 0.8, \\ 0 & \text{otherwise.} \end{cases}$$

(a) Write down the value of k.

(b) State the mean length.

(c) Calculate the variance of the length.

(d) Three offcuts are chosen at random. What is the probability that just two of them are greater than 0.6 m in length?

8 The random variable, X, has probability density function

$$f(x) = \begin{cases} kx^3 & 0 \leqslant x \leqslant 2, \\ 0 & \text{otherwise.} \end{cases}$$

(a) Find the value of k.   (b) Find $E(X)$.

(c) Find $\text{Var}(X)$.   (d) Find the median of the distribution.

(e) Find the probability that an observation lies within one standard deviation of the mean.

(f) Find the probability that out of four observations, two are greater than the mean and two are less than the mean.   (OCR, adapted)

9 The random variable, X, has probability density function

$$f(x) = \begin{cases} \lambda x^3 & 0 \leqslant x \leqslant 4, \\ 0 & \text{otherwise.} \end{cases}$$

(a) Find the value of λ.   (b) Find $E(X)$.

(c) Find $\text{Var}(X)$.   (d) Find the probability $P(1 < X < 2)$.   (OCR)

10 The continuous random variable, X, has probability density function

$$f(x) = \begin{cases} \dfrac{k}{x} & 1 \leqslant x \leqslant 2, \\ 0 & \text{otherwise.} \end{cases}$$

(a) Find the value of the constant, k.   (b) Find the mean, $E(X)$.

(c) Find the variance, $\text{Var}(X)$.   (d) Determine the median value of X.

(e) Show that the probability that X is less than the mean is $-\dfrac{\ln(\ln 2)}{\ln 2}$.   (OCR)

11 An internet surfer suggests that the time (t minutes) that he spends on the internet can be modelled by the probability density function

$$f(t) = \begin{cases} 0.1e^{-0.1t} & t \geqslant 0, \\ 0 & \text{otherwise.} \end{cases}$$

(a) Verify that this is a properly defined probability density function.

(b) Find the probability that the surfer spends less than 4 minutes on the internet.

(c) Find the probability that the surfer spends more than 10 minutes on the internet.

12 The random variable X has probability density function

$$f(x) = \begin{cases} ae^{-ax} & 0 \leqslant x, \\ 0 & \text{otherwise.} \end{cases}$$

(a) Find the median value of X.

The above distribution, with $a = 0.8$, is proposed as a model for the length of life, in years, of a species of bird.

(b) Find the expected number out of a total of 50 birds that would fall in the class interval 2–3 years.

13 The continuous random variable X has probability density function

$$f(x) = \begin{cases} (x-a)(2a-x) & a \leqslant x \leqslant 2a, \\ 0 & \text{otherwise.} \end{cases}$$

(a) Show that $a^3 = 6$.　　　　(b) Find $E(X)$.　　　　　　　　　　　　　(OCR)

14 A farmer needs to install a new water-pump. Pumps almost always run perfectly for the first year but thereafter if they fail they are not worth repairing and have to be replaced. They virtually never last more than 9 years. The length of time, in years, that the pumps last can be modelled by the continuous random variable X which has probability density function given by

$$f(x) = \begin{cases} \dfrac{k}{x} & 1 \leqslant x \leqslant 9, \\ 0 & \text{otherwise,} \end{cases}$$

where k is a constant.

(a) Show that $k = \dfrac{1}{2\ln 3}$.

(b) Find the median length of life of a pump.

(c) Find the probability that a pump lasts between 1 and 2 years only.　　　(OCR, adapted)

2 The normal distribution

This chapter investigates a very commonly occurring distribution, called the normal distribution. When you have completed it you should

- understand the use of the normal distribution to model a continuous random variable
- be able to use the cumulative normal distribution tables accurately
- be able to solve problems involving the normal distribution
- be able to find a relationship between x, μ and σ given the value of $P(X > x)$ or its equivalent
- recall conditions under which the normal distribution can be used as an approximation to the binomial distribution
- be able to solve problems using the normal approximation, with a continuity correction.

2.1 A bell-shaped distribution

You saw in Chapter 1 that the probability distribution of a continuous random variable can be modelled by a function, f(x), called the **probability density function**. This term is often abbreviated to the initials p.d.f. Recall that probability density functions have two defining properties:

- $f(x) \geqslant 0$ for all x,
- $\displaystyle\int_{-\infty}^{\infty} f(x)\, dx = 1$.

In this chapter you will be considering a particular family of distributions. When you collect real, continuous data and you represent the results in a histogram you find that one particular pattern occurs very frequently. The histogram in Fig. 2.2 shows this sort of pattern.

The data in Table 2.1 refer to the heights of 39 people taken from the 'Brain size' datafile in S1 Table 1.5. Fig. 2.2 is a histogram for these data.

Height, h (inches)	Class boundaries	Class width	Frequency	Frequency density
62–63	$61.5 \leqslant h < 63.5$	2	4	2
64–65	$63.5 \leqslant h < 65.5$	2	5	2.5
66–67	$65.5 \leqslant h < 67.5$	2	8	4
68–71	$67.5 \leqslant h < 71.5$	4	13	3.25
72–75	$71.5 \leqslant h < 75.5$	4	5	1.25
76–79	$75.5 \leqslant h < 79.5$	4	4	1

Table 2.1. Heights for 39 people from the datafile 'Brain size'.

Fig. 2.2 shows some features common to many histograms.

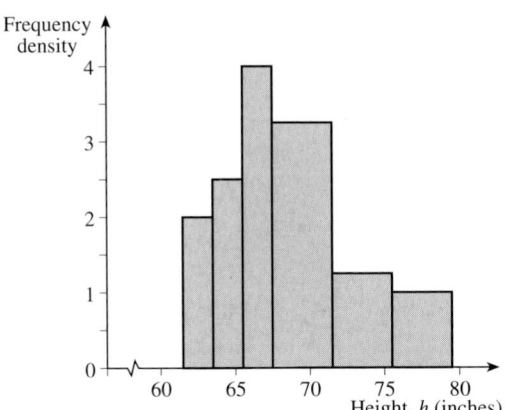

Fig. 2.2. Histogram for the data in Table 2.1.

(a) The distribution has a modal class somewhere in the middle of the range of values.

(b) The distribution is almost symmetrical.

(c) The frequency density tails off fairly rapidly as values of the variable move further away from the modal class.

Notice that it would not be true to say that the distribution shown in Fig. 2.2 is symmetrical. But remember it comes from a sample of only 39 values. You can imagine that for a larger sample the distribution might look more symmetrical. This example shows that real data do not always give you the ideal picture which you would expect.

You will have seen yourself many histograms for which the distribution is almost symmetrical. If the distribution were symmetrical then the mean and median would be 'in the middle' of the distribution and would be in the centre of the modal class. So for a symmetrical distribution it can be said that

mean = median = mode.

Note that the reverse is not necessarily true. If the mean, median and mode are equal, the distribution need not be symmetrical.

The probability density function for such an ideal distribution would have a bell shape similar to the one shown in Fig. 2.3.

Many continuous distributions have probability density functions which are approximately bell-shaped.

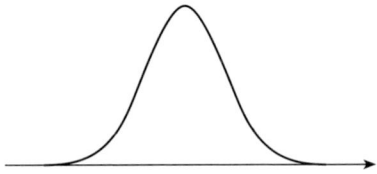

Fig. 2.3. Typical bell-shaped probability density function.

The height and weight of living objects commonly have distributions which are approximately bell-shaped. This is not really so surprising. Consider, for example, the height of adult females. A bell-shaped distribution would suggest that most females are about 'average' in terms of height and that a few are much taller and a few are much shorter. This picture tends to be confirmed by what you see in everyday life. It would be very useful, therefore, to find a function f(x) whose graph, when plotted, gives this typical bell shape.

Unfortunately it will not be enough to find one such function because, although the general bell shape applies to many different situations, the precise details of the bell vary from one distribution to another. For example, the heights of adult male humans may have a mean of 172 cm but the heights of adult male chimpanzees would not be centred around the same value.

Therefore you need a family of functions which give bell-shaped curves and there needs to be some parameter that you can vary which alters the line of symmetry of the curve.

Similarly the distributions for men and chimpanzees do not have the same amount of spread. There needs to be a second parameter which allows for different amounts of dispersion.

Although you do not need to learn the formula for this family of functions it is given for your information. It is

$$f(x) = \frac{1}{\sigma\sqrt{2\pi}}e^{-\frac{(x-\mu)^2}{2\sigma^2}} \qquad \text{for all real values of } x.$$

Any random variable whose distribution has this probability density function for some values of μ and σ^2 is said to have a **normal distribution** with parameters μ and σ^2. For a random variable X this is denoted by $X \sim N(\mu, \sigma^2)$.

If you have a graphic calculator, or if you have access to a graph drawing package on a computer, you might like to experiment with this function and draw the graphs for several values of μ and σ^2. You might have guessed what the symbols μ and σ^2 represent. The

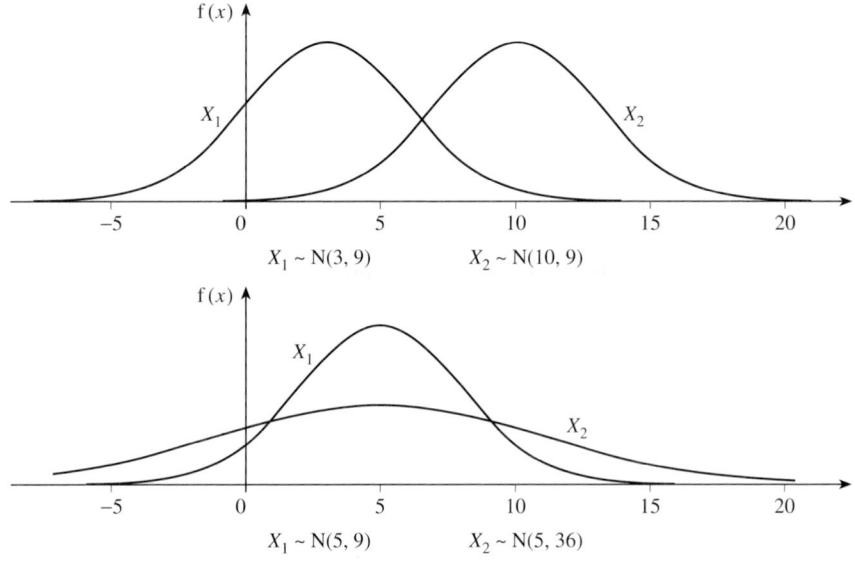

Fig. 2.4. Normal distributions with different values of μ and σ^2.

parameter μ gives the location of the mean of the distribution. In this case the mean is the same as the median and the mode since all three measures of location have the same value.

The line $x = \mu$ is the axis of symmetry for the curve whose equation is $y = f(x)$. Points of inflexion occur at the points on the curve where $x = \mu - \sigma$ and $x = \mu + \sigma$, so σ is a measure of the spread of the distribution. Although it is not possible to prove this at the moment, it will probably not surprise you to learn that σ^2 is the variance of the distribution.

You can see how the shape of the distribution varies with different values of μ and σ^2 by considering the diagrams in Fig. 2.4.

2.2   The standard normal distribution

If the random variable $Z \sim N(0, 1)$ then Z is said to have a **standard normal distribution**. In one sense this distribution has the probability density function with the 'simplest' equation. Because it is regarded as a special case, it is given its own notation. The letter Z is often reserved exclusively for a random variable with the $N(0, 1)$ distribution.

The probability density function for the $N(0, 1)$ distribution is

$$\phi(z) = \frac{1}{\sqrt{2\pi}} e^{-\frac{1}{2}z^2} \quad \text{for} -\infty < z < \infty.$$

where ϕ, pronounced 'fī', is the Greek letter f, and is used instead of the usual f for function.

The graph of $y = \phi(z)$ is drawn in Fig. 2.5.

Here is a summary of the properties of $\phi(z)$.

- $\phi(z)$ is symmetrical about the y-axis (the line $z = 0$),
- $\phi(z) \to 0$ (very quickly) as $z \to \pm\infty$, and $\phi(\pm 3) \approx 0$,
- for this distribution $E(Z) = 0$ and $Var(Z) = 1$,
- mean = median = mode = 0.

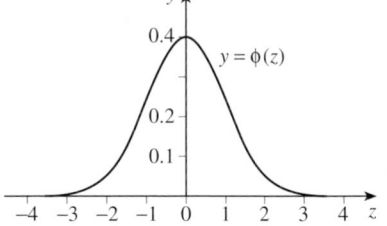

Fig. 2.5. Graph of the probability density function of the $N(0, 1)$ distribution.

Although you do not need to know the formula for $\phi(z)$, it is worth noting that $\dfrac{1}{\sqrt{2\pi}}$ is just the constant needed to ensure that the function has an area of one unit under its graph. It is not possible to show this by formal integration methods at this stage but you could verify that it is approximately true by using a numerical method such as the trapezium rule (see C2 Chapter 10).

2.3   Using normal distribution tables

If your calculator has a routine which gives you the area under the probability density function of the standard normal distribution, you may wish to omit this section. It is included to help those of you who do not have such a calculator and who must therefore rely on using normal distribution tables.

Unfortunately no simple formula exists for the indefinite integral $\int \phi(z)\,dz$, so areas under the graph of $\phi(z)$ have to be found numerically and then tabulated.

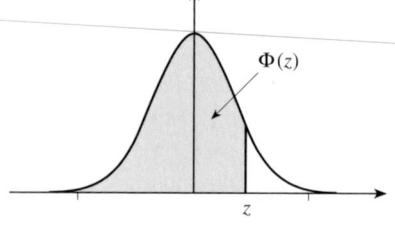

On page 178 there is a table of areas under the graph of $y = \phi(z)$. The area tabulated is shown by the shaded region in Fig. 2.6, and is given by

$$P(Z \leqslant z) = \int_{-\infty}^{z} \phi(x)\,dx.$$

Fig. 2.6. The function $\Phi(z)$.

The tabulated function is denoted by $\Phi(z)$, so

$$\Phi(z) = P(Z \leqslant z) = \int_{-\infty}^{z} \phi(x)\,dx.$$

Note that Φ is the capital Greek ϕ.

The function $\Phi(z)$ is called the **cumulative distribution function** of the standard normal distribution. The term cumulative distribution function is often abbreviated to c.d.f.

To see what the numbers in the cumulative normal distribution tables mean, consider the value $\Phi(2)$. From the table on page 178, $\Phi(2) = 0.9772$. This means that for a random variable Z with a N(0, 1) distribution, $P(Z \leqslant 2) = 0.9772$. Fig. 2.7 illustrates this situation.

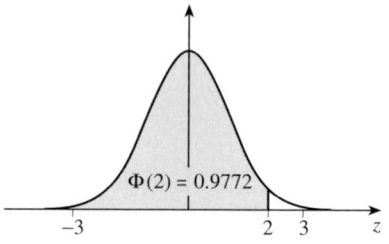

Fig. 2.7. $\Phi(2) = 0.9772$

The tables enable you to find $P(Z \leqslant z)$ for values of z, given correct to 3 decimal places, from $z = 0$ up to $z = 3$. Table 2.8 is taken from the table on page 178.

z	0	1	2	3	4	5	6	7	8	9	1	2	3	4	5	6	7	8	9
0.6	0.7257	0.7291	**0.7324**	0.7357	0.7389	0.7422	0.7454	0.7486	0.7517	0.7549	3	7	10	**13**	16	19	23	26	29

Table 2.8. Extract from the cumulative normal distribution table on page 178.

Suppose that you wish to find $P(Z \leqslant 0.624)$, where $Z \sim \text{N}(0, 1)$, using the tables. The first two digits 0.6 of 0.624 indicate that you must look in the row of the z-column labelled 0.6. The digit in the second decimal place is 2 so now look at the entry in the first column marked 2, giving the value 0.7324. The digit in the third decimal place is 4, so you must add 13 ten-thousandths to 0.7324, giving 0.7337. Thus

$$P(Z \leqslant 0.624) = 0.7337.$$

To find the area between two values, $z = a$ and $z = b$, use the fact that the area between $z = a$ and $z = b$ can be written as

(area between $z = a$ and $z = b$) = (area up to $z = b$) − (area up to $z = a$).

In symbols,

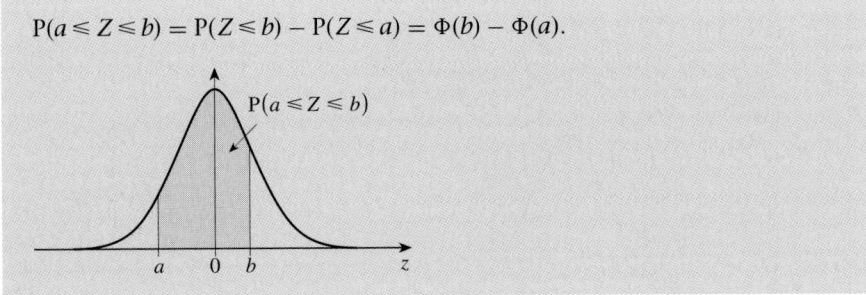

$$P(a \leq Z \leq b) = P(Z \leq b) - P(Z \leq a) = \Phi(b) - \Phi(a).$$

Recall from Section 1.2 that when calculating probabilities for a continuous distribution it makes no difference whether the sign is $\leq$ or $<$. So $P(a \leq Z \leq b) = P(a \leq Z < b) = P(a < Z \leq b) = P(a < Z < b)$.

For example,

$$P(1.20 \leq Z \leq 2.34) = \Phi(2.34) - \Phi(1.20) = 0.9904 - 0.8849 = 0.1055.$$

It is sensible to round all answers obtained from these tables to 3 decimal places since the entries are given correct to 4 decimal places. So write

$$
\begin{aligned}
P(1.20 \leq Z \leq 2.34) &= \Phi(2.34) - \Phi(1.20) \\
&= 0.9904 - 0.8849 \\
&= 0.1055 = 0.106, \text{ correct to 3 decimal places.}
\end{aligned}
$$

Notice that the tables do not give the values of $\Phi(z)$ for negative values of z. The reason is that you can deduce the value of $\Phi(z)$ for negative z from the symmetry of the graph of $\phi(z)$.

The diagrams in Fig. 2.9 show how to calculate $P(Z \leq -1.2)$.

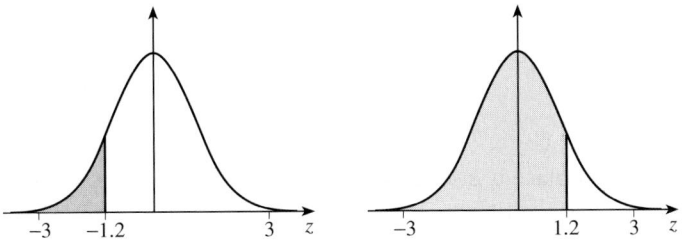

Fig. 2.9. Diagram showing how to calculate $\Phi(z)$ when z is negative.

Fig. 2.9 shows that the area shaded in the left diagram is equal to the area unshaded under the graph in the right diagram. Since the total area under the graph in each diagram, shaded and unshaded, is equal to 1,

$$
\begin{aligned}
\Phi(-1.2) &= 1 - \Phi(1.2) = 1 - 0.8849 \\
&= 0.1151 = 0.115, \text{ correct to 3 decimal places.}
\end{aligned}
$$

This is an example of the identity:

$$\Phi(-a) \equiv 1 - \Phi(a)$$

which applies for all values of a.

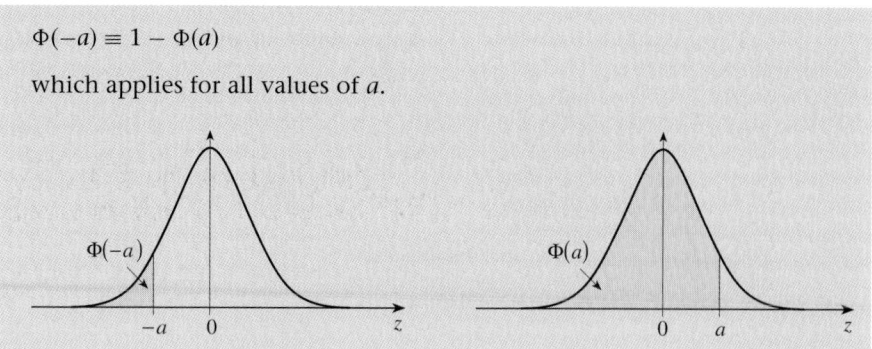

This identity means that it is not necessary to tabulate values of $\Phi(z)$ for negative values of z.

If you are using a calculator you may not need to use the formula $\Phi(-z) \equiv 1 - \Phi(z)$ because the calculator gives output for negative values of z. But whichever method you use, tables or calculator, make sure that you show your working clearly.

It will help to draw a sketch of the region whose area you are finding. These sketches will be drawn in this section, but omitted in following sections. However, you are advised always to make a sketch.

Example 2.3.1

The random variable Z is such that $Z \sim N(0, 1)$. Find the following probabilities.

(a) $P(0.7 \leqslant Z < 1.4)$ (b) $P(Z \leqslant -2.3)$ (c) $P(Z > 0.732)$ (d) $P(-1.4 \leqslant Z \leqslant 1)$

(a) $P(0.7 \leqslant Z < 1.4) = \Phi(1.4) - \Phi(0.7)$
$$= 0.9192 - 0.7580$$
$$= 0.1612$$
$$= 0.161, \text{ correct to 3 decimal places.}$$

(b) Using the identity $\Phi(-z) \equiv 1 - \Phi(z)$,

$$P(Z \leqslant -2.3) = 1 - P(Z \leqslant 2.3)$$
$$= 1 - \Phi(2.3)$$
$$= 1 - 0.9893$$
$$= 0.0107$$
$$= 0.011, \text{ correct to 3 decimal places.}$$

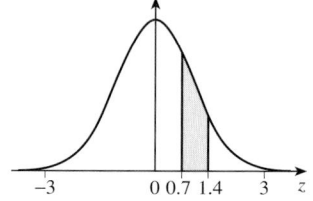

(c) $P(Z > 0.732) = 1 - P(Z \leqslant 0.732)$
$$= 1 - \Phi(0.732)$$
$$= 1 - (0.7673 + 0.0006)$$
$$= 1 - 0.7679 = 0.2321$$
$$= 0.232, \text{ correct to 3 decimal places.}$$

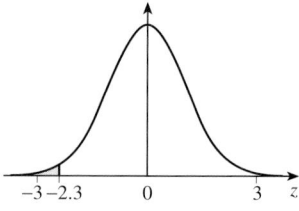

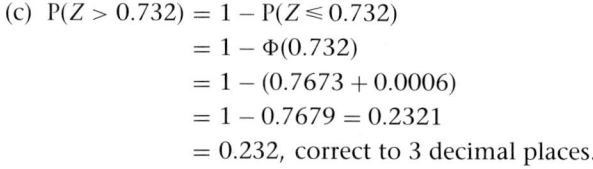

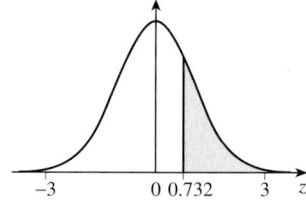

(d) $P(-1.4 \leqslant Z \leqslant 1) = P(Z \leqslant 1) - P(Z \leqslant -1.4)$
$= P(Z \leqslant 1) - (1 - P(Z \leqslant 1.4))$
$= P(Z \leqslant 1) - 1 + P(Z \leqslant 1.4)$
$= 0.8413 - 1 + 0.9192$
$= 0.7605$
$= 0.761$, correct to 3 decimal places.

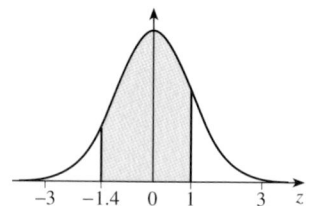

Notice how drawing a rough sketch of the graph of the N(0, 1) distribution with the ends of the sketch marked as -3 and 3 can give you some indication of whether your answer is approximately correct.

It is also sometimes necessary to use the tables 'in reverse'. For example, if you know the probability of $P(Z \leqslant k)$, you may need to find the corresponding value of k. As the function Φ is one-one (see C3 Section 2.7) you can always use the tables in this way.

Example 2.3.2
The random variable Z is such that $Z \sim N(0, 1)$. Use the cumulative normal distribution tables to find

(a) the value of s such that $P(Z \leqslant s) = 0.7$,

(b) the value of t such that $P(Z > t) = 0.8$.

(c) the value of w such that $P(Z < w) = 0.1$.

(a) In this case you need to use the tables in reverse. You know that $\Phi(s) = 0.7$ (shown in the diagram on the right).

From the tables,

$$\Phi(0.524) = 0.6999 \quad \text{and} \quad \Phi(0.525) = 0.7002,$$

so $s = 0.524$, correct to 3 decimal places.

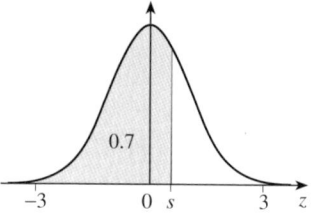

(b) From the diagram on the right it is clear that the value of t such that $P(Z > t) = 0.8$ is negative.

Since the value of t is negative, it cannot be found directly from the cumulative normal distribution tables.

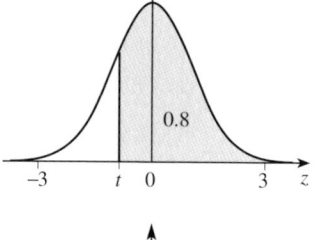

However, from the diagram below, $t = -v$ where $P(Z \leqslant v) = 0.8$, using symmetry.

You know that $\Phi(v) = 0.8$.

From the tables, $\Phi(0.842) = 0.8000$, so $v = 0.842$, and hence $t = -0.842$, correct to 3 decimal places.

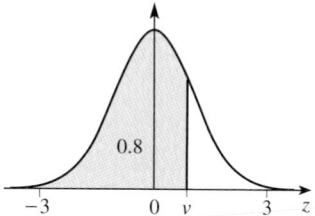

(c) From the diagram on the right it is clear that the value of w such that $P(Z < w) = 0.1$ is negative. However, from the diagram below, $w = -r$, where $P(Z \leqslant r) = 0.9$, using symmetry.

For this particular probability it is easier to find the value of r using the small table on page 179, rather than the main table in reverse. You will see from the small table that for $p = 0.90$, $z = 1.282$. So $r = 1.282$, and hence $w = -1.282$.

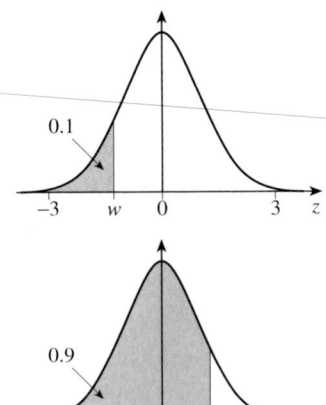

Exercise 2A

In this exercise use either your calculator or the tables on pages 178–9.

1 $Z \sim N(0, 1)$. Find the following probabilities.

(a) $P(Z < 1.23)$ (b) $P(Z \leqslant 2.468)$ (c) $P(Z < 0.157)$ (d) $P(Z \geqslant 1.236)$

(e) $P(Z > 2.378)$ (f) $P(Z \geqslant 0.588)$ (g) $P(Z > -1.83)$ (h) $P(Z \geqslant -2.057)$

(i) $P(Z > -0.067)$ (j) $P(Z \leqslant -1.83)$ (k) $P(Z < -2.755)$ (l) $P(Z \leqslant -0.206)$

(m) $P(Z < 1.645)$ (n) $P(Z \geqslant 1.645)$ (o) $P(Z > -1.645)$ (p) $P(Z \leqslant -1.645)$

2 The random variable Z is distributed such that $Z \sim N(0, 1)$. Find these probabilities.

(a) $P(1.15 < Z < 1.35)$ (b) $P(1.111 \leqslant Z \leqslant 2.222)$

(c) $P(0.387 < Z < 2.418)$ (d) $P(0 \leqslant Z < 1.55)$

(e) $P(-1.815 < Z < 2.333)$ (f) $P(-0.847 < Z \leqslant 2.034)$

(g) $P(-2.505 < Z < 1.089)$ (h) $P(-0.55 \leqslant Z \leqslant 0)$

(i) $P(-2.82 < Z < -1.82)$ (j) $P(-1.749 \leqslant Z \leqslant -0.999)$

(k) $P(-2.568 < Z < -0.123)$ (l) $P(-1.96 \leqslant Z < 1.96)$

(m) $P(-2.326 < Z < 2.326)$ (n) $P(|Z| \leqslant 1.3)$

(o) $P(|Z| > 2.4)$

3 The random variable $Z \sim N(0, 1)$. In each part, find the value of s, t, u or v.

(a) $P(Z < s) = 0.6700$ (b) $P(Z < t) = 0.8780$ (c) $P(Z < u) = 0.9842$

(d) $P(Z < v) = 0.8455$ (e) $P(Z > s) = 0.4052$ (f) $P(Z > t) = 0.1194$

(g) $P(Z > u) = 0.0071$ (h) $P(Z > v) = 0.2241$ (i) $P(Z > s) = 0.9977$

(j) $P(Z > t) = 0.9747$ (k) $P(Z > u) = 0.8496$ (l) $P(Z > v) = 0.5$

(m) $P(Z < s) = 0.0031$ (n) $P(Z < t) = 0.0142$ (o) $P(Z < u) = 0.0468$

(p) $P(Z < v) = 0.4778$ (q) $P(-s < Z < s) = 0.90$ (r) $P(-t < Z < t) = 0.80$

(s) $P(-u < Z < u) = 0.99$ (t) $P(|Z| < v) = 0.50$

2.4   Standardising a normal distribution

Suppose the random variable X has a normal distribution with parameters μ and σ^2. Then the bell-shaped graph of the normal distribution is centred on μ.

Let $Y = X - \mu$. The probability density function of Y will still have the typical bell shape but it will be centred on 0 rather than on μ. (See C1 Section 10.1.)

The spreads of the two distributions are identical, so $Y \sim \mathrm{N}(0, \sigma^2)$. Fig 2.10 shows the relation between the distributions of X and Y.

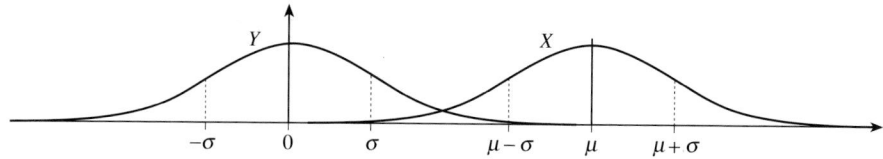

Fig. 2.10. Probability density functions of $X \sim \mathrm{N}(\mu, \sigma^2)$ and $Y \sim \mathrm{N}(0, \sigma^2)$, where $Y = X - \mu$.

Now let $Z = \dfrac{Y}{\sigma}$. This alters the spread of the distribution, so that when $Y = \pm\sigma$, then $Z = \pm 1$, but it does not alter the fact that the distribution has a characteristic bell shape. (See C1 Section 10.2.) So, as Fig. 2.11 shows, the probability density function of Z is an $\mathrm{N}(0,1)$ distribution.

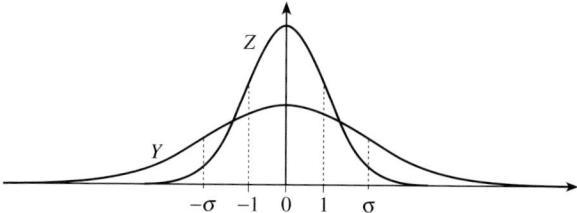

Fig. 2.11. Probability density functions of $Y \sim \mathrm{N}(0, \sigma^2)$ and $Z \sim \mathrm{N}(0, 1)$.

Summarising this discussion:

If $X \sim \mathrm{N}(\mu, \sigma^2)$ and $Z = \dfrac{X - \mu}{\sigma}$, then $Z \sim \mathrm{N}(0, 1)$.

This means that by using the transformation $Z = \dfrac{X - \mu}{\sigma}$ you can change a statement about an $\mathrm{N}(\mu, \sigma^2)$ distribution into an equivalent statement about an $\mathrm{N}(0, 1)$ distribution.

This process is called **standardisation** and the equation $Z = \dfrac{X - \mu}{\sigma}$ is called the **standardisation equation**.

To see how standardisation works, consider finding the probability $\mathrm{P}(X \leqslant 230)$, where $X \sim \mathrm{N}(205, 20^2)$

Using the standardisation equation $Z = \dfrac{X - 205}{20}$, you know that $Z \sim \mathrm{N}(0, 1)$. Then

$$P(X \leqslant 230) = P\left(Z \leqslant \frac{230-205}{20}\right) = P(Z \leqslant 1.25)$$
$$= \Phi(1.25) = 0.8944$$
$$= 0.894, \text{ correct to 3 decimal places.}$$

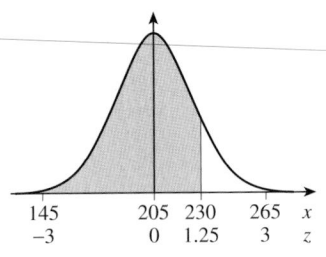

This probability is given by the shaded region in Fig. 2.12, which shows the distribution of X. The values of Z corresponding to the marked values of X are also shown. The lowest and highest marked values of X have been found by using the fact that the curve comes very close to the horizontal axis when $Z = \pm 3$. This corresponds to $X = \mu \pm 3\sigma = 205 \pm 3 \times 20$, that is 145 and 165.

Fig. 2.12

Example 2.4.1
Given that $X \sim N(4, 25)$, find the following probabilities.

(a) $P(X < 4.5)$ (b) $P(5 \leqslant X \leqslant 6)$ (c) $P(2 \leqslant X \leqslant 7)$ (d) $P(X > 1)$

Let $Z = \dfrac{X-4}{5}$. Then $Z \sim N(0, 1)$.

(a) $P(X < 4.5) = P\left(Z < \dfrac{4.5-4}{5}\right) = P(Z < 0.1)$
$$= \Phi(0.1) = 0.5398$$
$$= 0.540, \text{ correct to 3 decimal places.}$$

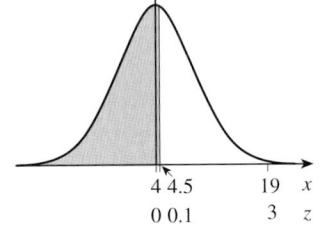

(b) $P(5 \leqslant X \leqslant 6) = P\left(\dfrac{5-4}{5} \leqslant Z \leqslant \dfrac{6-4}{5}\right)$
$$= P(0.2 \leqslant Z \leqslant 0.4)$$
$$= P(Z \leqslant 0.4) - P(Z \leqslant 0.2)$$
$$= \Phi(0.4) - \Phi(0.2)$$
$$= 0.6554 - 0.5793 = 0.0761$$
$$= 0.076, \text{ correct to 3 decimal places.}$$

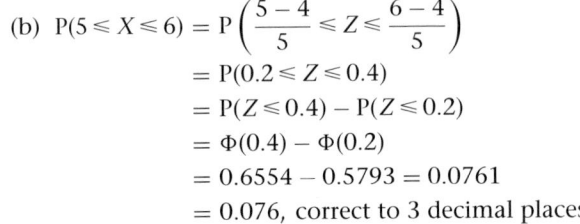
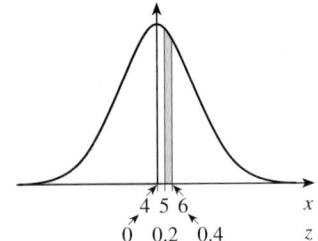

(c) $P(2 \leqslant X \leqslant 7) = P\left(\dfrac{2-4}{5} \leqslant Z \leqslant \dfrac{7-4}{5}\right)$
$$= P(-0.4 \leqslant Z \leqslant 0.6)$$
$$= P(Z \leqslant 0.6) - P(Z \leqslant -0.4)$$
$$= \Phi(0.6) - \Phi(-0.4)$$
$$= \Phi(0.6) - (1 - \Phi(0.4))$$
$$= 0.7257 - (1 - 0.6554) = 0.3811$$
$$= 0.381, \text{ correct to 3 decimal places.}$$

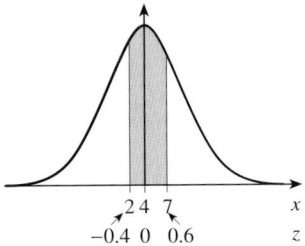

(d) $P(X > 1) = P\left(Z > \dfrac{1-4}{5}\right)$
$$= P(Z > -0.6)$$
$$= P(Z < 0.6) \qquad \text{(by symmetry)}$$
$$= \Phi(0.6)$$
$$= 0.7257$$
$$= 0.726, \text{ correct to 3 decimal places.}$$

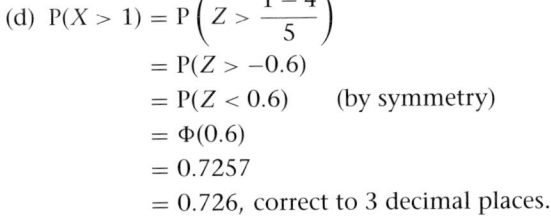
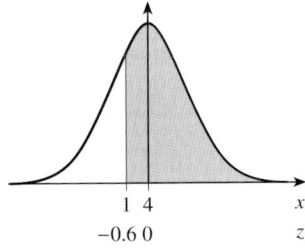

Example 2.4.2

Given that $X \sim N(6, 4)$, find, correct to 3 significant figures, the values of s and t such that

(a) $P(X \leqslant s) = 0.6500,$ (b) $P(X > t) = 0.8200.$

Let $Z = \dfrac{X - 6}{2}$. Then $Z \sim N(0, 1)$.

(a) The statement $P(X \leqslant s) = 0.6500$ is equivalent to
$$P\left(Z \leqslant \frac{s - 6}{2}\right) = 0.6500.$$

Therefore $\Phi\left(\dfrac{s - 6}{2}\right) = 0.6500.$

From the tables,

$$\Phi(0.385) = 0.6498 \quad \text{and} \quad \Phi(0.386) = 0.6502.$$

Therefore, by interpolation, $\Phi(0.3855) = 0.6500,$

so $\dfrac{s - 6}{2} = 0.3855$, giving

$$s = 6 + 2 \times 0.3855 = 6.771, \text{ which is } 6.77 \text{ correct to 3 significant figures.}$$

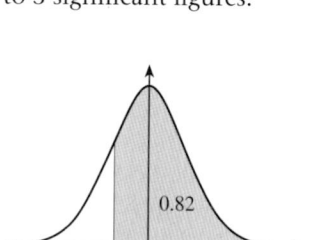

(b) The statement $P(X > t) = 0.8200$ is equivalent to
$$P\left(Z > \frac{t - 6}{2}\right) = 0.8200.$$

The problem is now similar to Example 2.3.2(b).
The value of $\dfrac{t - 6}{2}$ which you are looking for is
negative. First find w such that $P(Z \leqslant w) = 0.8200$.
From the tables, $w = 0.9155$. This means that
$\dfrac{t - 6}{2} = -0.9155$. Rearranging gives $t = 4.169$,
which is 4.17, correct to 3 significant figures.

Exercise 2B

You are strongly advised to draw rough sketches for these questions.

1 Given that $X \sim N(20, 16)$, find the following probabilities.
   (a) $P(X \leqslant 26)$ (b) $P(X > 30)$ (c) $P(X \geqslant 17)$ (d) $P(X < 13)$

2 Given that $X \sim N(24, 9)$, find the following probabilities.
   (a) $P(X \leqslant 29)$ (b) $P(X > 31)$ (c) $P(X \geqslant 22)$ (d) $P(X < 16)$

3 Given that $X \sim N(50, 16)$, find the following probabilities.
   (a) $P(54 \leqslant X \leqslant 58)$ (b) $P(40 < X \leqslant 44)$ (c) $P(47 < X < 57)$
   (d) $P(39 \leqslant X < 53)$ (e) $P(44 \leqslant X \leqslant 56)$

4 The random variable X can take negative and positive values. X is distributed normally with mean 3 and variance 4. Find the probability that X has a negative value.

5 The random variable X has a normal distribution. The mean is μ (where $\mu > 0$) and the variance is $\frac{1}{4}\mu^2$.

(a) Find $P(X > 1.5\mu)$. (b) Find the probability that X is negative.

6 Given that $X \sim N(44, 25)$, find s, t, u and v correct to 2 decimal places when

(a) $P(X \leqslant s) = 0.9808$, (b) $P(X \geqslant t) = 0.7704$,

(c) $P(X \geqslant u) = 0.0495$, (d) $P(X \leqslant v) = 0.3336$.

7 Given that $X \sim N(15, 4)$, find s, t, u, v and w correct to 2 decimal places when

(a) $P(X \leqslant s) = 0.9141$, (b) $P(X \geqslant t) = 0.5746$, (c) $P(X \geqslant u) = 0.1041$,

(d) $P(X \leqslant v) = 0.3924$, (e) $P(|X - 15| < w) = 0.9$.

8 Given that $X \sim N(35.4, 12.5)$, find the values of s, t, u and v correct to 1 decimal place when

(a) $P(X < s) = 0.96$, (b) $P(X > t) = 0.9391$,

(c) $P(X > u) = 0.2924$, (d) $P(X < v) = 0.1479$.

2.5 Modelling with the normal distribution

The normal distribution is often used as a model for practical situations. In the following examples, you need to translate the given information into the language of the normal distribution before you can solve the problem.

Example 2.5.1
Look back to the data on heights given in Table 2.1, and to the associated histogram in Fig. 2.2. Assuming that the distribution is normal, how many of the 39 people would you expect to be in the interval $61.5 \leqslant h < 63.5$?

You can check that the mean and the standard deviation of the data are 68.9 and 4.3. (If necessary, see S1 Sections 2.6 and 3.7.)

Using a random variable, H, with an $N(68.9, 4.3^2)$ distribution you can calculate the expected frequency for each class.

Given that $H \sim N(68.9, 4.3^2)$, let $Z = \dfrac{H - 68.9}{4.3}$. Then $Z \sim N(0, 1)$.

$$P(61.5 \leqslant H < 63.5) = P\left(\frac{61.5 - 68.9}{4.3} \leqslant Z < \frac{63.5 - 68.9}{4.3}\right)$$
$$= P(-1.72\ldots \leqslant Z < -1.25\ldots)$$
$$= \Phi(-1.25\ldots) - \Phi(-1.72\ldots)$$
$$= \Phi(1.72\ldots) - \Phi(1.25\ldots) \quad \text{(using symmetry)}$$
$$= 0.9574 - 0.8955 = 0.0619.$$

This means that the expected frequency for the class $61.5 \leqslant h < 63.5$ is $39 \times 0.0619 = 2.4$, correct to 1 decimal place.

Therefore in the group of 39 people you would expect roughly 2 people to have heights in the class $61.5 \leqslant h < 63.5$.

The observed frequency was actually 4. Does this mean that the N(68.9, 4.3²) distribution is a poor model for these data? To answer this question sensibly, you really need to calculate the expected frequencies for all six classes.

> Using the method shown above find the expected frequencies for the remaining five classes and then review the results to consider whether the N(68.9, 4.3²) distribution is a suitable model for these data.

Example 2.5.2

Two friends Sarah and Hannah often go to the Post Office together. They travel in Sarah's car. Sarah always drives Hannah to the Post Office and drops her off there. Sarah then drives around until she is ready to pick Hannah up some time later. Their experience has been that the time Hannah takes in the Post Office can be approximated by a normal distribution with mean 6 minutes and standard deviation 1.3 minutes. How many minutes after having dropped Hannah off should Sarah return if she wants to be at least 95% certain that Hannah will not keep her waiting?

Let T be the time Hannah takes in the Post Office on a randomly chosen trip. Then $T \sim N(6, 1.3^2)$.

Let t be the number of minutes after dropping Hannah off when Sarah returns; you then need to find t such that $P(T \leqslant t) \geqslant 0.95$.

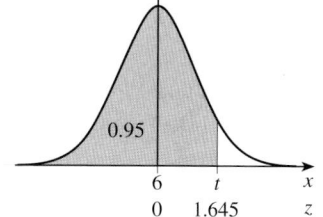

After standardising, this expression becomes

$$P\left(Z \leqslant \frac{t-6}{1.3}\right) \geqslant 0.95 \quad \text{or} \quad \Phi\left(\frac{t-6}{1.3}\right) \geqslant 0.95.$$

From the tables on pages 178–9, $\Phi(1.645) = 0.95$.

Therefore $\dfrac{t-6}{1.3} \geqslant 1.645$, which, on rearranging, gives $t \geqslant 8.1385\ldots$

Sarah should not return for at least 8.14 minutes, correct to 3 significant figures, if she wants to be at least 95% sure that Hannah will not keep her waiting.

2.6 Practical activities

1 Leaves Collect about 50 fallen leaves from a bush and measure the length of each leaf. You may need to consider what 'length' means, but any consistently applied definition should be satisfactory. Summarise the data in a grouped frequency table similar to Table 2.1 and calculate estimates of the mean length and the standard deviation. Use a normal distribution with the estimated mean and standard deviation to calculate expected frequencies for each class and compare these expected frequencies with the observed frequencies. Was the normal distribution a good model? You could repeat this experiment with a larger number of leaves, say 100. Has this any effect upon your conclusions?

2 Other situations You can investigate a number of other situations to see whether or not they show normal characteristics: weight, height, foot length, finger length etc. for people of the same age and gender; masses of pebbles in samples of gravel, lengths of nails of the 'same' size; heights jumped in the practical activities for S1 Section 1.5; the error (plus or minus) in bisecting a line 30 cm long by eye; masses of coins of various ages (measured very accurately on a scientific balance); lengths of songs in minutes taken from a CD.

Exercise 2C

1 The time spent waiting for a prescription to be prepared at a chemist's shop is normally distributed with mean 15 minutes and standard deviation 2.8 minutes. Find the probability that the waiting time is

(a) more than 20 minutes,   (b) less than 8 minutes,

(c) between 10 minutes and 18 minutes.

2 The heights of a group of sixteen-year-old girls are normally distributed with mean 161.2 cm and standard deviation 4.7 cm. Find the probability that one of these girls will have height

(a) more than 165 cm,   (b) less than 150 cm,

(c) between 165 cm and 170 cm,   (d) between 150 cm and 163 cm.

In a sample of 500 girls of this age estimate how many will have heights in each of the above four ranges.

3 The lengths of replacement car wiper blades are normally distributed with mean of 25 cm and standard deviation 0.2 cm. For a batch of 200 wiper blades estimate how many would be expected to be

(a) 25.3 cm or more in length,   (b) between 24.89 cm and 25.11 cm in length,

(c) between 24.89 cm and 25.25 cm in length.

4 The time taken by a garage to replace worn-out brake pads follows a normal distribution with mean 90 minutes and standard deviation 5.8 minutes.

(a) Find the probability that the garage takes longer than 105 minutes.

(b) Find the probability that the garage takes less than 85 minutes.

(c) The garage claims to complete the replacements in 'a to b minutes'. If this claim is to be correct for 90% of the repairs, find a and b correct to 2 significant figures, based on a symmetrical interval centred on the mean.

5 The fluorescent light tubes made by the company Well-lit have lifetimes which are normally distributed with mean 2010 hours and standard deviation 20 hours. The company decides to promote its sales of the tubes by guaranteeing a minimum life of the tubes, replacing free of charge any tubes that fail to meet this minimum life. If the company wishes to have to replace free only 3% of the tubes sold, find the guaranteed minimum it must set.

A purchaser buys four of these fluorescent light tubes. What is the probability that one of the four fails before the guaranteed minimum lifetime?

6 The lengths of sweetpea flower stems are normally distributed with mean 18.2 cm and standard deviation 2.3 cm.

  (a) Find the probability that the length of a flower stem is between 16 cm and 20 cm.

  (b) 12% of the flower stems are longer than h cm. 20% of the flower stems are shorter than k cm. Find h and k.

  (c) Stem lengths less than 14 cm are unacceptable at a florist's shop. In a batch of 500 sweetpeas estimate how many would be unacceptable.

2.7 Problems that involve finding μ and σ

Sometimes you are given information about a normal distribution and are asked to use it to find the values of μ or σ (or both). Here are some examples.

Example 2.7.1

The diameters of washers produced by a machine are normally distributed with a standard deviation of 0.1 mm. The washers are inspected and discarded if their diameter exceeds 2.0 mm. What is the mean diameter of washers produced by the machine if 3% are discarded?

Let the mean diameter of the washers be μ. Then, if D is the diameter of a randomly chosen washer, $D \sim N\left(\mu, 0.1^2\right)$.

If 3% of washers are rejected because they are oversize

$$P(D > 2.0) = 0.03.$$

After standardising using $Z = \dfrac{D - \mu}{\sigma}$, this equation becomes

$$P\left(Z > \frac{2.0 - \mu}{0.1}\right) = 0.03.$$

Writing $\left(\dfrac{2.0 - \mu}{0.1}\right) = s$ this equation becomes

$$P(Z > s) = 0.03$$

or, in terms of the cumulative distribution function,

$$1 - \Phi(s) = 0.03.$$

On rearranging this gives

$$\Phi(s) = 1 - 0.03 = 0.97.$$

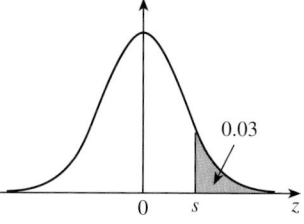

From the table on page 178, $s = 1.881$, so

$$\left(\frac{2.0 - \mu}{0.1}\right) = 1.881.$$

Solving this equation gives $\mu = 1.81$, correct to 3 significant figures.

Example 2.7.2

A dart player aiming at a vertical line finds that the perpendicular distance of a dart from the line is normally distributed with mean 0, where distances to the right of the line are taken as positive and those to the left of the line are taken as negative. Find the standard deviation of this distribution if there is a probability of 99% that a dart lands within 1 cm of the vertical line.

Let the standard deviation of the distribution be σ. Then, if X is the distance from the line of a randomly chosen dart, $X \sim N(0, \sigma^2)$.

If 99% of darts land within 1 cm of the line,

$$P(|X| \leq 1) = 0.99.$$

After standardising using $Z = \dfrac{X - \mu}{\sigma}$, this equation becomes

$$P\left(|Z| \leq \frac{1 - 0}{\sigma}\right) = 0.99.$$

Writing $\dfrac{1}{\sigma} = t$, this equation becomes

$$P(|Z| \leq t) = 0.99.$$

This probability is shown in the diagram on the right. In terms of the cumulative distribution function,

$$\Phi(t) = 0.99 + \tfrac{1}{2} \times 0.01 = 0.995.$$

From the table on page 179, $t = 2.576$, so

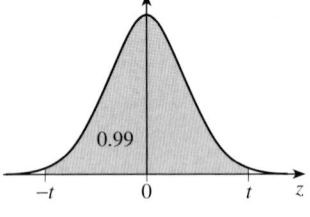

$$\frac{1}{\sigma} = 2.576.$$

Solving this equation gives $\sigma = 0.388$, correct to 3 significant figures.

Example 2.7.3

A biologist has been collecting data on the heights of a particular species of cactus (*Notocactus rutilans*). He has observed that 34.2% of the cacti are below 12 cm in height and 18.4% of the cacti are above 16 cm in height. He assumes that the heights are normally distributed. Find the mean and standard deviation of the distribution.

Let the mean and standard deviation of the distribution be μ and σ respectively. Then, if H is the height of a randomly chosen cactus of this species, $H \sim N(\mu, \sigma^2)$.

The biologist's observations can now be written

$$P(H < 12) = 0.342 \quad \text{and} \quad P(H > 16) = 0.184.$$

After standardising using $Z = \dfrac{H - \mu}{\sigma}$, these equations become

$$P\left(Z < \frac{12 - \mu}{\sigma}\right) = 0.342 \quad \text{and} \quad P\left(Z > \frac{16 - \mu}{\sigma}\right) = 0.184.$$

Writing $\dfrac{12 - \mu}{\sigma} = s$ and $\dfrac{16 - \mu}{\sigma} = t$, the two equations become

$$P(Z < s) = 0.342 \quad \text{and} \quad P(Z > t) = 0.184$$

or, in terms of the cumulative normal distribution function,

$$\Phi(s) = 0.342 \quad \text{and} \quad 1 - \Phi(t) = 0.184.$$

This information is summarised in the diagram.

Using the tables, after writing $s = -v$, gives $\Phi(v) = 0.658$, $v = 0.407$ and $s = -0.407$.

Since $1 - \Phi(t) = 0.184$, $\Phi(t) = 0.816$ giving $t = 0.900$.

Therefore $s = \dfrac{12 - \mu}{\sigma} = -0.407$ and $t = \dfrac{16 - \mu}{\sigma} = 0.900$.

These give the two simultaneous equations

$$12 - \mu = -0.407\sigma,$$
$$16 - \mu = 0.900\sigma.$$

Solving these equations gives $\mu = 13.2$ and $\sigma = 3.06$, correct to 3 significant figures.

Exercise 2D

1 X has a normal distribution with mean 32 and variance σ^2. Given that the probability that X is less than 33.14 is 0.6406, find σ^2. Give your answer correct to 2 decimal places.

2 X has a normal distribution, and $P(X > 73.05) = 0.0289$. Given that the variance of the distribution is 18, find the mean.

3 X is distributed normally, $P(X \geqslant 59.1) = 0.0218$ and $P(X \geqslant 29.2) = 0.9345$. Find the mean and standard deviation of the distribution, correct to 3 significant figures.

4 $X \sim N(\mu, \sigma^2)$, $P(X \geqslant 9.81) = 0.1587$ and $P(X \leqslant 8.82) = 0.0116$. Find μ and σ, correct to 3 significant figures.

5 The T-Q company makes a soft drink sold in '330 ml' cans. The actual volume of drink in the cans is distributed normally with standard deviation 2.5 ml.

To ensure that at least 99% of the cans contain more than 330 ml, find the volume that the company should supply in the cans on average.

6 The packets in which sugar is sold are labelled '1 kg packets'. In fact the mass of sugar in a packet is distributed normally with mean mass 1.08 kg.

Sampling of the packets of sugar shows that just 2.5% are 'underweight' (that is, contain less than the stated mass of 1 kg).

Find the standard deviation of the distribution.

7 The life of the Powerhouse battery has a normal distribution with mean 210 hours. It is found that 4% of these batteries operate for more than 222 hours.

Find the variance of the distribution, correct to 2 significant figures.

8 In a statistics examination, 15% of the candidates scored more than 63 marks and 10% of the candidates scored less than 32 marks. Assuming that the marks were distributed normally find the mean mark and the standard deviation.

2.8   The normal distribution as an approximation to the binomial distribution

If you were asked to estimate the probability that a school of 1000 students contains more than 150 left-handed students, how would you try to solve such a problem? Perhaps one sensible approach would be to take a reasonably large sample, say of size 50, and count the number of left-handed students in the sample. From this information you could estimate the probability that a randomly chosen student is left-handed.

For example, if your sample contains 8 left-handed people you would estimate the probability that a randomly chosen person is left-handed as $\frac{8}{50}$, or 0.16. If you define L as the number of left-handed people in a random sample of 1000 people, you could then use the distribution B(1000, 0.16) as a model for the distribution of L. (See S1 Section 7.1 for the binomial distribution.) You only need to find P($L > 150$). This is given by

$$P(L > 150) = 1 - P(L \leqslant 150) = 1 - P(L = 0) - P(L = 1) - P(L = 2) - \cdots - P(L = 150)$$

$$= 1 - \binom{1000}{0} 0.16^0 0.84^{1000} - \binom{1000}{1} 0.16^1 0.84^{999}$$

$$- \binom{1000}{2} 0.16^2 0.84^{998} - \cdots - \binom{1000}{150} 0.61^{150} 0.84^{850}.$$

To calculate this is horrendous; there are 151 separate calculations to be carried out.

Fortunately there is an approximate method which uses the normal distribution and involves far less work. This section shows how to carry out such approximations.

Fig. 2.13 shows bar charts of the binomial distribution for different values of n and p.

The diagrams in the top row of Fig. 2.13 show $p = 0.1$, with three values of n, 12, 20 and 60. When $n = 12$ and $p = 0.1$ the bar chart is positively skewed. However, as n gets larger, the bar chart becomes more symmetrical and bell-shaped in appearance.

The diagrams in the bottom row of Fig. 2.13 show that when $p = \frac{1}{2}$ the shape of the bar chart resembles the bell shape that you associate with a normal distribution. This is true even when n is quite small as the diagram for $n = 12$ and $p = \frac{1}{2}$ shows.

You should be able to see that if a third row of bar charts were drawn with $p = 0.9$ for the three values of n, 12, 20 and 60, then each bar chart would be the mirror image of the corresponding bar chart in the first row, about the vertical line $x = \frac{1}{2}n$. Thus, the bar chart for $n = 12$ and $p = 0.9$ is the mirror image of that for $n = 12$ and $p = 0.1$.

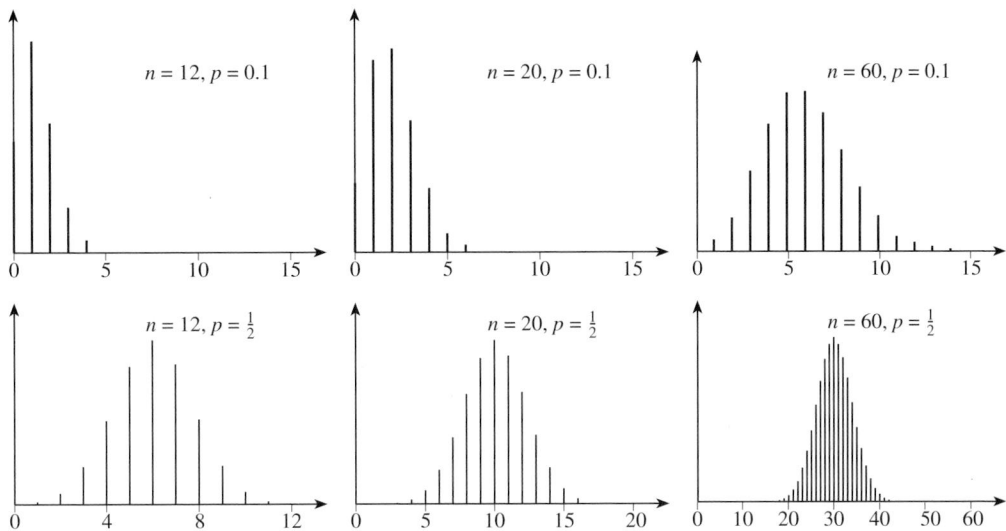

Fig. 2.13. Bar charts showing the binomial distribution for different values of n and p.

Summarising these observations you find that if $X \sim B(n, p)$ and n is sufficiently large then the distribution of X is approximately normal. If p is close to 0 or 1, then n must be larger than if p is close to $\frac{1}{2}$.

There is a simple condition which you can use to test whether a binomial distribution can reasonably be approximated by a normal distribution. This is that $np > 5$ and $nq > 5$ where $q = 1 - p$.

Notice that if $p = \frac{1}{2}$ then the conditions $np > 5$ and $nq > 5$ will be satisfied when $n > 10$. You saw that when $n = 12$ and $p = \frac{1}{2}$ the normal approximation would be reasonable.

On the other hand, if $p = 0.1$ or if $p = 0.9$, it is only when $n > 50$ that *both* $np > 5$ *and* $nq > 5$. You saw that for a $B(60, 0.1)$ distribution the normal approximation seemed satisfactory. A normal approximation would still be satisfactory for a $B(60, 0.9)$ distribution because the bar chart representing this distribution is a mirror image of the one representing a $B(60, 0.1)$ distribution.

If the normal distribution is a good approximation to a binomial distribution you would imagine that the normal curve would nearly pass through the tops of the bars on the bar chart. In this case it seems reasonable to suppose that the two distributions have the same mean and variance.

But you know that if $X \sim B(n, p)$ then $E(X) = np$ and $Var(X) = npq$ (see S1 Section 8.3.) The approximating normal distribution should therefore also have mean np and variance npq. That is, the distribution of X is approximated by an $N(np, npq)$ distribution.

For example, if $X \sim B\left(60, \frac{1}{2}\right)$ then the distribution of X can be approximated by the normal distribution with mean $\mu = 60 \times \frac{1}{2} = 30$ and variance $\sigma^2 = 60 \times \frac{1}{2} \times \frac{1}{2} = 15$. So the distribution $X \sim B\left(60, \frac{1}{2}\right)$ can be approximated by the distribution $V \sim N(30, 15)$.

See whether you can draw the bar charts in Fig. 2.13 using a spreadsheet. Experiment with values of n and p and check whether the bar charts look 'normally distributed' whenever the conditions $np > 5$ and $nq > 5$ are satisfied.

But how does the normal approximation work in practice? There seems immediately to be a problem since, for example,

$$P(X = 31) = \binom{60}{31} \times 0.5^{31} \times 0.5^{29}$$

whereas

$$P(V = 31) = 0$$

since V has a continuous distribution.

In fact, $P(V = v) = 0$ for any $v = 0, 1, 2, \ldots, 60$, so a little more work is needed in order to make the connection between the binomial distribution and the normal distribution useful.

Usually discrete distributions are represented by bar charts in which each bar is separate from the next bar and in which the height of the bar is proportional to the probability of that particular value, as in Fig. 2.14.

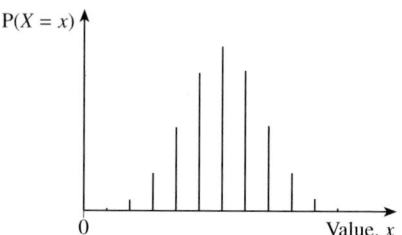

Fig. 2.14. Bar chart showing the distribution of a discrete random variable, X.

In order to compare the binomial distribution with the normal distribution it is more helpful to draw a bar chart that looks similar to a histogram. You widen each of the bars by a $\frac{1}{2}$ unit on either side so that each is still centred on an integer value but the blocks now touch. Each block has an area proportional to the probability of the integer on which it is centred. The resulting diagram is more suitable for comparison with the normal distribution, as you can see in Fig. 2.15.

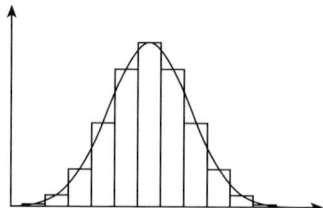

Fig. 2.15. Comparison between the binomial distribution and the normal distribution.

The possible values which a $B(n, p)$ distribution can take are $0, 1, 2, \ldots, n$ whereas the $N(np, npq)$ distribution can take all real values. In particular, this means that the normal distribution can take values greater than n or less than 0. This would seem to indicate that a normal distribution is not a satisfactory approximation to a binomial distribution. However, the area below the normal curve for x-values above n or below 0 will be very small indeed and so, although it is possible for the $N(np, npq)$ distribution to be greater than n or less than 0, it is very unlikely indeed and you do not need to worry about the fact that a normal distribution can take all real values.

Fig. 2.16a and Fig. 2.16b show how you can make the relationship between the normal approximation and the binomial distribution more precise.

You can see that the probability which is represented by the shaded rectangular region in Fig. 2.16a can be approximated by the shaded region in Fig. 2.16b, which resembles a trapezium and which is the area under the normal curve between 30.5 and 31.5.

In other words, $P(X = 31) \approx P(30.5 < V < 31.5)$.

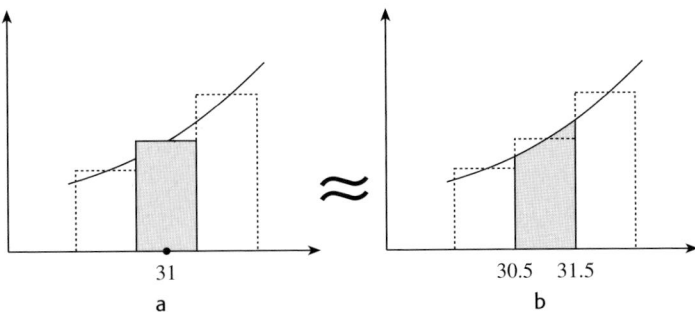

Fig. 2.16. The normal distribution approximates to the binomial distribution.

If you wanted to calculate $P(X \leqslant 26)$ you would calculate the total area of all the blocks up to and including the block at $x = 26$. This area is best approximated by the area under the normal curve up to $v = 26.5$. That is,

$$P(X \leqslant 26) \approx P(V \leqslant 26.5).$$

The 'extra' 0.5 which appears is necessary because you are approximating a discrete distribution by a continuous distribution. It is called a **continuity correction** and it is needed in order to make the approximation as accurate as possible.

Summarising:

> If $X \sim B(n, p)$, and if $np > 5$ and $nq > 5$, where $q = 1 - p$, then X can reasonably be approximated by $V \sim N(np, npq)$.
>
> A continuity correction must be applied.

> Note that nq is the expected number of failures, not the variance of the distribution.

Example 2.8.1

The random variable X has a $B\left(60, \frac{1}{2}\right)$ distribution. For each of the following binomial probabilities describe the region under the approximating normal curve whose area gives the best estimate.

(a) $P(X \leqslant 12)$ (b) $P(X = 16)$

(c) $P(X < 22)$ (d) $P(X > 18)$

(e) $P(12 < X \leqslant 34)$ (f) $P(12 \leqslant X < 21)$

Since $X \sim B\left(60, \frac{1}{2}\right)$, it can be approximated by the distribution of V where $V \sim N(30, 15)$.

(a) To find $P(X \leqslant 12)$ you need to find the total area of the blocks for $x = 0, 1, 2, \ldots, 12$. The area under the normal curve which best approximates to this is the area for which $v \leqslant 12.5$, so $P(X \leqslant 12) \approx P(V \leqslant 12.5)$.

(b) To find $P(X = 16)$ you need to find the total area of the block for $x = 16$. The area under the normal curve which best approximates to this is the area between $v = 15.5$ and $v = 16.5$, so $P(X = 16) \approx P(15.5 \leqslant V \leqslant 16.5)$.

(c) To find $P(X < 22)$ you need to find the total area of the blocks for $x = 0, 1, 2, \ldots, 21$. The area under the normal curve which best approximates to this is the area for which $v \leqslant 21.5$, so $P(X < 22) \approx P(V \leqslant 21.5)$.

(d) To find $P(X > 18)$ you need to find the total area of the blocks for $x = 19, \ldots, 60$. The area under the normal curve which best approximates to this is the area for which $v \geqslant 18.5$, so $P(X > 18) \approx P(V \geqslant 18.5)$.

(e) To find $P(12 < X \leqslant 34)$ you need to find the total area of the blocks for $x = 13, 14, \ldots, 34$. The area under the normal curve which best approximates to this is between $v = 12.5$ and $v = 34.5$, so $P(12 < X \leqslant 34) \approx P(12.5 \leqslant V \leqslant 34.5)$.

(f) To find $P(12 \leqslant X < 21)$ you need to find the total area of the blocks for $x = 12, 13, \ldots, 20$. The area under the normal curve which best approximates to this is between $v = 11.5$ and $v = 20.5$, so $P(12 \leqslant X < 21) \approx P(11.5 \leqslant V \leqslant 20.5)$.

The best way to work with the normal approximation to the binomial distribution using the continuity correction is to draw a sketch of the situation each time it arises. Do not try to learn the results in Example 2.8.1.

Notice that there was no need in Example 2.8.1 to test the validity of the normal approximation to the binomial distribution, because it had already been verified in the discussion which preceded the example. That is not the case in the next example.

Example 2.8.2
A random variable X has a binomial distribution with parameters $n = 80$ and $p = 0.4$. Use a suitable approximation to calculate the following probabilities.

(a) $P(X \leqslant 34)$ (b) $P(X \geqslant 26)$ (c) $P(X = 33)$ (d) $P(30 < X \leqslant 40)$.

The values of np and nq are given by $np = 80 \times 0.4 = 32$ and $nq = 80 \times (1 - 0.4) = 48$. Since these are both greater than 5 the normal distribution is a good approximation to the binomial distribution, so you can approximate to $X \sim B(80, 0.4)$ by $V \sim N(np, npq) = N(32, 19.2)$.

Now that you are working with a normal distribution, V, standardise by letting $Z = \dfrac{V - 32}{\sqrt{19.2}}$. Then $Z \sim N(0.1)$.

(a) $P(X \leqslant 34) \approx P(V \leqslant 34.5) = P\left(Z \leqslant \dfrac{34.5 - 32}{\sqrt{19.2}}\right) = P(Z \leqslant 0.570\ldots)$

$\qquad = \Phi(0.571) = 0.7160$

$\qquad = 0.716$, correct to 3 decimal places.

(b) $P(X \geqslant 26) \approx P(V \geqslant 25.5) = P\left(Z \geqslant \dfrac{25.5 - 32}{\sqrt{19.2}}\right) = P(Z \geqslant -1.483)$

$\qquad = 1 - \Phi(-1.483) = 1 - (1 - \Phi(1.483)) = \Phi(1.483)$

$\qquad = 0.9310 = 0.931$, correct to 3 decimal places.

(c) $P(X = 33) \approx P(32.5 \leqslant V \leqslant 33.5) = P\left(\dfrac{32.5 - 32}{\sqrt{19.2}}) \leqslant Z \leqslant \dfrac{33.5 - 32}{\sqrt{19.2}}\right)$

$\qquad = P(0.114 \leqslant Z \leqslant 0.342) = \Phi(0.342) - \Phi(0.114)$

$\qquad = 0.6338 - 0.5454 = 0.0884$

$\qquad = 0.088$, correct to 3 decimal places.

(d) $P(30 < X \leqslant 40) \approx P(30.5 \leqslant V \leqslant 40.5) = P\left(\dfrac{30.5 - 32}{\sqrt{19.2}} \leqslant Z \leqslant \dfrac{40.5 - 32}{\sqrt{19.2}}\right)$

$\qquad = P(-0.342 \leqslant Z \leqslant 1.940) = \Phi(1.940) - \Phi(-0.342)$

$\qquad = \Phi(1.940) - (1 - \Phi(0.342))$

$\qquad = 0.9738 - (1 - 0.6338) = 0.6076$

$\qquad = 0.608$, correct to 3 decimal places.

Example 2.8.3

A manufacturer of spice jars knows that 8% of the jars produced are defective. He supplies jars in cartons containing 12 jars. He supplies cartons of jars in crates of 60 cartons. In each case making clear the distribution that you are using, calculate the probability that

(a) a carton contains exactly 2 defective jars,

(b) a carton contains at least 1 defective jar,

(c) a crate contains between 39 and 44 (inclusive) cartons with at least 1 defective jar.

Let D be the number of defective jars in a randomly chosen box of 12 jars. Then $D \sim B(12, 0.08)$.

Since $np = 12 \times 0.08 = 0.96 < 5$ you cannot use the normal approximation. You must therefore use the binomial distribution.

(a) $P(D = 2) = \dbinom{12}{2} \times 0.08^2 \times 0.92^{10} = 0.1834\ldots$

The probability that a carton contains exactly 2 defective jars is 0.183, correct to 3 decimal places.

(b) $P(D \geqslant 1) = 1 - P(D = 0) = 1 - 0.92^{12} = 0.6323\ldots$

The probability that a carton contains at least 1 defective jar is 0.632, correct to 3 decimal places.

(c) Let C be the number of cartons containing at least 1 defective jar in a randomly chosen crate of 60 cartons.

Then C has a binomial distribution with $n = 60$. The probability of success, p, is the value found in part (b). So $p = 0.6323\ldots$

For this binomial distribution, $np = 60 \times 0.6323\ldots = 37.94\ldots$ and $nq = 60 \times (1 - 0.6323\ldots) = 22.06\ldots$ Since they are both greater than 5, the normal approximation is valid.

The distribution of C is approximately the same as the distribution of V where $V \sim N(60 \times 0.6323\ldots, 60 \times 0.6323\ldots \times (1 - 0.6323\ldots))$. That is, the distribution of C is approximately the same as $V \sim N(37.94, 13.95)$.

So $P(39 \leqslant C \leqslant 44) \approx P(38.5 \leqslant V \leqslant 44.5)$.

Let $Z = \dfrac{V - 37.94}{\sqrt{13.95}}$. Then $Z \sim N(0, 1)$.

$$P(39 \leqslant C \leqslant 44) \approx P(38.5 \leqslant V \leqslant 44.5) = P\left(\frac{38.5 - 37.94}{\sqrt{13.95}} \leqslant Z \leqslant \frac{44.5 - 37.94}{\sqrt{13.95}}\right)$$
$$= P(0.150 \leqslant Z \leqslant 1.756) = \Phi(1.756) - \Phi(0.150)$$
$$= 0.9604 - 0.5596 = 0.4008.$$

The probability that a crate contains between 39 and 44 (inclusive) cartons with at least 1 defective jar is 0.401, correct to 3 decimal places.

Returning to the problem posed at the beginning of this section, you can now use what you have learned to calculate an approximation to the probability of there being more than 150 left-handed students in a school of 1000 students.

Recall that the random variable L was defined as the number of left-handed people in a randomly chosen sample of 1000 people. The distribution of L was modelled by a B(1000, 0.16) distribution.

Now $np = 160$ and $nq = 840$ and both are much greater than 5 so it is valid to use the normal approximation. The distribution of L can be approximated by the random variable $V \sim N(160, 134.4)$ and therefore $P(L > 150) \approx P(V > 150.5)$.

Standardising, let $Z = \dfrac{V - 160}{\sqrt{134.4}}$. Then

$$P(V > 150.5) = P\left(Z > \frac{150.5 - 160}{\sqrt{134.4}}\right)$$
$$= P(Z > -0.819\ldots) = P(Z < 0.819\ldots)$$
$$= \Phi(0.819\ldots) = 0.7935$$
$$= 0.794, \text{ correct to 3 decimal places.}$$

Exercise 2E

1 State whether the following binomial distributions can or cannot reasonably be approximated by a normal distribution. Write down a brief calculation to justify your conclusion in each case.

(a) B(50, 0.2)   (b) B(60, 0.1)   (c) B(70, 0.01)   (d) B(30, 0.7)   (e) B(40, 0.9)

2 A random variable, X, has a binomial distribution with parameters $n = 40$ and $p = 0.3$. Use a suitable approximation, which you should show is valid, to calculate the following probabilities.

(a) $P(X \geqslant 18)$ (b) $P(X < 9)$ (c) $P(X = 15)$ (d) $P(11 < X < 15)$

3 The mass production of a cheap pen results in there being 1 defective pen in 20 on average. Use an approximation, which you should show is valid, to find, in a batch of 300 of these pens, the probability of there being

(a) 24 or more defective pens,   (b) 10 or fewer defective pens.

4 A fair coin is tossed 18 times.

(a) Use the binomial distribution to find the probability of obtaining 14 heads.

(b) Use a normal approximation to find the probability of obtaining 14 heads, and to find the probability of obtaining 14 or more heads. Show that the approximation is valid.

5 In a certain county 12% of people have green eyes. If 50 of these people are inspected, find the probability that

(a) 12 or more of them have green eyes,

(b) between 3 and 10 (inclusive) of them have green eyes.

Show that your approximation is valid.

6 Fred attempts to dial a connection to the internet for his email each day. He is successful on his first attempt 8 times out of 10. Use a normal approximation, showing first that it is valid, to find the probability that Fred is successful on his first attempt at dialling a connection on 36 days or more over a period of 40 days.

7 (a) An unbiased dice is thrown 60 times. Find the probability that a five is obtained on 12 to 18 (inclusive) of these throws.

(b) In a game two unbiased dice are thrown. A winning score on each throw is a total of 5, 6, 7 or 8. Find the probability of a win on 70 or more throws out of 120 throws.

8 At an election there are two parties, X and Y. On past experience twice as many people voted for party X as for party Y.

An opinion poll researcher samples 90 voters. Find the probability that 70 or more say they will vote for party X at the next election.

If 2000 researchers each questioned 90 voters, how many of these researchers would be expected to record '70 or more for party X' results?

9 A manufacturer states that '3 out of 4 people prefer my product (Acme) to a competitor's product'. To test this claim a researcher asks 80 people about their liking for Acme. Assuming that the manufacturer is correct, find the probability that fewer than 53 prefer Acme. If 1000 researchers each questioned 80 people, how many of these researchers would be expected to record 'fewer than 53 prefer Acme' results?

10 Videos are packed in a box which contains 20 videos. 5% of the videos are faulty. The boxes are packed in crates which contain 50 boxes. Find the probabilities of the following events, clearly stating which distribution you are using and why.

(a) A box contains 2 faulty videos.

(b) A box contains at least 1 faulty video.

(c) A crate contains between 35 and 39 (inclusive) boxes with at least 1 faulty video.

Miscellaneous exercise 2

1 Given that $X \sim N(10, 2.25)$, find $P(X > 12)$. (OCR)

2 The random variable X has the distribution $X \sim N(10, 8)$. Find $P(X > 6)$. (OCR)

3 A random variable X has an N(m, 4) distribution. Its associated normal curve is shown in the diagram. Find the value of m such that the shaded area is 0.800, giving your answer correct to 3 significant figures. (OCR)

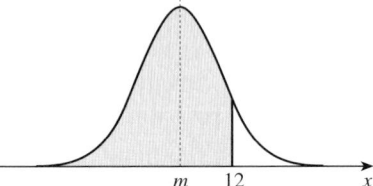

4 The number of hours of sunshine at a resort has been recorded for each month for many years. One year is selected at random and H is the number of hours of sunshine in August of that year. H can be modelled by a normal variable with mean 130.

(a) Given that $P(H < 179) = 0.975$, calculate the standard deviation of H.

(b) Calculate $P(100 < H < 150)$. (OCR)

5 An ordinary unbiased dice is thrown 900 times. Using a suitable approximation, find the probability of obtaining at least 160 sixes. (OCR)

6 W is a normally distributed random variable with mean 0.58 and standard deviation 0.12. Find $P(W < 0.79)$. (OCR)

7 X is a random variable with the distribution $X \sim N(140, 56.25)$. Find the probability that X is greater than 128.75. (OCR)

8 The manufacturers of a new model of car state that, when travelling at 56 miles per hour, the petrol consumption has a mean value of 32.4 miles per gallon with standard deviation 1.4 miles per gallon. Assuming a normal distribution, calculate the probability that a randomly chosen car of that model will have a petrol consumption greater than 30 miles per gallon when travelling at 56 miles per hour. (OCR)

9 A normally distributed random variable, X, has mean 20.0 and variance 4.15. Find the probability that $18.0 < X < 21.0$. (OCR)

10 The lifetime of a Fotobrite light bulb is normally distributed with mean 1020 hours and standard deviation 85 hours. Find the probability that a Fotobrite bulb chosen at random has a lifetime between 1003 and 1088 hours. (OCR)

11 It is given that 40% of the population support the Gamboge Party. One hundred and fifty members of the population are selected at random. Use a suitable approximation to find the probability that more than 55 out of the 150 support the Gamboge Party.   (OCR)

12 The playing time, T minutes, of classical compact discs is modelled by a normal variable with mean 61.3 minutes. Calculate the standard deviation of T if 5% of discs have playing times greater than 78 minutes.   (OCR)

13 The random variable Y has the distribution $N(\mu, 16)$. Given that $P(Y > 57.50) = 0.1401$, find the value of μ giving your answer correct to 2 decimal places.   (OCR)

14 The area that can be painted using one litre of Luxibrite paint is normally distributed with mean 13.2 m^2 and standard deviation 0.197 m^2. The corresponding figures for one litre of Maxigloss paint are 13.4 m^2 and 0.343 m^2. It is required to paint an area of 12.9 m^2. Find which paint gives the greater probability that one litre will be sufficient, and obtain this probability.   (OCR)

15 The time required to complete a certain car journey has been found from experience to have mean 2 hours 20 minutes and standard deviation 15 minutes.

(a) Use a normal model to calculate the probability that, on one day chosen at random, the journey requires between 1 hour 50 minutes and 2 hours 40 minutes.

(b) It is known that delays occur rarely on this journey, but that when they do occur they are lengthy. Give a reason why this information suggests that a normal distribution might not be a good model.   (OCR)

16 The weights of eggs, measured in grams, can be modelled by an $X \sim N(85.0, 36)$ distribution. Eggs are classified as large, medium or small, where a large egg weighs 90.0 grams or more, and 25% of eggs are classified as small. Calculate

(a) the percentage of eggs which are classified as large,

(b) the maximum weight of a small egg.   (OCR)

17 The random variable X is normally distributed with standard deviation 3.2. The probability that X is less than 74 is 0.8944.

(a) Find the mean of X.

(b) Fifty independent observations of X are made. Find the expected number of observations that are less than 74.

(c) Three independent observations of X are made. What is the probability that exactly one observation is less than 74?   (OCR, adapted)

18 A machine cuts a very long plastic tube into short tubes. The length of the short tubes is modelled by a normal distribution with mean m and standard deviation 0.25 cm. The value of m can be set by adjusting the machine. Find the value of m for which the probability is 0.1 that the length of a short tube, picked at random, is less than 6.50 cm. The machine is adjusted so that $m = 6.40$, the standard deviation remaining unchanged. Find the probability that a tube picked at random is between 6.30 and 6.60 cm long.   (OCR)

19 The random variable X is normally distributed with mean and standard deviation both equal to a.

Given that $P(X < 3) = 0.2$, find the value of a. (OCR)

20 A university classifies its degrees as Class 1, Class 2.1, Class 2.2, Class 3, Pass and Fail. Degrees are awarded on the basis of marks which may be taken as continuous and modelled by a normal distribution with mean 57.0 and standard deviation 10.0. In a particular year, the lowest mark for a Class 1 degree was 70.0, the lowest mark for a Class 2.1 degree was 60.0, and 4.5% of students failed. Calculate

(a) the percentage of students who obtained a Class 1 degree,

(b) the percentage of students who obtained a Class 2.1 degree,

(c) the lowest possible mark for a student who obtained a Pass degree. (OCR)

21 The mass of grapes sold per day in a supermarket can be modelled by a normal distribution. It is found that, over a long period, the mean mass sold per day is 35.0 kg, and that, on average, less than 15.0 kg are sold on one day in twenty.

(a) Show that the standard deviation of the mass of grapes sold per day is 12.2 kg, correct to 3 significant figures.

(b) Calculate the probability that, on a day chosen at random, more than 53.0 kg are sold. (OCR)

22 The random variable X is normally distributed with mean μ and variance σ^2. It is given that $P(X > 81.89) = 0.010$ and $P(X < 27.77) = 0.100$. Calculate the values of μ and σ. (OCR)

23 Two firms, Goodline and Megadelay, produce delay lines for use in communications. The delay time for a delay line is measured in nanoseconds (ns).

(a) The delay times for the output of Goodline may be modelled by a normal distribution with mean 283 ns and standard deviation 8 ns. What is the probability that the delay time of one line selected at random from Goodline's output is between 275 and 286 ns?

(b) It is found that, in the output of Megadelay, 10% of the delay times are less than 274.6 ns and 7.5% are more than 288.2 ns. Again assuming a normal distribution, calculate the mean and standard deviation of the delay times for Megadelay. Give your answers correct to 3 significant figures. (OCR)

24 State conditions under which a binomial probability model can be well approximated by a normal model.

X is a random variable with the distribution $X \sim B(12, 0.42)$.

(a) Anne uses the binomial distribution to calculate the probability that $X < 4$ and gives 4 significant figures in her answer. What answer should she get?

(b) Ben uses a normal distribution to calculate an approximation for the probability that $X < 4$ and gives 4 significant figures in his answer. What answer should he get?

(c) Given that Ben's working is correct, calculate the percentage error in his answer. (OCR)

25 The diameters of corks for wine bottles of a particular kind are normally distributed with mean 1.90 cm. In order to be acceptable, the diameter must be between 1.80 cm and 2.00 cm. The proportion of corks that are acceptable is 90%. Calculate the standard deviation of the diameters.

A sample of n corks is selected. Give a condition under which the number of acceptable corks in the sample can be modelled by a binomial distribution.

Assuming this condition holds,

(a) for the case $n = 6$, calculate the probability of obtaining exactly 5 acceptable corks,

(b) for the case $n = 80$, use a suitable approximation to estimate the probability that 70 or fewer corks will be acceptable. (OCR)

26 A large box contains many plastic syringes, but previous experience indicates that 10% of the syringes in the box are defective. 5 syringes are taken at random from the box. Use a binomial model to calculate, giving your answers correct to three decimal places, the probability that

(a) none of the 5 syringes is defective,

(b) at least 2 syringes out of the 5 are defective.

Discuss the validity of the binomial model in this context.

Instead of removing 5 syringes, 100 syringes are picked at random and removed. A normal distribution may be used to estimate the probability that at least 15 out of the 100 syringes are defective. Give a reason why it may be convenient to use a normal distribution to do this, and calculate the required estimate. (OCR)

27 On average my train is late on 45 journeys out of 100. Next week I shall be making 5 train journeys. Let X denote the number of times my train will be late.

(a) State one assumption which must be made for X to be modelled by a binomial distribution.

(b) Find the probability that my train will be late on all of the 5 journeys.

(c) Find the probability that my train will be late on 2 or more out of the 5 journeys.

Approximate your binomial model by a suitable normal model to estimate the probability that my train is late on 20 or more out of 50 journeys. (OCR)

28 It is estimated that, on average, one match in five in the Football League is drawn, and that one match in two is a home win.

(a) Twelve matches are selected at random. Calculate the probability that the number of drawn matches is

(i) exactly three, (ii) at least four.

(b) Ninety matches are selected at random. Use a suitable approximation to calculate the probability that between 13 and 20 (inclusive) of the matches are drawn.

(c) Twenty matches are selected at random. The random variables D and H are the numbers of drawn matches and home wins, respectively, in these matches. State, with a reason, which of D and H can be better approximated by a normal variable. (OCR)

29 The random variable Y is such that $Y \sim N(8, 25)$. Show that, correct to 3 decimal places, $P(|Y - 8| < 6.2) = 0.785$.

Three random observations of Y are made. Find the probability that exactly two observations will lie in the interval defined by $|Y - 8| < 6.2$.   (OCR)

30 Squash balls, dropped onto a concrete floor from a given point, rebound to heights which can be modelled by a normal distribution with mean 0.8 m and standard deviation 0.2 m. The balls are classified by height of rebound, in order of decreasing height, into these categories: Fast, Medium, Slow, Super-Slow and Rejected.

(a) Balls which rebound to heights between 0.65 m and 0.9 m are classified as Slow. Calculate the percentage of balls classified as Slow.

(b) Given that 9% of balls are classified as Rejected, calculate the maximum height of rebound of these balls.

(c) The percentages of balls classified as Fast and as Medium are equal. Calculate the minimum height of rebound of a ball classified as Fast, giving your answer correct to 2 decimal places.   (OCR)

3 The Poisson distribution

This chapter introduces a discrete probability distribution which is used for modelling random events. When you have completed it you should

- be able to calculate probabilities for the Poisson distribution both directly and by using tables of cumulative Poisson probabilities
- understand the relevance of the Poisson distribution to the distribution of random events
- be able to use the result that the mean and variance of a Poisson distribution are equal
- be able to use the Poisson distribution as an approximation to the binomial distribution where appropriate
- be able to use the normal distribution, with a continuity correction, as an approximation to the Poisson distribution where appropriate.

If you have not yet met the mathematical constant e in C3, then you could leave this chapter and tackle it between Chapters 4 and 5, or Chapters 5 and 6.

3.1 The Poisson probability formula

Situations often arise where the variable of interest is the number of occurrences of a particular event in a given interval of space or time. An example is given in Table 3.1. This shows the frequency of 0, 1, 2 etc. phone calls arriving at a switchboard in 100 consecutive time intervals of 5 minutes. In this case the 'event' is the arrival of a phone call and the 'given interval' is a time interval of 5 minutes.

Number of calls	0	1	2	3	4 or more
Frequency	71	23	4	2	0

Table 3.1. Frequency distribution of number of telephone calls in 5-minute intervals.

Some other examples are

- the number of cars passing a point on a motorway in a time interval of 1 minute,
- the number of misprints on each page of a book,
- the number of radioactive particles emitted by a radioactive source in a time interval of 1 second.

Further examples can be found in the practical activities in Section 3.4.

The probability distribution which is used to model these situations is called the **Poisson distribution** after the French mathematician and physicist Siméon-Denis Poisson (1781–1840). The distribution is defined by the probability formula

$$P(X = x) = e^{-\lambda} \frac{\lambda^x}{x!}, \qquad x = 0, 1, 2, \dots$$

This formula involves the mathematical constant e which you may have already met in module C3. If you have not, then it is enough for you to know at this stage that the approximate value of e is 2.718 and that powers of e can be found using your calculator. Check that you can use your calculator to show that $e^{-2} = 0.135\ldots$ and $e^{-0.1} = 0.904\ldots$

The method by which Poisson arrived at this formula will be outlined in Section 3.2.

This formula involves only one parameter, λ. (λ, pronounced 'lambda', is the Greek letter l.) You will see later that λ is the mean of the distribution. The notation for indicating that a random variable X has a Poisson distribution with mean λ is $X \sim \text{Po}(\lambda)$. Once λ is known you can calculate $P(X = 0)$, $P(X = 1)$ etc. Note that there is no upper limit on the value of X.

Example 3.1.1
The number of particles emitted per second by a radioactive source has a Poisson distribution with mean 5. Calculate the probabilities of

(a) 0,   (b) 1,   (c) 2,   (d) 3 or more

emissions in a time interval of 1 second.

(a) Let X be the random variable 'the number of particles emitted in 1 second'. Then $X \sim \text{Po}(5)$. Using the Poisson probability formula $P(X = x) = e^{-\lambda} \dfrac{\lambda^x}{x!}$ with $\lambda = 5$,

$$P(X = 0) = e^{-5} \frac{5^0}{0!} = 0.006737\ldots = 0.00674, \text{ correct to 3 significant figures.}$$

A reminder: $0! = 1$. See C2 Section 2.3.

(b) $P(X = 1) = e^{-5} \dfrac{5^1}{1!} = 0.03368\ldots = 0.0337$, correct to 3 significant figures.

(c) $P(X = 2) = e^{-5} \dfrac{5^2}{2!} = 0.08422\ldots = 0.0842$, correct to 3 significant figures.

(d) Since there is no upper limit on the value of X the probability of 3 or more emissions must be found by subtraction.

$$\begin{aligned} P(X \geqslant 3) &= 1 - P(X = 0) - P(X = 1) - P(X = 2) \\ &= 1 - 0.006737\ldots - 0.0337\ldots - 0.08422\ldots \\ &= 0.875, \text{ correct to 3 significant figures.} \end{aligned}$$

Example 3.1.2
The number of demands for taxis to a taxi firm is Poisson distributed with, on average, four demands every 30 minutes. Find the probabilities of

(a) no demand in 30 minutes,

(b) 1 demand in 1 hour,

(c) fewer than 2 demands in 15 minutes.

(a) Let X be the random variable 'the number of demands in a 30-minute interval'. Then $X \sim \text{Po}(4)$. Using the Poisson formula with $\lambda = 4$,

$$P(X = 0) = e^{-4}\frac{4^0}{0!} = 0.0183, \text{ correct to 3 significant figures.}$$

(b) Let Y be the random variable 'the number of demands in a 1-hour interval'. As the time interval being considered has changed from 30 minutes to 1 hour, you must change the value of λ to equal the mean for this new time interval, that is to 8, giving $Y \sim \text{Po}(8)$. Using the Poisson formula with $\lambda = 8$,

$$P(Y = 1) = e^{-8}\frac{8^1}{1!} = 0.00268, \text{ correct to 3 significant figures.}$$

(c) Again the time interval has been altered. Now the appropriate value for λ is 2. Let W be the number of demands in 15 minutes. Then $W \sim \text{Po}(2)$.

$$P(W < 2) = P(W = 0) + P(W = 1) = e^{-2}\frac{2^0}{0!} + e^{-2}\frac{2^1}{1!} = 0.406,$$

correct to 3 significant figures.

You can often simplify the calculation of Poisson probabilities by using cumulative probability tables, similar to those which you met for the binomial distribution in S1. These tables give $P(X \leqslant x)$ for different values of λ. You will find cumulative Poisson probability tables on pages 174–7 of this book for values of λ up to 19. Your calculator may give individual and cumulative Poisson probabilities.

Example 3.1.3

The number of organic particles suspended in a volume V ml of water from a particular pond follows a Poisson distribution with mean $0.2V$. Using tables or a calculator, find the probability that

(a) a volume of 50 ml contains fewer than 8 particles,

(b) a volume of 30 ml contains more than 2 particles,

(c) a volume of 10 ml contains 3 particles,

(d) the value of x such that the probability that there are more than x particles in a volume of 80 ml is 0.2577.

(a) For $V = 50$, $\lambda = 0.2 \times 50 = 10$. Note first that $P(X < 8) = P(X \leqslant 7)$. Then, From the table on page 177, $P(X \leqslant 7) = 0.2202 = 0.220$, correct to 3 significant figures.

(b) For $V = 30$, $\lambda = 0.2 \times 30 = 6$. Note that $P(X > 2) = 1 - P(X \leqslant 2)$. From the table on page 176, $1 - P(X \leqslant 2) = 1 - 0.0620 = 0.938$, correct to 3 significant figures.

(c) For $V = 10$, $\lambda = 0.2 \times 10 = 2$.

Using the probability formula $P(X = x) = e^{-\lambda}\frac{\lambda^x}{x!}$,

$$P(X = 3) = e^{-2}\frac{2^3}{3!} = 0.180, \text{ correct to 3 significant figures.}$$

Alternatively, using the cumulative probability tables,

$$P(X = 3) = P(X \leqslant 3) - P(X \leqslant 2) = 0.8571 - 0.6767$$
$$= 0.180, \text{ correct to 3 significant figures.}$$

(d) For $V = 80$, $\lambda = 0.2 \times 80 = 16$.

You require x such that $P(X > x) = 0.2577$. This means that

$$P(X \leqslant x) = 1 - 0.2577 = 0.7423.$$

From the table on page 177, $P(X \leqslant x) = 0.7423$ when $x = 18$.

Here is a summary of the results of this section.

> The **Poisson distribution** is used as a model for the number, X, of events in a given interval of space or time. It has the probability formula
>
> $$P(X = x) = e^{-\lambda}\frac{\lambda^x}{x!}, \qquad x = 0, 1, 2, \ldots,$$
>
> where λ is equal to the mean number of events in the given interval.
>
> The notation $X \sim \text{Po}(\lambda)$ indicates that X has a Poisson distribution with mean λ.

Some books use μ rather than λ to denote the parameter of a Poisson distribution.

Exercise 3A

1 The random variable T has a Poisson distribution with mean 3. Calculate
    (a) $P(T = 2)$,   (b) $P(T \leqslant 1)$,   (c) $P(T \geqslant 3)$.

2 Given that $U \sim \text{Po}(3.25)$, calculate
    (a) $P(U = 3)$,   (b) $P(U \leqslant 2)$,   (c) $P(U \geqslant 2)$.

3 The random variable W has a Poisson distribution with mean 2.4. Use the tables of cumulative Poisson probabilities to calculate
    (a) $P(W \leqslant 3)$,   (b) $P(W \geqslant 2)$,   (c) $P(W = 3)$.

4 Accidents on a busy urban motorway occur at a mean rate of 2 per week. Assuming that the number of accidents per week follows a Poisson distribution, calculate the probability that
    (a) there will be no accidents in a particular week,
    (b) there will be exactly 2 accidents in a particular week,
    (c) there will be fewer than 3 accidents in a given two-week period.

5 On average, 15 customers a minute arrive at the check-outs of a busy supermarket. Assuming that a Poisson distribution is appropriate, calculate

(a) the probability that no customers arrive at the check-outs in a given 10-second interval,

(b) the probability that more than 3 customers arrive at the check-outs in a 15-second interval,

(c) the number of customers, x, such that the probability that x or more customers arrive in a minute is 0.1805.

6 During April of this year, I received 15 telephone calls. Assuming that the number of telephone calls I receive in April of next year follows a Poisson distribution with the same mean number of calls per day, calculate the probability that

(a) on a given day in April next year I will receive no telephone calls,

(b) in a given 7-day week next April I will receive more than 3 telephone calls.

7 Assume that cars arrive at a motorway service area at a rate of 100 per hour and that a Poisson distribution is appropriate.

(a) What is the probability that during a 3-minute period no cars will arrive at the service area?

(b) What time interval is such that the probability is at least 0.25 that no car will arrive at the service area during that interval?

8* A radioactive source emits particles at an average rate of 1 per second. Assume that the number of emissions follows a Poisson distribution.

(a) Calculate the probability that 0 or 1 particle will be emitted in 4 seconds.

(b) The emission rate changes such that the probability of 0 or 1 emission in 4 seconds becomes 0.8. What is the new emission rate?

3.2   Modelling random events

The examples which you have already met in this chapter have assumed that the variable you are dealing with has a Poisson distribution. How can you decide whether the Poisson distribution is a suitable model if you are not told? The answer to this question can be found by considering the way in which the Poisson distribution is related to the binomial distribution in the situation where the number of trials is very large and the probability of success is very small.

Table 3.2 reproduces Table 3.1 giving the frequency distribution of phone calls in 100 5-minute intervals.

Number of calls	0	1	2	3	4 or more
Frequency	71	23	4	2	0

Table 3.2. Frequency distribution of number of telephone calls in 5-minute intervals.

If these calls were plotted on a time axis you might see something which looked like Fig. 3.3.

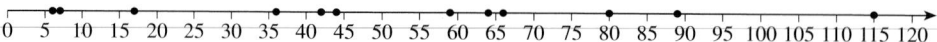

Fig. 3.3. Times of arrival of telephone calls at a switchboard.

The time axis has been divided into 5-minute intervals (only 24 are shown) and these intervals can contain 0, 1, 2 etc. phone calls. Suppose now that you assume that the phone calls occur *independently* of each other and *randomly* in time. In order to make the terms in italics clearer consider the following. Imagine the time axis is divided up into very small intervals of width δt (where δ is used in the same way as it is in pure mathematics). These intervals are so small that they never contain more than one call. If the calls are *random* then the probability that one of these intervals contains a call does not depend on which interval is considered; that is, it is constant. If the calls are *independent* then whether or not one interval contains a call has no effect on whether any other interval contains a call.

Looking at each interval of width δt in turn to see whether it contains a call or not gives a series of trials, each with two possible outcomes. This is just the kind of situation which is described by the binomial distribution. These trials also satisfy the conditions for the binomial distribution that they should be independent and have a fixed probability of success.

Suppose that a 5-minute interval contains n intervals of width δt. If there are, on average, λ calls every 5 minutes then the proportion of intervals which contain a call will be equal to $\dfrac{\lambda}{n}$. The probability, p, that one of these intervals contains a call is therefore equal to $\dfrac{\lambda}{n}$. Since δt is small, n is large and $\dfrac{\lambda}{n}$ is small. You can verify from Table 3.2 that the mean number of calls in a 5-minute interval is 0.37 so the distribution of X, the number of calls in a 5-minute interval is $B\left(n, \dfrac{0.37}{n}\right)$.

Finding P($X = 0$)   Using the binomial probability formula $P(X = x) = \dbinom{n}{x} p^x q^{n-x}$, you can calculate, for example, the probability of zero calls in a 5-minute interval as

$$P(X = 0) = \binom{n}{0}\left(\frac{0.37}{n}\right)^0\left(1 - \frac{0.37}{n}\right)^n.$$

In order to proceed you need a value for n. Recall that n must be large enough to ensure that the δt-intervals never contain more than one call. Suppose $n = 1000$. This gives

$$P(X = 0) = \binom{1000}{0}\left(\frac{0.37}{1000}\right)^0\left(1 - \frac{0.37}{1000}\right)^{1000} = 0.690\,68\ldots$$

However, even with such a large number of intervals there is still a chance that one of the δt-intervals could contain more than one call, so a larger value of n would be better. Try $n = 10\,000$ giving

$$P(X = 0) = \binom{10\,000}{0}\left(\frac{0.37}{10\,000}\right)^0\left(1 - \frac{0.37}{10\,000}\right)^{10\,000} = 0.690\,72\ldots$$

Explore for yourself what happens as you increase the value of n still further. You should find that your answers tend towards the value $0.690\,73\ldots$ This is equal to $e^{-0.37}$, which is the value the Poisson probability formula gives for $P(X = 0)$ when $\lambda = 0.37$.

This is an example of the general result that $\left(1 - \dfrac{x}{n}\right)^n$ tends to the value e^{-x} as n tends to infinity.

Provided that two events cannot occur simultaneously, allowing n to tend to infinity will ensure that not more than one event can occur in a δt-interval.

Finding P($X = 1$)   In a similar way you can find the probability of one call in a 5-minute interval by starting from the binomial formula and allowing n to increase as follows.

$$P(X = 1) = \binom{n}{1}\left(\frac{0.37}{n}\right)^1\left(1 - \frac{0.37}{n}\right)^{n-1} = 0.37\left(1 - \frac{0.37}{n}\right)^{n-1}.$$

Putting $n = 1000$,

$$P(X = 1) = 0.37\left(1 - \frac{0.37}{1000}\right)^{999} = 0.37 \times 0.690\,94\ldots = 0.255\,64\ldots$$

Putting $n = 10\,000$,

$$P(X = 1) = 0.37\left(1 - \frac{0.37}{10\,000}\right)^{9999} = 0.37 \times 0.690\,75\ldots = 0.255\,579\ldots$$

Again, you should find that as n increases the probability tends towards the value given by the Poisson probability formula,

$$P(X = 1) = 0.37 \times e^{-0.37} = 0.255\,57\ldots$$

Finding P($X = 2$), P($X = 3$), etc.   You could verify for yourself that similar results are obtained when the probabilities of $X = 2, 3$ etc. are calculated by a similar method. A spreadsheet program or a programmable calculator would be helpful.

The general result for $P(X = x)$ can be derived as follows. Starting with $X \sim B\left(n, \dfrac{\lambda}{n}\right)$.

$$P(X = x) = \binom{n}{x}\left(\frac{\lambda}{n}\right)^x\left(1 - \frac{\lambda}{n}\right)^{n-x}$$

$$= \frac{n(n-1)(n-2)\ldots(n-x+1)}{x!} \times \frac{\lambda^x}{n^x}\left(1 - \frac{\lambda}{n}\right)^{n-x}$$

$$= \frac{\lambda^x}{x!} \times \frac{n-1}{n} \times \frac{n-2}{n} \times \cdots \times \frac{n-x+1}{n} \times \left(1 - \frac{\lambda}{n}\right)^{n-x}.$$

Now consider what happens as n gets larger. The fractions $\dfrac{n-1}{n}$, $\dfrac{n-2}{n}$ etc. tend towards 1. The term $\left(1 - \dfrac{\lambda}{n}\right)^{n-x}$ can be approximated by $\left(1 - \dfrac{\lambda}{n}\right)^n$ since x, a constant, is negligible compared with n and, as you have seen previously, this tends towards $e^{-\lambda}$. Combining these results gives

$$P(X = x) = \frac{\lambda^x}{x!}e^{-\lambda}.$$

The assumptions made in the derivation above give the conditions that a set of events must satisfy for the Poisson distribution to be a suitable model. They are listed below.

> The Poisson distribution is a suitable model for events which
> - occur randomly in space or time,
> - occur singly, that is events cannot occur simultaneously,
> - occur independently, and
> - occur at a constant rate, that is the mean number of events in a given time interval is proportional to the size of the interval.

Example 3.2.1

For each of the following situations state whether the Poisson distribution would provide a suitable model. Give reasons for your answers.

(a) The number of cars per minute in the outside lane passing under a motorway bridge between 10 a.m. and 11 a.m. when the traffic is flowing freely.

(b) The number of cars per minute entering a city-centre carpark on a busy Saturday between 9 a.m. and 10 a.m.

(c) The number of particles emitted per second by a radioactive source.

(d) The number of currants in Chelsea buns sold at a particular baker's shop on a particular day.

(e) The number of blood cells per ml in a dilute solution of blood which has been left standing for 24 hours.

(f) The number of blood cells per ml in a dilute solution of blood which has been well shaken.

    (a) The Poisson distribution should be a good model for this situation as the appropriate conditions should be met: since the traffic is flowing freely the cars should pass independently and at random; it is not possible for cars to pass simultaneously; the average rate of traffic flow is likely to be constant over the time interval given.

    (b) The Poisson distribution is unlikely to be a good model: if it is a busy day the cars will be queuing for the carpark and so they will not be moving independently.

    (c) The Poisson distribution should be a good model provided that the time period over which the measurements are made is much longer than the lifetime of the source: this will ensure that the average rate at which the particles are emitted is constant. Radioactive particles are emitted independently and at random and, for practical purposes, they can be considered to be emitted singly.

    (d) The Poisson distribution should be a good model provided that the following conditions are met: all the buns are prepared from the same mixture so that the average number of currants per bun is constant; the mixture is well stirred so that the currants are distributed at random; the currants do not stick to each other or touch each other so that they are positioned independently.

(e) The Poisson distribution will not be a good model because the blood cells will have tended to sink towards the bottom of the solution. Thus the average number of blood cells per ml will be greater at the bottom than the top.

(f) If the solution has been well shaken the Poisson distribution will be a suitable model. The blood cells will be distributed at random and at a constant average rate. Since the solution is dilute the blood cells will not be touching and so will be positioned independently.

3.3   The variance of a Poisson distribution

In Section 3.2 the Poisson probability formula was deduced from the distribution of $X \sim B\left(n, \dfrac{\lambda}{n}\right)$ by considering what happens as n tends to infinity. The variance of a Poisson distribution can be obtained by considering what happens to the variance of the distribution of $X \sim B\left(n, \dfrac{\lambda}{n}\right)$ as n gets very large. In module S1 you met the formula $\text{Var}(X) = npq$ for the variance of a binomial distribution. Substituting for p and q gives

$$\text{Var}(X) = n \times \frac{\lambda}{n}\left(1 - \frac{\lambda}{n}\right) = \lambda\left(1 - \frac{\lambda}{n}\right).$$

As n gets very large the term $\dfrac{\lambda}{n}$ tends to zero. This gives λ as the variance of the Poisson distribution. Thus the Poisson distribution has the interesting property that its mean and variance are equal.

> For a Poisson distribution $X \sim \text{Po}(\lambda)$
>
> $$\text{mean} = \mu = E(X) = \lambda,$$
> $$\text{variance} = \sigma^2 = \text{Var}(X) = \lambda.$$
>
> The mean and variance of a Poisson distribution are equal.

The equality of the mean and variance of a Poisson distribution gives a simple way of testing whether a variable might be modelled by a Poisson distribution. The mean of the data in Table 3.2 has already been used and is equal to 0.37. You can verify that the variance of these data is 0.4331. These values, which are both 0.4 to 1 decimal place, are sufficiently close to indicate that the Poisson distribution may be a suitable model for the number of phone calls in a 5-minute interval. This is confirmed by Table 3.4 below, which shows that the relative frequencies calculated from Table 3.2 are close to the theoretical probabilities found by assuming that $X \sim \text{Po}(0.37)$. (The values for the probabilities are given to 3 decimal places and the value for $P(X \geqslant 4)$ has been found by subtraction.)

Note that if the mean and variance are not approximately equal then the Poisson distribution is not a suitable model. If they are equal then the Poisson distribution may be a suitable model, but is not necessarily so.

x	Frequency	Relative frequency	$P(X = x)$
0	71	0.71	$e^{-0.37} = 0.691$
1	23	0.23	$e^{-0.37}0.37 = 0.256$
2	4	0.04	$e^{-0.37}\dfrac{0.37^2}{2!} = 0.047$
3	2	0.02	$e^{-0.37}\dfrac{0.37^3}{3!} = 0.006$
≥ 4	0	0	0
Totals	100	1	1

Table 3.4. Comparison of theoretical Poisson probabilities and relative frequencies for the data in Table 3.2.

Exercise 3B

1 For each of the following situations, say whether or not the Poisson distribution might provide a suitable model.

(a) The number of raindrops that fall into a milk bottle left on a doorstep for collection in a period of 1 minute during a shower.

(b) The number of occupants of vehicles that pass a given point on a busy road in 1 minute.

(c) The number of flaws in a given length of material of constant width.

(d) The number of claims made to an insurance company in a month.

2 Some conservationists recorded the number of hedgehogs found run over by cars on a country lane for 13 weeks. The weekly figures were

$$8 \quad 9 \quad 7 \quad 11 \quad 5 \quad 4 \quad 12 \quad 10 \quad 7 \quad 6 \quad 11 \quad 3 \quad 11$$

(a) Calculate the mean and variance of these data and comment on whether the Poisson distribution might be a suitable model.

(b) Use the Poisson distribution with the mean found in part (a) to calculate the probability of 7 or more hedgehogs being found run over in a given week.

(c) A bypass was built reducing the probability of 7 or more hedgehogs being run over to 0.0244. Use tables to find the new mean number of hedgehogs run over per week.

3 The number of telephone calls I received during the month of March is summarised in the table.

Number of telephone phone calls received per day (x)	0	1	2	3	4
Number of days	9	12	5	4	1

(a) Calculate the relative frequency for each of $x = 0, 1, 2, 3, 4$.

(b) Calculate the mean and variance of the distribution. (Give your answers correct to 2 decimal places.) Comment on the suitability of the Poisson distribution as a model for this situation.

(c) Use the Poisson distribution to calculate P($X = x$), for $x = 0$, 1, 2, 3 and 4 using the mean calculated in part (b).

(d) Compare the theoretical probabilities and the relative frequencies found in part (a). Do these figures support the comment made in part (b)?

4 The number of goals scored by a football team during a season gave the following results.

Number of goals per match	0	1	2	3	4	5	6	7
Number of matches	5	19	9	5	2	1	0	1

Calculate the mean and variance of the distribution and the relative frequencies and theoretical probabilities, assuming a Poisson distribution with the same mean. Do you think, in the light of your calculations, that the Poisson distribution provides a suitable model for the number of goals scored per match?

5 The number of cars passing a given point in 100 10-second intervals was observed as follows.

Number of cars	0	1	2	3	4	5
Number of intervals	47	33	16	3	0	1

Do you think that a Poisson distribution is a suitable model for these data?

3.4 Practical activities

1 Traffic flow   In order to carry out this activity you will need to make your observations on a road where the traffic flows freely, preferably away from traffic lights, junctions etc. The best results will be obtained if the rate of flow is one to two cars per minute on average.

(a) Count the number of cars which pass each minute over a period of one hour and assemble your results into a frequency table.

(b) Calculate the mean and variance of the number of cars per minute. Comment on your results.

(c) Compare the relative frequencies with the Poisson probabilities calculated by taking λ equal to the mean of your data. Comment on the agreement between the two sets of values.

2 Random rice   For this activity you need a chessboard and a few tablespoonfuls of uncooked rice.

(a) Scatter the rice 'at random' on to the chessboard. This can be achieved by holding your hand about 50 cm above the board and moving it around as you drop the rice. Drop sufficient rice to result in two to three grains of rice per square on average.

(b) Count the number of grains of rice in each square and assemble your results into a frequency table.

(c) Calculate the mean and variance of the number of grains per square. If these are reasonably close then go on to part (d). If not, see if you can improve your technique for scattering rice 'at random'!

(d) Compare the relative frequencies with the Poisson probabilities calculated taking λ equal to the mean of your data. Comment on the agreement between the two sets of values.

3 Background radiation   For this activity you need a Geiger counter with a digital display. When the Geiger counter is switched on it will record the background radiation.

(a) Prepare a table in which you can record the reading on the Geiger counter every 5 seconds for total time of 5 minutes.

(b) Switch the counter on and record the reading every 5 seconds.

(c) Plot a graph of the reading on the counter against time taking values every 30 seconds. Does this graph suggest that the background rate is constant?

(d) The number of counts in each 5 second interval can be found by taking the difference between successive values in the table which you made in parts (a) and (b). Find these values and assemble them into a frequency table.

(e) Calculate the mean and variance of the number of counts per 5 seconds. Comment on your results.

(f) Compare the relative frequencies with the Poisson probabilities calculated by taking λ equal to the mean of your data. Comment on the agreement between the two sets of values.

4 Football goals   For this activity you need details of the results of the football matches in the FA Carling Premiership and Nationwide First, Second and Third Divisions for one particular week.

(a) Make a frequency table of the number of goals scored by each team.

(b) Calculate the mean and variance of the number of goals scored.

(c) Compare the relative frequencies with the Poisson probabilities calculated by taking λ equal to the mean of your data.

(d) Discuss whether the variable 'number of goals scored by each team' satisfies the conditions required for the Poisson distribution to be a suitable model. Comment on the results you obtained in part (b) and part (c) in the light of your answer.

3.5   The Poisson distribution as an approximation to the binomial distribution

In certain circumstances it is possible to use the Poisson distribution rather than the binomial distribution in order to make the calculation of probabilities easier.

Consider items coming off a production line. Suppose that some of the items are defective and that defective items occur at random with a constant probability of 0.03. The items are packed in boxes of 200 and you want to find the probability that a box contains two or fewer defective items. The number, X, of defective items in box has a binomial distribution since there are

- a fixed number (200) of items in each box,
- each item is either defective or not,
- the probability of a defective item is constant and equal to 0.03,
- defective items occur independently of each other.

This means that $X \sim \mathrm{B}(200, 0.03)$. The probability that a box contains two or fewer defective items can be calculated exactly using the binomial distribution as follows.

$$P(X \leqslant 2) = P(X = 0) + P(X = 1) + P(X = 2)$$
$$= 0.97^{200} + \binom{200}{1}0.97^{199}0.03 + \binom{200}{2}0.97^{198}0.03^2$$
$$= 0.002\,261\ldots + 0.013\,987\ldots + 0.043\,042\ldots$$
$$= 0.0592, \text{ correct to 3 significant figures.}$$

This binomial distribution has a large value of n and a small value of p. This is exactly the situation which applied in Section 3.2 when the Poisson distribution was treated as a limiting case of the binomial distribution. In these circumstances, that is large n and small p, the probabilities can be calculated approximately using a Poisson distribution whose mean is equal to the mean of the binomial distribution. The mean of the binomial distribution is given by $np = 200 \times 0.03 = 6$ (see S1 Section 8.3). Using $X \sim \mathrm{Po}(6)$ gives for the required probability

$$P(X \leqslant 2) = P(X = 0) + P(X = 1) + P(X = 2)$$
$$= e^{-6} + e^{-6}6 + e^{-6}\frac{6^2}{2!}$$
$$= 0.002\,478\ldots + 0.014\,872\ldots + 0.044\,617\ldots$$
$$= 0.0620, \text{ correct to 3 significant figures.}$$

Alternatively the answer to the second calculation could be found by using cumulative Poisson probability tables (see page 176).

If you follow though the calculations using a calculator you will find that the calculation using the Poisson distribution is much easier to perform. Using the Poisson distribution only gives an approximate answer. In this case the answers for the individual probabilities and the value for $P(X \leqslant 2)$ agree to 1 significant figure. This is often good enough for practical purposes.

It is important to remember that the approximate method using the Poisson distribution will only give reasonable agreement with the exact method using the binomial distribution when n is large and p is small. The larger n and the smaller p, the better the agreement between the two answers. In practice you should not use the approximate method unless n is large and p is small. A useful rule of thumb is that $n > 50$ and $np < 5$.

> If $X \sim \mathrm{B}(n,\ p)$, and if $n > 50$ and $np < 5$, then X can reasonably be approximated by the Poisson distribution $W \sim \mathrm{Po}(np)$. The larger n and the smaller p, the better the approximation.

Example 3.5.1

Calculate the following probabilities, using a suitable approximation where appropriate.

(a) $P(X < 3)$ given that $X \sim B(100, 0.02)$.

(b) $P(X < 10)$ given that $X \sim B(60, 0.3)$.

(c) $P(X < 2)$ given that $X \sim B(10, 0.01)$.

(a) Here n is large (that is, greater than 50) and p is small, which suggests that a Poisson approximation may be appropriate. As a check calculate $np = 100 \times 0.02 = 2$. Since $np < 5$ the Poisson approximation, $W \sim Po(2)$ may be used. From the cumulative Poisson probability tables

$$P(W < 3) = P(W \leqslant 2) = 0.6767.$$

(b) Here n is still large (that is greater than 50) but p is not small enough to make $np\,(= 60 \times 0.03 = 18)$ less than 5. However $np\,(= 18)$ and $nq\,(= 60 \times 0.7 = 42)$ are both greater than 5 so the normal approximation to the binomial distribution, which you met in Section 2.8, may be used. The mean of the binomial distribution is 18 and the variance is $npq = 60 \times 0.3 \times 0.7 = 12.6$, so $X \sim B(60, 0.3)$ is approximated by $V \sim N(18, 12.6)$ with a continuity correction.

$$P(X < 10) = P(V \leqslant 9.5)$$
$$= P\left(Z \leqslant \frac{9.5 - 18}{\sqrt{12.6}}\right)$$
$$= P(Z \leqslant -2.395)$$
$$= 1 - \Phi(2.395)$$
$$= 1 - 0.9917$$
$$= 0.008, \text{ correct to 3 decimal places.}$$

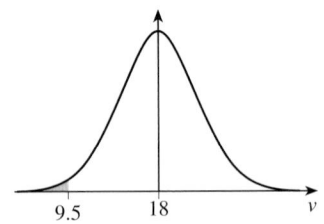

(c) Here p is small but n is not large enough to use the Poisson approximation. The normal approximation should not be used either since $np = 10 \times 0.01 = 0.1$ is not greater than 5. In fact it is not appropriate to use an approximation at all. The required probability must be calculated using the binomial probability formula as follows.

$$P(X < 2) = P(X = 0) + P(X = 1)$$
$$= \binom{10}{0}0.99^{10}0.01^0 + \binom{10}{1}0.99^9 0.01^1$$
$$= 0.9043\ldots + 0.091\,35\ldots$$
$$= 0.996, \text{ correct to 3 significant figures.}$$

Exercise 3C

1 (a) There are 1000 pupils in a school. Find the probability that exactly 3 of them have their birthdays on January 1st, by using

(i) $B\left(1000, \dfrac{1}{365}\right)$,   (ii) $Po\left(\dfrac{1000}{365}\right)$.

(b) There are 5000 students in a university. Calculate the probability that exactly 15 of them have their birthdays on January 1st, by using

    (i) a suitable binomial distribution,   (ii) a suitable Poisson approximation.

For the rest of the exercise, use, where appropriate, the Poisson approximation to the binomial distribution.

2 If $X \sim B(300, 0.004)$ find

    (a) $P(X < 3)$,   (b) $P(X > 4)$.

3 The probability that a patient has a particular disease is 0.008. One day 80 people go to their doctor.

    (a) What is the probability that exactly 2 of them have the disease?

    (b) What is the probability that 3 or more of them have the disease?

4 The probability of success in an experiment is 0.01. Find the probability of 4 or more successes in 100 trials of the experiment.

5 When eggs are packed in boxes the probability that an egg is broken is 0.008.

    (a) What is the probability that in a box of 6 eggs there are no broken eggs?

    (b) Calculate the probability that in a consignment of 500 eggs fewer than 4 eggs are broken.

6 (a) The probability of winning exactly £10 in a lottery is 0.01765. If I buy 100 tickets, what is the probability that I do not win a £10 prize?

    (b) The probability of winning the jackpot in the lottery is 7.15×10^{-8}. How many tickets do I need to buy to have at least a 10% chance of winning the jackpot?

3.6 The normal distribution as an approximation to the Poisson distribution

Example 3.5.1(b) gave a reminder of the method for using the normal distribution as an approximation to the binomial distribution. The normal distribution may be used in a similar way as an approximation to the Poisson distribution provided that the mean of the Poisson distribution is sufficiently large.

Fig. 3.5 shows why such an approximation is valid: as the value of λ increases, the shape of the Poisson distribution becomes more like the characteristic bell shape of the normal distribution.

> You can use a spreadsheet to draw these diagrams for yourself.

Since the variance of a Poisson distribution is equal to its mean, both the mean and variance of the normal distribution which is used as an approximation are taken to be equal to λ. Just as for the normal approximation to the binomial distribution, a continuity correction is needed because a discrete distribution is being approximated by a continuous one. As a

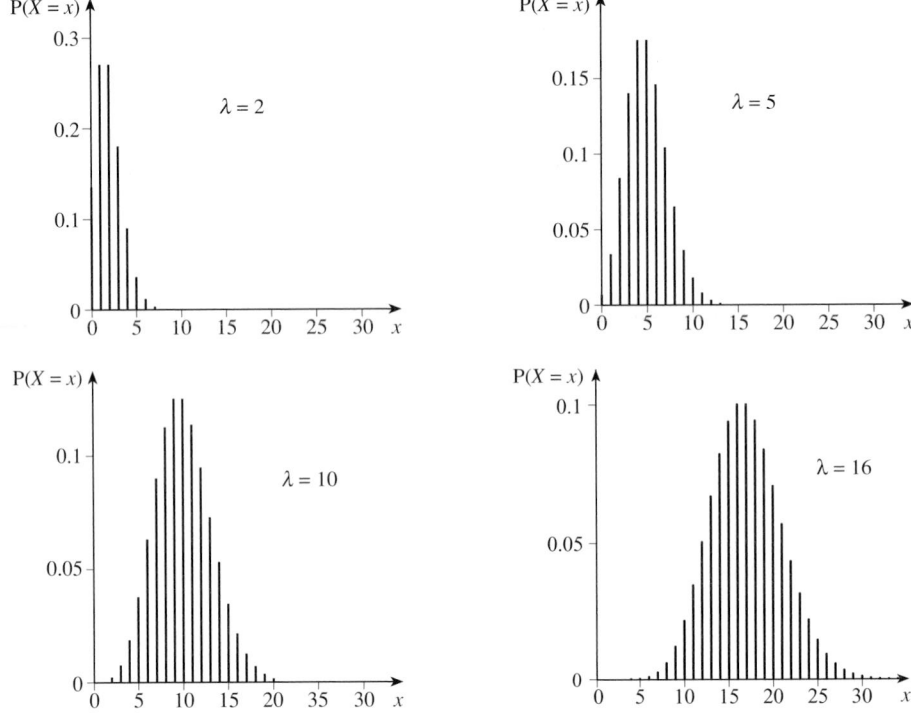

Fig. 3.5. Bar charts showing the Poisson distribution for different values of λ.

rule-of-thumb the normal approximation to the Poisson distribution should only be used if $\lambda > 15$. You can see from the last diagram in Fig. 3.5 that this looks very reasonable.

> If $X \sim \text{Po}(\lambda)$ and if $\lambda > 15$ then X may reasonably be approximated by the normal distribution $Y \sim \text{N}(\lambda, \lambda)$.
>
> A continuity correction must be applied.
>
> The larger λ the better the approximation.

Example 3.6.1

It is thought that the number of serious accidents, X, in a time interval of t weeks, on a given stretch of motorway, can be modelled by a Poisson distribution with mean $0.4t$. Find the probability of

(a) one or fewer accidents in a randomly chosen fortnight,

(b) 12 or more accidents in a randomly chosen year.

   (a) For a time interval of one fortnight, $\lambda = 0.4 \times 2 = 0.8$.

   From the cumulative Poisson probability tables $P(X \leqslant 1) = 0.8088$.

Note that, since $\lambda \leqslant 15$, the normal approximation is not appropriate.

(b) For a time interval of 1 year, $\lambda = 0.4 \times 52 = 20.8$.

Since $\lambda > 15$, a normal approximation is appropriate. $X \sim \text{Po}(20.8)$ is approximated by $Y \sim \text{N}(20.8, \ 20.8)$, with a continuity correction.

$$P(X \geqslant 12) = P(Y > 11.5) = P\left(Z > \frac{11.5 - 20.8}{\sqrt{20.8}}\right) = P(Z > -2.039)$$
$$= P(Z \leqslant 2.039) = \Phi(2.039)$$
$$= 0.9792 = 0.979, \text{ correct to 3 decimal places.}$$

Exercise 3D

Use the normal approximation to the Poisson distribution, where appropriate.

1 If $X \sim \text{Po}(30)$ find

(a) $P(X \leqslant 31)$, (b) $P(35 \leqslant X \leqslant 40)$, (c) $P(29 < X \leqslant 32)$.

2 Accidents occur in a factory at an average rate of 5 per month. Find the probabilities that

(a) there will be fewer than 4 in a month, (b) there will be exactly 62 in a year.

3 The number of accidents on a motorway follows a Poisson distribution with a mean of 8 per week. Find the probability that in a year (assumed to be 52 weeks) there will be fewer than 400 accidents.

4 Daisies grow at random positions in a lawn at a mean rate of 8 per m^2. The lawn is a rectangle of length 8 m and width 5 m. Calculate the probability that there are more than 350 daisies growing in the lawn.

5 Water taken from a river contains on average 16 bacteria per ml. Assuming a Poisson distribution find the probability that 5 ml of the water contains

(a) from 65 to 85 (inclusive) bacteria, (b) exactly 80 bacteria.

6 A small telesales firm receives an average of 40 telephone calls an hour. The number of calls follows a Poisson distribution.

(a) Find the probability that there are from 35 to 50 calls (inclusive) in a given hour.

(b) Find the probability that there are exactly 42 calls in a given hour.

7 Given that $X \sim \text{Po}(50)$ and $P(X > x) \leqslant 0.05$, use a normal approximation with a continuity correction to find the minimum integral value of x.

8 Sales of dog-biscuits bought in a shop during a week follow a Poisson distribution with mean 100. How many dog-biscuits should be kept in stock to be at least 99% certain that supply will be able to meet demand?

Miscellaneous exercise 3

1 Between the hours of 0800 and 2200, cars arrive at a certain petrol station at an average rate of 0.8 per minute. Assuming that arrival times are random, calculate the probability that at least 2 cars will arrive during a particular minute between 0800 and 2200. (OCR)

2 The proportion of patients who suffer an allergic reaction to a certain drug used to treat a particular medical condition is assumed to be 0.045.

Each of a random sample of 90 patients with the condition is given the drug and X is the number who suffer an allergic reaction. Assuming independence, explain why X can be modelled approximately by a Poisson distribution and calculate $P(X = 4)$. (OCR)

3 The number of night calls to a fire station in a small town can be modelled by a Poisson distribution with mean 4.2 per night. Find the probability that on a particular night there will be 3 or more calls to the fire station.

State what needs to be assumed about the calls to the fire station in order to justify a Poisson model. (OCR)

4 A shop sells two brands of television sets. The average number of Kubla sets sold per week is 1.8, and the corresponding figure for Xanadu sets is 2.7. Sales take place independently at random times.

(a) Find the probability that exactly 2 Kubla sets are sold in a given week.

(b) Find the probability that exactly 4 Xanadu sets are sold in a given two-week period. (OCR, adapted)

5 A householder wishes to sow part of her garden with grass seed. She scatters seed randomly so that the number of seeds falling on any particular region is a random variable having a Poisson distribution, with its mean proportional to the area of the region. The part of the garden that she intends to sow has area 50 m^2 and she estimates that she will sow 10^6 seeds. Calculate the expected number of seeds falling on a region, R, of area 1 cm^2, and show that the probability that no seeds fall on R is 0.135, correct to three significant figures.

The number of seeds falling on R is denoted by X. Find the probability that either $X = 0$ or $X > 4$.

The number of seeds falling on a region of area 100 cm^2 is denoted by Y. Using a normal approximation, find $P(175 \leqslant Y \leqslant 225)$. (OCR)

6 It is given that 93% of children in the UK have been immunised against whooping cough. The number of children in a random sample of 60 children who have been immunised is X, and the number not immunised is Y. State, with justification, which of X or Y has a distribution which can be approximated by a Poisson distribution.

Using a Poisson approximation, estimate the probability that at least 58 children from the sample have been immunised against whooping cough. (OCR)

7 A firm investigated the number of employees suffering injuries whilst at work. The results recorded below were obtained for a 52-week period.

Number of employees injured in a week	0	1	2	3	4 or more
Number of weeks	31	17	3	1	0

Give reasons why one might expect this distribution to approximate to a Poisson distribution. Evaluate the mean and variance of the data and explain why this gives further evidence in favour of a Poisson distribution.

Using the calculated value of the mean, find the theoretical frequencies of a Poisson distribution for the number of weeks in which 0, 1, 2, 3, 4 or more employees were injured.   (OCR)

8 Analysis of the scores in football matches in a local league suggests that the total number of goals scored in a randomly chosen match may be modelled by the Poisson distribution with parameter 2.7. The number of goals scored in different matches are independent of one another.

(a) Find the probability that a match will end with no goals scored.

(b) Find the probability that 4 or more goals will be scored in a match.

One Saturday afternoon, 11 matches are played in the league.

(c) State the expected number of matches in which no goals are scored giving your answer to the nearest whole number.

(d) Find the probability that there are goals scored in all 11 matches.

(e) State the distribution for the total number of goals scored in the 11 matches. Using a suitable approximating distribution, or otherwise, find the probability that more than 30 goals are scored in total.   (MEI)

9 The discrete random variable X has probability distribution as shown in the table below, where p is a constant.

x	0	1	2	3
$P(X = x)$	p	$\frac{1}{2}p$	$\frac{1}{4}p$	$\frac{1}{20}p$

Show that $p = \frac{5}{9}$.

One hundred independent observations of X are made, and the random variable Y denotes the number of occasions on which $X = 3$. Explain briefly why the distribution of Y may be approximated by a suitable Poisson distribution, and state the mean of this Poisson distribution.

Find $P(Y = 2)$ and $P(Y \geqslant 4)$, giving your answers to 3 significant figures.   (OCR)

10 Data files on computers have sizes measured in megabytes. When files are sent from one computer to another down a communications link, the number of errors has a Poisson distribution. On average, there is one error for every 10 megabytes of data.

(a) Find the probability that a 3 megabyte file is transmitted

  (i) without error,   (ii) with 2 or more errors.

(b) Show that a file which has a 95% chance of being transmitted without error is a little over half a megabyte in size.

A commercial organisation transmits 1000 megabytes of data per day.

(c) State how many errors per day they will incur on average.

  Using a suitable approximating distribution, show that the number of errors on any randomly chosen day is virtually certain to be between 70 and 130.   (MEI)

11 A manufacturer produces an integrated electronic unit which contains 36 separate pressure sensors. Due to difficulties in manufacture, it happens very often that not all the sensors in a unit are operational. 100 units are tested and the number N of pressure sensors which function correctly are distributed according to the table.

N	36	35	34	33	32	31	30	29	28	$\leqslant 27$
Number of units	5	15	22	22	17	11	5	2	1	0

Calculate the mean number of sensors which are faulty.

The manufacturer only markets those units which have at least 32 of their 36 sensors operational. Estimate, using the Poisson distribution, the percentage of units which are not marketed.   (OCR)

12 An aircraft has 116 seats. The airline has found, from long experience, that on average 2.5% of people with tickets for a particular flight do not arrive for that flight. If the airline sells 120 seats for a particular flight determine, using a suitable approximation, the probability that more than 116 people arrive for that flight. Determine also the probability that there are empty seats on the flight.   (OCR)

4 Sampling

This chapter looks at the ways of selecting a sample from a population. When you have completed it you should

- understand the distinction between a sample and a population
- understand how to select a random sample from a population
- appreciate the benefits of choosing a random sample
- recognise that a sample mean can be a random variable and use the facts that $E(\overline{X}) = \mu$ and that $Var(\overline{X}) = \dfrac{\sigma^2}{n}$
- use the fact that $\overline{X}$ has a normal distribution if X has a normal distribution
- understand the meaning of the central limit theorem and be able to use it in calculations
- understand the term 'unbiased' with reference to an estimator of the mean or variance of a population.

4.1 Populations and samples

In statistics you usually wish to study a certain collection of individuals or items. The collection is known as the **population**. The term 'population' makes you think that the objects under consideration are living but this does not need to be true. For example, in S1 Section 1.1 you studied a set of data taken from the internet about breakfast cereals. Breakfast cereals were the population in this case. It would have been useful to have information about all breakfast cereals produced from anywhere in the world, but this is unrealistic since it would take too long to do such an investigation and it would cost too much to employ people to do such a large survey. Therefore a more realistic aim would be to take a subsection of the population. The term used to describe a subsection of a population is a **sample**.

Ideally a sample should have all the characteristics of the larger population. In other words, it should be a miniature version of the population with identical properties. Unfortunately it is almost impossible for any sample of any population to possess all the characteristics of the population. For example, in the investigation into breakfast cereals the information was collected in the US, so many breakfast cereals produced in the UK were not represented. It is quite likely that UK cereals have different properties from those produced and sold in the US but no information was available for UK cereals. Occasionally you may have the time, money and resources to investigate a population completely. Such an investigation is called a **census**. For example, the UK government does a census of the population of the UK once every ten years.

In general the selection of a sample is preferable to a census, because it takes too much time and costs too much money to do a census. There are several other reasons why you might prefer to take a sample rather than carry out a census.

- There are likely to be fewer recording errors when a sample is taken because it will probably involve fewer people. Those people are likely to have more time to carry out the measurement and recording for the survey because the size and complexity of the task will not be as great as with a census.

- The analysis of the results can be carried out more speedily.

- Sometimes measurement on an individual sample member may result in its destruction. For example, if you were recording the lifetimes of batteries of a certain brand, then every battery which was selected would be used until it no longer worked. If a census were done then every battery ever made by that manufacturer would be destroyed. It is unlikely that any manufacturer would be willing to agree to such a census!

When you take a sample from a population you want to try to ensure that your method of selection is done in such a way that no feature of the population is over-represented or under-represented in the sample.

For example, suppose you were selecting students from a secondary school with the aim of determining the mean height of all the students in the school. You would not choose a sample consisting entirely of Year 7 students because you would expect that such a sample would underestimate the true mean height. When a sampling method does over-represent or under-represent a feature of the population it is said to be **biased**. Any good selection method should try to reduce the chance of bias as far as possible.

The most common approach to the task of avoiding bias is to select a **random sample**.

> A random sample of size n is a sample chosen in such a way that each possible group of size n which could be taken from the population has the same chance of being picked.

4.2   Choosing a random sample

In order to select a random sample you need a list of all the members of the population. This list is called a **sampling frame**.

Suppose, for example, that the population consists of 450 different objects and that you want to take a random sample of size 20. You would assign each member of the population a unique identification number between 1 and 450 inclusive. You would then write each of the numbers between 1 and 450 on separate tickets and put them into a large hat. To obtain a random sample of size 20 you draw out 20 tickets from the hat, one after another, just as you would in a lottery competition. You must ensure that the tickets are thoroughly shuffled between each selection and you select the tickets without replacement.

The method described above is rather time-consuming if the size of the population is large and so it is more common to adopt alternative methods which use random number tables or the random number facility on a calculator or computer.

The random number facility on a calculator provides a decimal number between 0 and 1 given to a fixed number of decimal places. The number of decimal places given varies depending on the make of calculator. Some makes give the decimal with 10 digits after the decimal point. To get your calculator to produce this random decimal you will probably need to look for the command [rand] or [rnd] on your calculator. Each time you give the calculator this command it will produce a 10 digit decimal number between 0.00000 00000 and 0.99999 99999 inclusive. A different 10 digit decimal appears each time you use [rand]. Strictly speaking, the decimals produced in this way are not random because the calculator uses a system of rules to produce each decimal and if you knew the rules you could predict each decimal number. This means that the digits produced are not really independent of one another. For a truly random sequence of digits, the process which produces the digits should ensure that each digit in the sequence is equally likely to be any of the digits 0, 1, 2, . . . , 9, independently of any of the other digits. Nevertheless the sequences produced in this way do have some of the properties of random digits and they are usually considered to be acceptable as an alternative to a truly random sequence of digits.

In this book, random numbers will be written in blocks of five digits.

A **random number table** is a list of integers 0, 1, 2, . . . , 9 which is produced so that each digit is equally likely to appear in any position in the list. This list of digits has been taken from a set of random number tables.

$$24359 \quad 74025 \quad 90831 \quad 88610$$
$$14668 \quad 78292 \quad 51470 \quad 17505$$
$$40580 \quad 96418 \quad 73381 \quad 23112$$

Although the tables have been arranged in blocks of five digits, you can regard the digits as forming a single long list. The procedure for selecting a random sample is given below. The population size is 450 and each member of the population has a unique identification number between 1 and 450 inclusive.

- Choose some starting point in the tables at random (by using a dice or by some similar method). The digit in bold font shows the randomly chosen starting point.

$$24359 \quad 74025 \quad 90831 \quad 88610$$
$$14668 \quad 78292 \quad 5\mathbf{1}470 \quad 17505$$
$$40580 \quad 96418 \quad 73381 \quad 23112$$

- The population size is a three-digit number so read off the first three digits starting with the bold-faced digit, obtaining the number 147. This means that the first object in your sample is the object whose identification number is 147.

- Since the sample is to be of size 20, you need to choose 19 more objects from the population. Take the next block of three digits, 017, and select the object numbered 17. The third block is 505; this does not correspond to the identification number of any member of the population, so ignore it and move on to the next block, 405. Continue in this way, selecting blocks of three digits until you have a sample of 20 objects. If a three-digit block occurs more than once, ignore any later occurrence and move to the next block.

You may think that it is wasteful to discard all the blocks of digits which give numbers greater than 450. You can avoid this wastage by allocating a second block of three digits to each member of the population. Then 900 of the 1000 possible three-digit combinations would correspond to objects in your population. You cannot allocate the remaining 100 blocks to members of the population because that would give some members of the population a greater chance of being chosen than others. For a random sample every member of the population must have an equal chance of being selected.

There are many ways in which you can allocate two blocks to each member of the population. Ideally you want a way which makes it easy to identify which member of the population has been selected. Table 4.1 shows one possible way.

Number identifying population member	Random digit blocks
1	001 002
2	003 004
$\vdots$	$\vdots$
450	899 900

Table 4.1. Allocating random numbers to a population.

It is easy to identify which member of the population has been selected using the system in Table 4.1. For an even-numbered block you halve its value to find the appropriate member of the population and for an odd-numbered block you add one and then halve the number. For example, block 420 corresponds to object number $\frac{1}{2} \times 420 = 210$ and block 555 corresponds to object number $\frac{1}{2} \times (555 + 1) = 278$.

If the population size is greater than 1000 but less than 10 000 you can adapt the sampling method described by taking blocks containing four random digits rather than three.

It is easy to adjust the method if you are using the random number facility on a calculator. Suppose, for example, you obtain the random decimal 0.33936 62525. You can ignore the decimal point and treat the 10 digits as 10 random digits 33936 62525. After that you can use the method which was given for use with random number tables.

You should realise that even when you have taken a random sample you are not guaranteed that your sample will be representative. For example, upon selecting a random sample of 10 students from a secondary school with the aim of estimating their mean height you might find that every member of the sample is a Year 7 student. It is not very likely but it is certainly possible. The method of random sampling does not guarantee that the chosen sample is representative. What is guaranteed is that the **method of selection** is free from bias.

You should also realise that it is not always possible to select a random sample. You will recall that you need a sampling frame before you can select a random sample from a population. Sometimes this is not possible. For example, suppose that your population is all women in the UK with blonde hair. No list is available for this population so a random sample cannot be taken. Other, non-random methods have been devised to take sensible samples in such cases.

Example 4.2.1

An insurance company receives a large number of claims for storm damage. Following a spell of particularly stormy weather 42 claims are received on a single day. Sufficient staff are available to investigate only 6 of these. The claims are numbered 01 to 42 and several suggestions are made as to how the sample of 6 should be selected. Comment on each of the following methods, including an explanation of whether it would yield a random sample or not. In each case 6 claims are required.

(a) Choose the six largest claims.

(b) Select two-digit random numbers, ignoring 00 and any number greater than 42. When six distinct numbers have been obtained choose the corresponding claims.

(c) Select two-digit random numbers. Divide each one by 42, take the remainder, add 1 and choose the corresponding claims. (For example, if 44 is selected then claim number 03 would be chosen.)

(d) As part (c), but when selecting the original random numbers ignore 84 and over.

(e) Select a single digit at random, ignoring 0, 8 and 9. Choose the claim corresponding to this number and every seventh claim thereafter. (For example, if 3 is selected choose claims numbered 03, 10, 17, 24, 31, 38).   (OCR, adapted)

(a) Choosing the six largest claims would be a good idea if the insurance company has any doubts about the claims, as the company would not want to pay out large amounts if the claims were not valid. However, this method does not give every one of the 42 claims an equal chance of being chosen so it is not a random sampling method.

(b) This method will provide a random sample. However, many of the random digit pairs will be ignored since it is quite likely that some of the pairs will be greater than 42, so the method is inefficient and wasteful.

(c) This method will give results between 1 and 42 inclusive but not all of the numbers between 1 and 42 have an equal chance of being chosen. For example, claim 1 has three possible random digit pairs which correspond to it. They are 00, 42 and 84. Claim 30 only has two random digit pairs with which it corresponds, 29 and 71. Therefore the suggested method will not provide a random sample.

(d) The objection that some of the pairs will occur more often than others is no longer valid. The method, as described, will provide a random sample.

(e) This method is usually known as a systematic sample. Each individual claim has an equal chance of being chosen but the method nevertheless does not provide a random sample. For a random sample every possible group of 6 claims needs to have an equal chance of being chosen. Using this method, however, it would be impossible, for example, to select the first 6 claims. Providing the list of claims is not arranged in any particular order this may well be a very reasonable method of selecting a sample, but it does not provide a truly random sample according to the strict definition of a random sample.

4.3   The sampling distribution of the mean

In order to investigate the relation between a population and samples taken from it, it is helpful to start with a simple practical situation.

Suppose that you are sampling throws of a fair cubical dice. The best way to do this randomly is to roll dice. If you want a sample of size one you would roll a single dice; if you want a sample of size two you would roll two dice, which is the same as rolling a single dice two times in sequence. For a sample of size n, you would roll n dice, or a single dice n times in sequence. To make things clear, imagine the following situation, starting with the simplest case.

Samples of size one

Suppose that you are playing a game in which you receive a prize, in £, equal to the score obtained on one dice throw. Before you start to play the game you do not know exactly what the value of your prize will be, so your prize is a random variable.

For a single throw of the dice the score, X, has the probability distribution given in Table 4.2.

Value, x	1	2	3	4	5	6
$P(X = x)$	$\frac{1}{6}$	$\frac{1}{6}$	$\frac{1}{6}$	$\frac{1}{6}$	$\frac{1}{6}$	$\frac{1}{6}$

Table 4.2. Probability distribution for X, the score when a single fair dice is thrown.

The mean, μ, of the distribution of X, is equal to $3\frac{1}{2}$. You can see that this is true by considering the symmetry of the distribution.

To find the variance of X, use the formula $\sigma^2 = \operatorname{Var} X = \sum x_i^2 p_i - \mu^2$ from S1 Section 8.2. In this case

$$\sigma^2 = \operatorname{Var}(X) = 1^2 \times \tfrac{1}{6} + 2^2 \times \tfrac{1}{6} + 3^2 \times \tfrac{1}{6} + 4^2 \times \tfrac{1}{6} + 5^2 \times \tfrac{1}{6} + 6^2 \times \tfrac{1}{6} - \left(3\tfrac{1}{2}\right)^2$$
$$= (1^2 + 2^2 + 3^2 + 4^2 + 5^2 + 6^2) \times \tfrac{1}{6} - \left(3\tfrac{1}{2}\right)^2$$
$$= \tfrac{91}{2} - \tfrac{49}{4} = \tfrac{35}{12}.$$

Samples of size two

Suppose now that the rule of the game is that you receive a prize, in £, equal to the mean of the scores obtained on two dice throws. For example, if it turned out that you threw a 4 and then a 1 your prize would be £2.50, whereas if you scored 6 and 4 your prize would be £5. Before you start to play the game you do not know exactly what the value of your prize will be, so the value of your prize is a random variable.

If you let X_1 be the score on the first dice throw and X_2 be the score on the second dice throw, then the mean score can be expressed in terms of X_1 and X_2 as $\frac{1}{2}(X_1 + X_2)$. Notice that each of X_1 and X_2 has a distribution identical to the distribution of X above.

So in this example $\frac{1}{2}(X_1 + X_2)$ is a mean but it is also a random variable because it depends on the two separate scores, which are themselves random. The natural symbol to use for this random variable is $\overline{X}$. (Notice that you saw the symbol $\bar{x}$ before, in S1 Section 3.7, but here the symbol is given in upper case (capitals) because it is a random variable.) In this chapter, where there is discussion about the size of the sample, it will be called $\overline{X}(2)$ as it represents the mean of two dice scores, or equivalently the mean value of a sample of size two drawn from the distribution of X.

Since $\overline{X}(2)$ is a random variable, it has a probability distribution associated with it. Table 4.3 shows all 36 equally likely possible outcomes of two fair dice throws. The entries represent the mean scores of the 36 possible pairs.

		x_2, Value of X_2					
		1	2	3	4	5	6
x_1, Value of X_1	1	1	$1\frac{1}{2}$	2	$2\frac{1}{2}$	3	$3\frac{1}{2}$
	2	$1\frac{1}{2}$	2	$2\frac{1}{2}$	3	$3\frac{1}{2}$	4
	3	2	$2\frac{1}{2}$	3	$3\frac{1}{2}$	4	$4\frac{1}{2}$
	4	$2\frac{1}{2}$	3	$3\frac{1}{2}$	4	$4\frac{1}{2}$	5
	5	3	$3\frac{1}{2}$	4	$4\frac{1}{2}$	5	$5\frac{1}{2}$
	6	$3\frac{1}{2}$	4	$4\frac{1}{2}$	5	$5\frac{1}{2}$	6

Table 4.3. Possible mean scores when two fair dice are thrown.

Of the 36 possible pairs, (x_1, x_2), there are four cases for which the mean score is $2\frac{1}{2}$. The four cases are (1, 4), (2, 3), (3, 2) and (4, 1). So the probability $P\left(\overline{X}(2) = 2\frac{1}{2}\right) = \frac{4}{36} = \frac{1}{9}$. By counting all (x_1, x_2) pairs that give the 11 possible mean scores you should be able to verify that Table 4.4 gives the probability distribution for $\overline{X}(2)$. This distribution is called the **sampling distribution of the mean**, in this case for the mean of two throws of a fair dice.

Value, x	1	$1\frac{1}{2}$	2	$2\frac{1}{2}$	3	$3\frac{1}{2}$	4	$4\frac{1}{2}$	5	$5\frac{1}{2}$	6
$P(\overline{X}(2) = x)$	$\frac{1}{36}$	$\frac{2}{36}$	$\frac{3}{36}$	$\frac{4}{36}$	$\frac{5}{36}$	$\frac{6}{36}$	$\frac{5}{36}$	$\frac{4}{36}$	$\frac{3}{36}$	$\frac{2}{36}$	$\frac{1}{36}$

Table 4.4. Probability distribution of the mean score when two fair dice are thrown.

There is a connection between the mean, μ, of the distribution of X and the mean of the distribution of $\overline{X}(2)$. From the symmetry of the distribution, $E(\overline{X}(2)) = 3\frac{1}{2}$, so $E(\overline{X}(2)) = \mu$.

The variances of X and $\overline{X}(2)$ are also connected. The variance of $\overline{X}(2)$ is given by

$$\text{Var}(\overline{X}(2)) = 1^2 \times \frac{1}{36} + \left(1\frac{1}{2}\right)^2 \times \frac{2}{36} + 2^2 \times \frac{3}{36} + \cdots + 6^2 \times \frac{1}{36} - \left(3\frac{1}{2}\right)^2$$
$$= \frac{35}{24}. \quad \text{(after some calculation)}$$

You can see from this result that, as $\sigma^2 = \frac{35}{12}$, $\text{Var}(\overline{X}(2)) = \frac{1}{2}\sigma^2$.

Summarising, and returning to the language of samples, for samples of size two $E(\overline{X}(2)) = \mu$ and $\text{Var}(\overline{X}(2)) = \frac{1}{2}\sigma^2$, where $E(X) = \mu$ and $\text{Var}(X) = \sigma^2$.

Samples of size three

Perhaps you can now predict the values of $E(\overline{X}(3))$ and $Var(\overline{X}(3))$ in terms of μ and σ^2 for samples of size three, or, equivalently, three dice throws? Let $\overline{X}(3)$ denote the mean score on three dice throws.

Let X_1, X_2 and X_3 be the scores on the first, second and third throws respectively. Then the mean $\overline{X}(3) = \frac{1}{3}(X_1 + X_2 + X_3)$.

Again $\overline{X}(3)$ is a random variable because X_1, X_2 and X_3 are random variables.

There are four different combinations of scores which give a mean score of $2\frac{1}{3}$: they are $(1, 1, 5)$, $(1, 2, 4)$, $(1, 3, 3)$ and $(2, 2, 3)$. The combination $(1, 1, 5)$ can occur in any of 3 different orders: $(1, 1, 5)$, $(1, 5, 1)$, $(5, 1, 1)$; similarly $(1, 2, 4)$ can occur in 6 orders: $(1, 2, 4)$, $(1, 4, 2)$, $(2, 1, 4)$, $(2, 4, 1)$, $(4, 1, 2)$, $(4, 2, 1)$; $(1, 3, 3)$ can occur in 3 orders: $(1, 3, 3)$, $(3, 1, 3)$, $(3, 3, 1)$; and $(2, 2, 3)$ can occur in 3 orders: $(2, 2, 3)$, $(2, 3, 2)$, $(3, 2, 2)$.

From these results, you can see that

$$P\left(\overline{X}(3) = 2\tfrac{1}{3}\right) = \tfrac{3}{216} + \tfrac{6}{216} + \tfrac{3}{216} + \tfrac{3}{216} = \tfrac{15}{216}.$$

By considering all (x_1, x_2, x_3) triples that give each of the 16 possible mean scores, you can derive the probability distribution of $\overline{X}(3)$. This is given in Table 4.5. This is the sampling distribution of the mean for samples of 3 throws of a fair dice.

Value, x	$P(\overline{X}(3) = x)$	Value, x	$P(\overline{X}(3) = x)$
1	$\frac{1}{216}$	$3\frac{2}{3}$	$\frac{27}{216}$
$1\frac{1}{3}$	$\frac{3}{216}$	4	$\frac{25}{216}$
$1\frac{2}{3}$	$\frac{6}{216}$	$4\frac{1}{3}$	$\frac{21}{216}$
2	$\frac{10}{216}$	$4\frac{2}{3}$	$\frac{15}{216}$
$2\frac{1}{3}$	$\frac{15}{216}$	5	$\frac{10}{216}$
$2\frac{2}{3}$	$\frac{21}{216}$	$5\frac{1}{3}$	$\frac{6}{216}$
3	$\frac{25}{216}$	$5\frac{2}{3}$	$\frac{3}{216}$
$3\frac{1}{3}$	$\frac{27}{216}$	6	$\frac{1}{216}$

Table 4.5. Probability distribution of the mean score when three fair dice are thrown.

From the symmetry of the distribution, the expected value, $E(\overline{X}(3))$, is again $3\frac{1}{2}$.

The variance is given by

$$Var(\overline{X}(3)) = 1^2 \times \tfrac{1}{216} + \left(1\tfrac{1}{3}\right)^2 \times \tfrac{3}{216} + \left(1\tfrac{2}{3}\right)^2 \times \tfrac{6}{216} + \cdots + 6^2 \times \tfrac{1}{216} - \left(3\tfrac{1}{2}\right)^2$$
$$= \left(1 + \tfrac{16}{9} \times 3 + \tfrac{25}{9} \times 6 + \cdots + 36\right) \times \tfrac{1}{216} - \left(3\tfrac{1}{2}\right)^2$$
$$= \tfrac{35}{36}. \quad \text{(after some calculation)}$$

So this time $Var(\overline{X}(3)) = \frac{1}{3}\sigma^2$.

Summarising, and generalising, the observations which have been made so far: if $\overline{X}(n)$ represents the mean score on n dice throws, then $E(\overline{X}(n)) = \mu$ and $Var(\overline{X}(n)) = \dfrac{\mu^2}{n}$, where $\mu = E(X)$ is the mean score on a single dice throw and $\sigma^2 = Var(X)$ is the variance of the score on a single dice throw.

You can check, if you persevere, whether these observations are plausible by considering the distribution of the mean score on four fair dice throws. If $\overline{X}(4)$ denotes the mean score, then $\overline{X}(4) = \frac{1}{4}(X_1 + X_2 + X_3 + X_4)$, where X_1 denotes the score on the first dice, and so on.

In fact the results given above are true generally.

> If a random sample consists of n observations of a random variable X, and the mean $\overline{X}$ is found, then $E(\overline{X}(n)) = \mu$ and $Var(\overline{X}(n)) = \dfrac{\sigma^2}{n}$, where $\mu = E(X)$ and $\sigma^2 = Var(X)$.

Example 4.3.1
A biased coin for which the probability of turning up heads is $\frac{2}{3}$ is spun 20 times. Let $\overline{X}$ denote the mean number of heads per spin.

Calculate   (a) μ and σ^2,   (b) $E(\overline{X})$ and $Var(\overline{X})$.

(a) The random variable X in this case represents the number of heads in one spin of the coin. The distribution of X is given in the table.

Value	0	1
$P(X = x)$	$\frac{1}{3}$	$\frac{2}{3}$

The mean is $\mu = E(X) = 0 \times \frac{1}{3} + 1 \times \frac{2}{3} = \frac{2}{3}$ and the variance is given by

$$\sigma^2 = Var(X) = 0^2 \times \tfrac{1}{3} + 1^2 \times \tfrac{2}{3} - \left(\tfrac{2}{3}\right)^2 = \tfrac{2}{9}.$$

(b) Using the result in the blue box,

$$E(\overline{X}(20)) = \mu = \tfrac{2}{3} \quad \text{and} \quad Var(\overline{X}(20)) = \frac{\sigma^2}{20} = \tfrac{1}{20} \times \tfrac{2}{9} = \tfrac{1}{90}.$$

4.4 The central limit theorem

In the previous section you saw the distribution of the score when one fair dice was thrown. This was given in Table 4.2 and it is reproduced here.

Value, x	1	2	3	4	5	6
$P(X = x)$	$\frac{1}{6}$	$\frac{1}{6}$	$\frac{1}{6}$	$\frac{1}{6}$	$\frac{1}{6}$	$\frac{1}{6}$

Table 4.6. Probability distribution for X, the score when a single fair dice is thrown.

Fig. 4.7 shows the distribution of P($X = x$) in a bar chart.

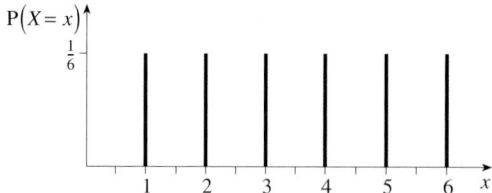

Fig. 4.7. Bar chart showing the distribution of P($X = x$).

Notice that the distribution of X in the bar chart is uniform. All the bars have the same height.

You also saw in the previous section the distribution of $\overline{X}(2)$, the mean score when two fair dice were thrown. This was given in Table 4.4 and it is reproduced here as Table 4.8.

Value, x	1	$1\frac{1}{2}$	2	$2\frac{1}{2}$	3	$3\frac{1}{2}$	4	$4\frac{1}{2}$	5	$5\frac{1}{2}$	6
P($\overline{X}(2) = x$)	$\frac{1}{36}$	$\frac{2}{36}$	$\frac{3}{36}$	$\frac{4}{36}$	$\frac{5}{36}$	$\frac{6}{36}$	$\frac{5}{36}$	$\frac{4}{36}$	$\frac{3}{36}$	$\frac{2}{36}$	$\frac{1}{36}$

Table 4.8. Probability distribution of the mean score when two fair dice are thrown.

Fig. 4.9 shows a bar chart of the distribution of $\overline{X}(2)$.

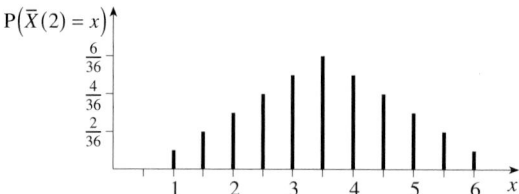

Fig. 4.9. Bar chart showing the distribution of P($\overline{X}(2) = x$).

Notice that the distribution of $\overline{X}(2)$ is not uniform. There is a 'peak' in the middle and the values in the centre of the range, 3, $3\frac{1}{2}$ and 4, are more likely to occur than other values.

You also saw in the previous section the distribution of $\overline{X}(3)$, the mean score when three fair dice were thrown. This was given in Table 4.5 and it is reproduced here as Table 4.10.

Value, x	P($\overline{X}(3) = x$)	Value, x	P($\overline{X}(3) = x$)
1	$\frac{1}{216}$	$3\frac{2}{3}$	$\frac{27}{216}$
$1\frac{1}{3}$	$\frac{3}{216}$	4	$\frac{25}{216}$
$1\frac{2}{3}$	$\frac{6}{216}$	$4\frac{1}{3}$	$\frac{21}{216}$
2	$\frac{10}{216}$	$4\frac{2}{3}$	$\frac{15}{216}$
$2\frac{1}{3}$	$\frac{15}{216}$	5	$\frac{10}{216}$
$2\frac{2}{3}$	$\frac{21}{216}$	$5\frac{1}{3}$	$\frac{6}{216}$
3	$\frac{25}{216}$	$5\frac{2}{3}$	$\frac{3}{216}$
$3\frac{1}{3}$	$\frac{27}{216}$	6	$\frac{1}{216}$

Table 4.10. Probability distribution of the mean score when three fair dice are thrown.

Fig 4.11 shows a bar chart of the distribution of $\overline{X}(3)$.

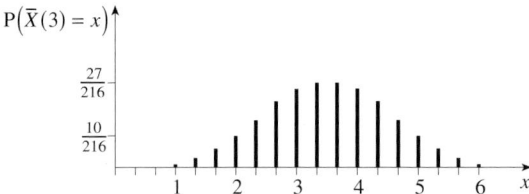

Fig. 4.11. Bar chart showing the distribution of $P(\overline{X}(3) = x)$.

If you compare Fig. 4.11 with Fig. 4.9, the chart for the mean score when only two dice are thrown, you can see that the central values occur much more often than the extreme values this time. In fact, this bar chart looks similar to the graphs of the normal distribution, which you studied in Chapter 2.

If you found the distribution for the mean score of four fair dice throws, you can check that this also looks like a normal distribution. You should now be able to see that as n gets larger the distribution of $\overline{X}(n)$ becomes more and more like a normal distribution.

Fig. 4.12 shows the results of a simulation using a spreadsheet for a sample of size 50. It confirms the impression that the distribution of $\overline{X}(n)$ becomes more like a normal distribution for large values of n.

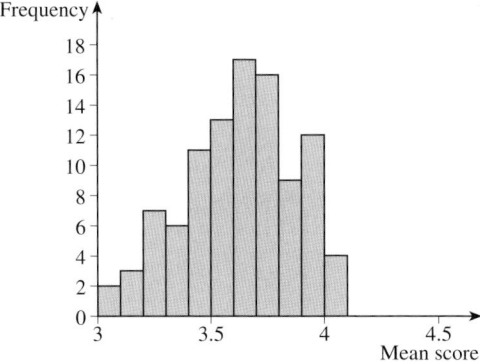

Fig. 4.12. Diagram showing the frequency
distribution of the mean of 50 throws of a fair dice
for 100 simulations on a spreadsheet.

You can try such a simulation for yourself. With an even larger number of simulations the shape of the diagram will be found to be more clearly normal.

So, from the examples you have considered, it would seem reasonable to conclude that the distribution of $\overline{X}(n)$ is approximately normal for large values of n. From the previous section,
$E(\overline{X}(n)) = \mu$ and $Var(\overline{X}(n)) = \dfrac{\sigma^2}{n}$.

The results above are special cases of a more general theorem called the **central limit theorem**.

> **The central limit theorem** For any sequence of independent identically distributed random variables $X_1, X_2, \ldots, X_n$, with finite mean μ and non-zero variance σ^2, then, provided n is sufficiently large, $\overline{X}$ has approximately a normal distribution with mean μ and variance $\dfrac{\sigma^2}{n}$, where $\overline{X} = \dfrac{X_1 + X_2 + \cdots + X_n}{n}$.
>
> In symbols, $\overline{X} \sim \mathrm{N}\left(\mu, \dfrac{\sigma^2}{n}\right)$.

Notice that the sample size n has been omitted from $\overline{X}$ because it is usually clear from the context how large the sample is.

You may have been wondering just how large n has to be for the normal distribution to be reasonably close to the distribution of $\overline{X}$. Unfortunately there is no simple answer. It depends on the distribution of X itself. If the distribution of X has some of the features of a normal distribution then n will probably not need to be very large at all. On the other hand, if the distribution of X is very skewed then n might need to be quite large. In solving problems you can usually judge whether it is appropriate to invoke the central limit theorem. A sensible rule of thumb is to apply the theorem when n is greater than about 30.

This theorem is a fundamental result in the theory of statistics and it explains why the normal distribution is so widely studied. The essential point is that it does not matter what distribution $X_1, X_2, \ldots, X_n$ have individually: provided they all have the same distribution and are independent of one another, the distribution of the mean $\overline{X}$ will be approximately normal as long as n is sufficiently large. The central limit theorem is too complicated to prove rigorously here; however, the previous discussion of the mean scores on one, two, three and four dice shows that the theorem is reasonable. The following examples show how the theorem applies to other random variables.

Example 4.4.1
A continuous random variable, X, has a probability density function, f(x), given by

$$\mathrm{f}(x) = \begin{cases} 2x & \text{for } 0 \leqslant x \leqslant 1, \\ 0 & \text{otherwise.} \end{cases}$$

Find   (a) the mean, μ,   (b) the variance, σ^2, of this distribution.

A random sample of 100 observations is taken from this distribution, and the mean $\overline{X}$ is found.

(c) Find the mean and variance of $\overline{X}$.   (d) Calculate the probability $P(\overline{X} < 0.68)$.

   (a) Using the definition of the mean of a continuous random variable given in Section 1.4,

$$\mu = \int_0^1 x \times 2x \, dx = \int_0^1 2x^2 \, dx = \left[\tfrac{2}{3}x^3\right]_0^1 = \tfrac{2}{3}.$$

(b) $\sigma^2 = \int_0^1 x^2 \times 2x \, dx - \left(\frac{2}{3}\right)^2 = \int_0^1 2x^3 \, dx - \left(\frac{2}{3}\right)^2$

$= \left[\frac{2}{4}x^4\right]_0^1 - \left(\frac{2}{3}\right)^2 = \frac{1}{2} - \frac{4}{9} = \frac{1}{18}.$

(c) $E(\overline{X}) = \mu = \frac{2}{3}$ and $Var(\overline{X}) = \dfrac{\sigma^2}{n} = \dfrac{\frac{1}{18}}{100} = \frac{1}{1800}.$

(d) By the central limit theorem, the distribution of
$\overline{X}$ is approximately $N(\frac{2}{3}, \frac{1}{1800})$. Standardising, using

$Z = \dfrac{\overline{X} - \frac{2}{3}}{\sqrt{\frac{1}{1800}}}$, it follows that

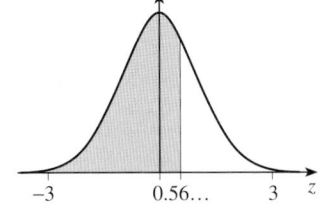

$$P(\overline{X} < 0.68) \approx P\left(Z < \dfrac{0.68 - \frac{2}{3}}{\sqrt{\frac{1}{1800}}} \right)$$

$= P(Z < 0.565\,68\ldots) = 0.7143$

$= 0.714$, correct to 3 significant figures.

Example 4.4.2

(a) If X denotes the number of sixes obtained when a fair dice is thrown 12 times, determine $E(X)$ and $Var(X)$.

(b) Forty students each threw a fair cubical dice 12 times. Each student then recorded the number of times that a six occurred in their own 12 throws. The students' lecturer then calculated the mean number of sixes obtained per student. Give an approximate distribution for this mean and hence find the probability that this mean exceeds 2.2.

(a) X satisfies the conditions for a binomial distribution to apply. The parameters of the binomial distribution in this case are $n = 12$ and $p = \frac{1}{6}$.

Recall from S1 Section 8.3 that for a random variable X which has a binomial distribution, $\mu = np$ and $\sigma^2 = npq$. So, in this case, $\mu = 12 \times \frac{1}{6} = 2$ and $\sigma^2 = 12 \times \frac{1}{6} \times \frac{5}{6} = \frac{5}{3}.$

(b) If $\overline{X}$ denotes the mean of the students' scores, then $E(\overline{X}) = \mu = 2$ and
$Var(\overline{X}) = \dfrac{\sigma^2}{n} = \dfrac{\frac{5}{3}}{40} = \frac{1}{24}.$

Using the central limit theorem, $\overline{X} \sim N\left(2, \dfrac{\frac{5}{3}}{40} \right) = N(2, \frac{1}{24})$, approximately.

$\overline{X}$ represents the mean of 40 binomial variables, so it can be written in terms of $X_1, X_2, \ldots, X_{40}$ as $\overline{X} = \frac{1}{40}(X_1 + X_2 + \cdots + X_{40})$, where X_i is the number of sixes obtained by student i for $i = 1, 2, \ldots, 40$.

You want to find $P(\overline{X} > 2.2)$. This can be written in terms of T, the total of the 40 variables, where $T = X_1 + X_2 + \cdots + X_{40}$.

$P(\overline{X} > 2.2)$ is equivalent to $P(T > 40 \times 2.2)$, which is $P(T > 88)$. However, T is the total number of sixes gained in 480 throws of a fair dice, so $T \sim B\left(480, \frac{1}{6}\right)$.

From Section 2.8, when you use a normal distribution to approximate to a binomial distribution, you need a continuity correction, so $P(T > 88)$ is approximately equal to $P(V > 88 + 0.5)$, where V is the appropriate normal approximation.

Expressing this in terms of $\overline{X}$, you want $P\left(\overline{X} > 2.2 + \frac{1}{80}\right)$.

So here, when it is applied to the mean, $\overline{X}$, of a set of n discrete variables, the continuity correction is $\dfrac{1}{2n}$, rather than $\frac{1}{2}$.

Standardising $\overline{X}$ using the usual equation gives $Z = \dfrac{\overline{X} - 2}{\sqrt{\frac{1}{24}}}$, so $Z \sim N(0, 1)$.

Then
$$P(\overline{X} > 2.2 + \tfrac{1}{80}) = P(Z > 0.2125\sqrt{24}) = P(Z > 1.041\ldots)$$
$$= 1 - \Phi(1.041\ldots) = 0.1490\ldots$$
$$= 0.149, \text{ correct to 3 significant figures.}$$

> When a discrete distribution is approximated by a continuous distribution, the continuity correction for the sample mean, $\overline{X}$, is $\dfrac{1}{2n}$ for a sample of size n.

4.5 Practical activities

1 Playing cards Take a pack of playing cards and discard the picture cards, that is the jack, queen and king, of each suit. Shuffle the cards and deal out 10 of them. Calculate the mean score by adding together the 10 face values and dividing by 10. Put the 10 cards back in the pack and shuffle again. Deal out a further 10 cards and calculate the mean score again. Repeat this to give 100 observations, each of which is the mean score of 10 cards. Calculate the mean and the variance of these scores. Compare these values with the ones you would expect from the theoretical results.

2 Central limit theorem

(a) Use a spreadsheet to produce a random number, r, between 0 and 1 in one cell.

(b) In a second cell calculate $n = \frac{1}{2}\left(1 + \sqrt[3]{2r - 1}\right)$.

(c) Repeat this in a large number of pairs of cells (say 500) to get 500 observations of n.

(d) Use your spreadsheet to draw a histogram of the values of n. This should give you a U-shaped distribution.

(e) Using a new spreadsheet calculate 50 values of n using the same formula as in part (b) and find their mean. Repeat this to get at least 100 means of 50 values of n.

(f) Draw a histogram of these 100 means. You should be able to see that the distribution of the means is not U-shaped like the original distribution. The distribution of the means should more nearly resemble a normal distribution.

Exercise 4A

1 A random sample of 200 adults from a particular residential section of a city is required. Explain clearly and concisely what is meant by a *random sample* in this context and suggest a method for obtaining such a sample.

One suggested method was firstly to select 200 households at random and secondly to select one adult at random from each household. Explain briefly why this method will not produce a random sample.   (OCR)

2 The following is a sequence of 50 random digits.

       28566 86259 00958 67172 09612 87941 86435 70383 10287 06202

Use these to select the following random samples, explaining your method.

(a) Two hours from the 24 in the day, chosen without replacement.

(b) Three students from a group of 400 students, chosen without replacement.

3 A manufacturer of a new soap powder wishes to predict the likely volume of sales in a town. Four schemes, as below, are proposed for selecting people for a questionnaire. Discuss the merits of each and choose one, explaining why you think it is the best.

(a) Take every 20th name on the electoral register of the town.

(b) Choose people entering a supermarket, ensuring that the numbers in each sex, age and social class category are proportional to the number in the population.

(c) Select houses at random from a town plan and interview one person from each.

(d) Choose at random one name from each page of the telephone directory and ring them up.   (OCR)

4 A random variable X has mean 50 and variance 1000. A random sample of 40 observations of X is taken and the mean, $\overline{X}$, of these observations is calculated. How, approximately, is $\overline{X}$ distributed?

Find

(a) $P(\overline{X} < 55)$,   (b) $P(\overline{X} > 40)$,   (c) $P(40 < \overline{X} < 55)$.

5 A discrete random variable, Y, has the probability distribution shown below.

y	1	2	3	4
$P(Y = y)$	0.1	0.2	0.5	0.2

For this distribution, find

(a) the mean, μ,   (b) the variance, σ^2.

A random sample of 50 observations of Y is taken. Find

(c) $P(\overline{Y} < 2.6)$,   (d) $P(|\overline{Y} - \mu| < 0.2)$.

6 An unbiased dice is thrown once. Write down the probability distribution of the score X and show that $\text{Var}(X) = \frac{35}{12}$.

The same dice is thrown 70 times.

(a) Find the probability that the mean score is less than 3.3.

(b) Find the probability that the mean score exceeds 3.8.

7 A rectangular field is gridded into squares of side 1 m. At one time of the year the number of snails in the field can be modelled by a Poisson distribution with mean 2.25 per m^2.

(a) A random sample of 120 squares is observed and the number of snails in each square is counted. Find the probability that the sample mean number of snails is at most 2.5.

(b) A random sample of 100 squares is observed and the number of snails in each square is counted. Find the probability that the sample mean number of snails is at least 2.

8 The random variable X has a B(40, 0.3) distribution. The mean of a random sample of n observations of X is denoted by $\overline{X}$. Find

(a) $\text{P}(\overline{X} \geqslant 13)$, assuming a sample size of 49,

(b) the smallest value of n for which $\text{P}(\overline{X} \geqslant 13) < 0.001$.

9 At a charity garden fete a simple game is played by throwing an unbiased dice until a six is thrown, when the game ends. The player donates 10p to the charity for each throw taken. Show that if 500 games are played then the organiser can be about 95% sure that for this sample the mean takings per game will exceed 56p.

(Note that if $X \sim \text{Geo}(p)$, S1 Section 7.3, then $\text{E}(X) = \dfrac{1}{p}$ and $\text{Var}(X) = \dfrac{1-p}{p^2}$.)

10 The number of tickets sold each day at a city railway station during the winter has mean 512 and variance 1600. For a randomly chosen period of 60 winter days, find the probability that the mean number of tickets sold per day over this period is less than 500.

11 The proportion of faulty plastic cups made by a factory machine is 0.08. The cups, including faulty ones, are packed in boxes of 100. About 4000 cups are required for an outdoor concert and the manager orders 44 boxes. Find the probability that these boxes will provide more than 4000 perfect cups.

12 A firm of caterers wishes to buy wine for a wedding reception of 200 guests. They estimate that, on average, each guest will drink 45 cl of wine. The volume of wine in the bottles they buy may be assumed to have a distribution with mean 70.5 cl and standard deviation 1.2 cl. Show that if they buy 128 bottles then the caterers can be more than 95% certain that their requirements will be met.

13 A random sample of $2n$ observations is taken of the random variable X, where $X \sim \text{B}(n, p)$ and $p > 0.5$. The sample mean is denoted by $\overline{X}$. It is given that $\text{Var}(\overline{X}) = 0.08$ and $\text{E}(\overline{X}) = 64$. Find

(a) the values of p and n,   (b) $\text{P}(\overline{X} > 64.5)$.

4.6 The distribution of $\overline{X}$ when $X_1, X_2, \ldots, X_n$ have an $N(\mu, \sigma^2)$ distribution

The central limit theorem states that the distribution of $\overline{X}$ is approximately $N\left(\mu, \dfrac{\sigma^2}{n}\right)$ when $X_1, X_2, \ldots, X_n$ are independent identically distributed random variables with finite mean μ and finite non-zero variance σ^2. It is necessary for the value of n to be quite large for this approximation to be reasonable. However, if the variables are normally distributed, the sample mean is normally distributed for samples of any size.

> If the distributions of $X_1, X_2, \ldots, X_n$, are independent $N(\mu, \sigma^2)$ variables, then the distribution of $\overline{X}$ is **exactly** $N\left(\mu, \dfrac{\sigma^2}{n}\right)$ no matter what size n is.

This point is used in Example 4.6.1.

Example 4.6.1
The mass of a randomly chosen male student in Year 10 at a large secondary school may be modelled by a normal distribution with mean 55 kg and standard deviation 2.2 kg. Four students are chosen at random from this year group. Calculate the probability that the mean mass of the four students is   (a) less than 58 kg,   (b) between 52 kg and 57.5 kg.

Let M_1, M_2, M_3 and M_4 be the masses of four randomly chosen male Year 10 students. Then

$$M_i \sim N(55, 2.2^2) \text{ for } i = 1, 2, 3, 4.$$

Therefore $\overline{M} \sim N\left(55, \dfrac{2.2^2}{4}\right) = N(55, 1.21).$

Note that, although n is very small, as the distribution for each M_i is normal the mean of $\overline{M}$ is normal.

Standardise by letting $Z = \dfrac{\overline{M} - 55}{1.1}$, then $Z \sim N(0, 1)$.

(a) $P(\overline{M} < 58) = P\left(Z < \dfrac{58 - 55}{1.1}\right)$

$\qquad = P(Z < 2.727\ldots)$

$\qquad = \Phi(2.727\ldots)$

$\qquad = 0.9968$

$\qquad = 0.997$, correct to 3 significant figures.

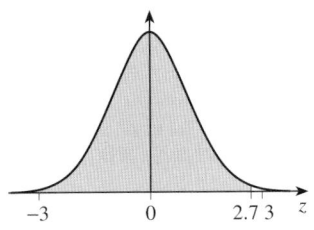

(b) $P(52 < \overline{M} < 57.5)$

$\qquad = P\left(\dfrac{52 - 55}{1.1} < Z < \dfrac{57.5 - 55}{1.1}\right)$

$\qquad = P(-2.727\ldots < Z < 2.272\ldots)$

$\qquad = \Phi(2.272\ldots) - \Phi(-2.727\ldots)$

$\qquad = 0.9884 - (1 - 0.9968)$

$\qquad = 0.985$, correct to 3 significant figures.

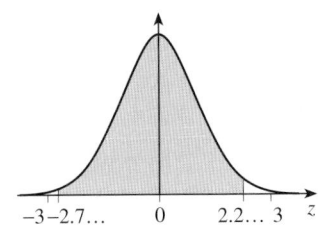

Example 4.6.2

A second sample of size n is chosen from the male Year 10 students. How large does n have to be for there to be at most a 2% chance that the mean mass of the sample differs from the mean mass of the population by more than 0.6 kg?

Let $M_1, M_2, \ldots, M_n$ be the masses of n randomly chosen Year 10 male students. Then

$$\overline{M} \sim N\left(55, \frac{2.2^2}{n}\right)$$

Then the minimum value of n is required for which

$$P(54.4 \leqslant \overline{M} \leqslant 55.6) \geqslant 0.98.$$

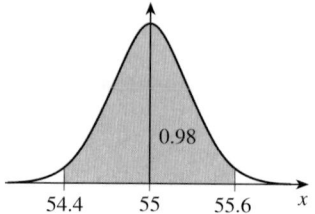

Standardising this gives

$$P\left(\frac{-0.6}{2.2/\sqrt{n}} \leqslant Z \leqslant \frac{0.6}{2.2/\sqrt{n}}\right) \geqslant 0.98.$$

Expressing this in terms of the cumulative distribution function gives

$$\Phi\left(\frac{0.6}{2.2/\sqrt{n}}\right) - \Phi\left(\frac{-0.6}{2.2/\sqrt{n}}\right) \geqslant 0.98.$$

Therefore $\Phi\left(\dfrac{0.6}{2.2/\sqrt{n}}\right) - \left(1 - \Phi\left(\dfrac{0.6}{2.2/\sqrt{n}}\right)\right) \geqslant 0.98.$

Solving this gives $\Phi\left(\dfrac{0.6}{2.2/\sqrt{n}}\right) \geqslant 0.99.$

Taking the inverse function $\dfrac{0.6}{2.2/\sqrt{n}} \geqslant \Phi^{-1}(0.99).$

From the tables, this gives $\dfrac{0.6}{2.2/\sqrt{n}} \geqslant 2.326.$

Rearranging this equation gives $\sqrt{n} \geqslant 8.528\ldots$, so $n \geqslant 72.7\ldots$

Since n must be an integer, it has to be greater than or equal to 73. So the sample needs to contain at least 73 students for its mean mass to approximate the population's mean mass with the accuracy and certainty desired.

Exercise 4B

1 The body length of a species of ant is normally distributed with mean 3.1 mm and standard deviation 0.2 mm.

  (a) What is the probability that an ant of this species chosen at random has a body length greater than 3.12 mm?

  (b) What is the probability that the mean body length of a sample of

   (i) 9 ants   (ii) 100 ants

   is greater than 3.12 mm?

2 The random variable X has mean μ and variance σ^2. State whether or not each of the following statements relating to the distribution of the mean $\overline{X}$ of a random sample of n observations of X is true. Correct any false statement.

(a) The central limit theorem states that $\overline{X}$ has a normal distribution for any distribution of X.

(b) $E(\overline{X}) = \mu$ and $Var(\overline{X}) = \dfrac{\sigma^2}{n}$ are true for any distribution of X and any value of n.

(c) The central limit theorem states that the sample is normally distributed for large values of n.

(d) If $X \sim N(\mu, \sigma^2)$ then $\overline{X} \sim N\left(\mu, \dfrac{\sigma^2}{n}\right)$ only for large values of n.

3 Random samples of three are drawn from a population of beetles whose lengths have a normal distribution with mean 2.4 cm and standard deviation 0.36 cm. The mean length $\overline{X}$ is calculated for each sample.

(a) State the distribution of $\overline{X}$, giving the values of its parameters.

(b) Find $P(\overline{X} > 2.5)$.

State which of the numerical values above, if any, depend on the central limit theorem.

4 The masses of kilogram bags of flour produced in a factory have a normal distribution with mean 1.005 kg and standard deviation 0.0082 kg. A shelf in a store is loaded with 22 of these bags, assumed to be a random sample.

(a) Find the probability that a randomly chosen bag has a mass of less than 1 kg.

(b) Find the probability that the mean mass of the 22 bags is less than 1 kg.

State, giving a reason, which of the above answers would be little changed if the distribution of masses were not normal.

5 The mean of a random sample of 500 observations of the random variable X, where $X \sim N(25, 18)$, is denoted by $\overline{X}$. Find the value of a for which $P(\overline{X} < a) = 0.25$.

Does your answer depend on the central limit theorem?

6 The life of Powerlong batteries, sold in packs of 6, may be assumed to have a normal distribution with mean 32 hours and standard deviation σ hours. Find the value of σ so that for one pack in 100 (on average) the mean life of the batteries is less than 30 hours.

7* A liquid drug is marketed in phials containing a nominal 1.5 ml but the amounts can vary slightly. The volume in each phial may be modelled by a normal distribution with mean 1.55 ml and standard deviation σ ml. The phials are sold in packs of 5 randomly chosen phials. It is required that in less than $\frac{1}{2}$% of packs will the total volume of the drug be less than 7.5 ml. Find the value of σ.

8* A goods lift can carry up to 5000 kg and is to be loaded with crates whose masses are normally distributed with mean 79.2 kg and standard deviation 5.5 kg. Show that

(a) it is highly likely that the lift can take 62 randomly selected crates without being overloaded,

(b) 65 randomly selected crates would almost certainly overload the lift.

4.7   Unbiased estimates

One of the main aims in the study of statistics is to be able to estimate the value of population parameters without going to the trouble of taking a census.

Consider the example of a hospital administrator who is concerned that the hospital sometimes does not have enough beds to cater for all of its patients. She wants to estimate μ, the mean time for which a patient stays in a hospital bed during a particular week. She takes a random sample of the patients who are admitted during that week and records the length of time, in days, for which each patient in the sample stays in hospital. She must now consider how to use the data that she has collected in order to estimate μ. For example, suppose she has collected the times for 10 patients. The results might be something like

$$7, 5, 5, 9, 3, 11, 6, 4, 2, 20.$$

What calculation should she carry out on these values to estimate μ? You may think that the answer is obvious. It makes sense to estimate μ by taking the mean of the sample. So in this case the estimate of μ would be $\frac{72}{10} = 7.2$. But is this the only sensible estimate that can be made from these data? What would be wrong, for instance, with taking the first time, 7 days, as an estimate of μ? It may be that the real mean, μ, is nearer to 7 than to 7.2. It is clear that you need a strategy for deciding which method is better.

To make a decision you need to think in detail about what the administrator is trying to do. Imagine that she has not yet taken her sample of 10 times. So at present the times are random variables because it is not certain which patients she will choose. Suppose that you call these random variables $X_1, X_2, \ldots, X_{10}$. Two possible methods for estimating μ have been suggested.

Method 1   Use the mean of the 10 sample values. Call this value M_1. Then $M_1 = \frac{1}{10}(X_1 + X_2 + \cdots + X_{10})$. Recall that this may also be called $\overline{X}$.

Method 2   Use the first value selected. Call this value M_2. So $M_2 = X_1$.

The values obtained in these ways are themselves random variables and are usually called **estimators**. M_1 and M_2 are both estimators of μ, the mean time for which a patient stays in a hospital bed during a particular week. The value that an estimator gives for a particular sample is called an **estimate**.

Suppose that there were N patients in the hospital during that week and suppose further that the times for which each patient stayed in hospital are $y_1, y_2, \ldots, y_N$. Of course, these times are unknown. However the mean, μ, can be expressed in terms of $y_1, y_2, \ldots, y_N$ as

$$\mu = \frac{y_1 + y_2 + \cdots + y_N}{N}.$$

Now X_1 can take any of the values $y_1, y_2, \ldots, y_N$. The probability distribution for X_1 is given in Table 4.13.

Value, x	y_1	y_2	$\cdots$	y_N
$P(X = x)$	$\dfrac{1}{N}$	$\dfrac{1}{N}$	$\cdots$	$\dfrac{1}{N}$

Table 4.13. Probability distribution of X_1.

Therefore

$$E(X_1) = y_1 \times \frac{1}{N} + y_2 \times \frac{1}{N} + \cdots + y_n \times \frac{1}{N}$$
$$= (y_1 + y_2 + \cdots + y_N) \times \frac{1}{N} = N\mu \times \frac{1}{N} = \mu.$$

It should be clear that $X_2, X_3, \ldots, X_{10}$ all have the same distribution as X_1, so each variable also has the expected value μ. You saw in Section 4.3 that if $X_1, X_2, \ldots, X_{10}$ is a set of random variables with the same mean, μ, then $E(\overline{X}) = \mu$.

Therefore, for both of the suggested methods, $E(M_1) = E(M_2) = \mu$.

What exactly does this statement tell you? It says that if you took all possible samples of size 10 and calculated the value of M_1 for each sample, then the mean of these values would be equal to μ, the quantity that the administrator is trying to estimate. The same is true of M_2. This means that both estimators are **unbiased**.

> For an unknown population parameter α, the estimator M is unbiased if $E(M) = \alpha$, where the expected value is taken over all possible samples of a given size.

Fig. 4.14 represents a way of understanding the idea of unbiasedness.

The line is the real number line and the crosses represent the values which an estimator gives for each sample of a population. If the estimator is unbiased then the mean value of all the points represented by the crosses will be the population parameter α.

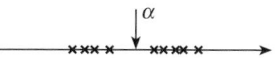

Fig. 4.14. Representation of unbiasedness.

Clearly you want an estimator to be unbiased because when this is the case the parameter of interest, α, is in effect the 'focus' of all the possible values that the estimator can take. Of course, this is only of theoretical importance here because the administrator has only one sample, and since both estimators are unbiased she needs some other means of deciding which estimator is the better one.

Suppose that the variance of X_1 is denoted by σ^2. Then σ^2 can be expressed in terms of $y_1, y_2, \ldots, y_N$ as

$$Var(X_1) = \sigma^2 = y_1^2 \times \frac{1}{N} + y_2^2 \times \frac{1}{N} + \cdots + y_N^2 \times \frac{1}{N} - \mu^2.$$

If the number of patients in the hospital during the week is a large number then you can assume that the distributions of $X_1, X_2, \ldots, X_{10}$ are independent. You saw in Section 4.3 that under these conditions $Var(\overline{X}) = \frac{1}{10}\sigma^2$.

This means that the estimates found from $M_1 = \overline{X}$ will on average be closer to μ than those found from $M_2 = X_1$. Fig. 4.15 shows a comparison between the two estimators.

Fig. 4.15. Closer estimates are found by larger samples.

You can see that the crosses are clustered more closely around μ in the first case. This confirms what you may have guessed from the start: it is better to use the estimator $M_1 = \overline{X}$ because it uses all of the information in the sample, whereas using only $M_2 = X_1$ discards 90% of the information gained by taking the sample.

In general it can be shown that $\overline{X}$ is always an unbiased estimator of μ. In other words, a sensible method of estimating the population mean is to take a random sample and use its mean as the estimate.

So is this true of all population parameters? To estimate the median of a population would you take the median of a random sample, or to estimate the mode of a population would you take the mode of a random sample? The previous example would seem to suggest that this is a sensible procedure but consider the following example.

Example 4.7.1
A jar contains a very large number of discs, 90% of which have the number 0 written on them and the remaining 10% of which have the number 1 on them. Tom does not know what numbers are written on the discs. He takes a random sample of two discs from the jar. Tom wishes to estimate the largest number written on any disc in the jar. He decides that his method of estimating the maximum will be to take the larger of the numbers on the two discs in his sample. If both discs have the same number written on them then he takes that value as his estimate of the maximum. Decide whether the proposed method gives an unbiased estimator of the population maximum.

Let the maximum value in the sample be M.

Tom's method is to take the sample maximum, M, as an estimator of the population maximum. Table 4.16 gives all possible samples of size two and the value of M for each sample together with the probability of that sample being chosen.

Since the jar is said to contain a large number of discs it is reasonable to suppose that the chances of selecting a 0 or 1 remain constant for each selection.

Sample values	m, Value of M	Probability
0, 0	0	$0.9 \times 0.9 = 0.81$
0, 1	1	$0.9 \times 0.1 = 0.09$
1, 0	1	$0.1 \times 0.9 = 0.09$
1, 1	1	$0.1 \times 0.1 = 0.01$

Table 4.16. Possible sample values for a sample of size two.

The probability distribution for M is given in Table 4.17.

Value, m	0	1
$P(M = m)$	0.81	0.19

Table 4.17. Probability distribution for M.

Therefore $E(M) = 0 \times 0.81 + 1 \times 0.19 = 0.19$.

But the population maximum is 1 and so the sample maximum, which is Tom's estimator, underestimates the population maximum on average. Therefore the sample maximum is a biased estimator of the population maximum.

You have now seen that it is not always sensible to use the sample version of a statistic as an estimator of the population version of the same statistic. There is a particularly important case where this warning applies. The case in question is the estimation of population variance. Consider the following example.

Example 4.7.2
A jar contains a large number of discs, 40% of which are numbered 1, 40% numbered 2 and 20% numbered 3. A random sample of size three is taken from the jar. By considering all possible values for samples of size three, determine whether the variance of the sample is an unbiased estimator of the variance of the population.

The mean of the population is

$$\mu = 1 \times 0.4 + 2 \times 0.4 + 3 \times 0.2 = 1.8.$$

The variance of the population is

$$\sigma^2 = 1^2 \times 0.4 + 2^2 \times 0.4 + 3^2 \times 0.2 - 1.8^2$$
$$= 0.56.$$

Consider the possible values of samples of size three. One such sample value is 1, 1, 2.

The variance of this sample is $\frac{1}{3}(1^2 + 1^2 + 2^2) - \left(\frac{4}{3}\right)^2 = \frac{2}{9}$.

The chance of selecting this particular sample is $0.4 \times 0.4 \times 0.4 = 0.064$.

You can repeat this calculation for all 27 possible sample values. Table 4.18 (below and on the next page) shows all possible sample values. It also shows the sample variance, V, and the probability of selecting that particular sample.

Sample values	Variance	Probability
1, 1, 1	0	$0.4^3 = 0.064$
2, 2, 2	0	$0.4^3 = 0.064$
3, 3, 3	0	$0.2^3 = 0.008$
1, 1, 2	$\frac{2}{9}$	$0.4^3 = 0.064$
2, 1, 1	$\frac{2}{9}$	$0.4^3 = 0.064$
1, 2, 1	$\frac{2}{9}$	$0.4^3 = 0.064$
1, 2, 2	$\frac{2}{9}$	$0.4^3 = 0.064$
2, 1, 2	$\frac{2}{9}$	$0.4^3 = 0.064$
2, 2, 1	$\frac{2}{9}$	$0.4^3 = 0.064$
1, 1, 3	$\frac{8}{9}$	$0.4^2 \times 0.2 = 0.032$
1, 3, 1	$\frac{8}{9}$	$0.4^2 \times 0.2 = 0.032$
3, 1, 1	$\frac{8}{9}$	$0.4^2 \times 0.2 = 0.032$
1, 3, 3	$\frac{8}{9}$	$0.4 \times 0.2^2 = 0.016$

Table 4.18. Possible sample values and sample variance for a sample of size three.

Sample values	Variance	Probability
3, 1, 3	$\frac{8}{9}$	$0.4 \times 0.2^2 = 0.016$
3, 3, 1	$\frac{8}{9}$	$0.4 \times 0.2^2 = 0.016$
2, 2, 3	$\frac{2}{9}$	$0.4^2 \times 0.2 = 0.032$
2, 3, 2	$\frac{2}{9}$	$0.4^2 \times 0.2 = 0.032$
3, 2, 2	$\frac{2}{9}$	$0.4^2 \times 0.2 = 0.032$
2, 3, 3	$\frac{2}{9}$	$0.4 \times 0.2^2 = 0.016$
3, 2, 3	$\frac{2}{9}$	$0.4 \times 0.2^2 = 0.016$
3, 3, 2	$\frac{2}{9}$	$0.4 \times 0.2^2 = 0.016$
1, 2, 3	$\frac{6}{9}$	$0.4^2 \times 0.2 = 0.032$
1, 3, 2	$\frac{6}{9}$	$0.4^2 \times 0.2 = 0.032$
2, 1, 3	$\frac{6}{9}$	$0.4^2 \times 0.2 = 0.032$
2, 3, 1	$\frac{6}{9}$	$0.4^2 \times 0.2 = 0.032$
3, 1, 2	$\frac{6}{9}$	$0.4^2 \times 0.2 = 0.032$
3, 2, 1	$\frac{6}{9}$	$0.4^2 \times 0.2 = 0.032$

Table 4.18. (*cont.*)

From this table you can construct the probability distribution of V, as in Table 4.19.

Value, v	0	$\frac{2}{9}$	$\frac{6}{9}$	$\frac{8}{9}$
$P(V = v)$	0.136	0.528	0.192	0.144

Table 4.19. Probability distribution table for *V*.

Now $E(V) = 0 \times 0.136 + \frac{2}{9} \times 0.528 + \frac{6}{9} \times 0.192 + \frac{8}{9} \times 0.144 = 0.3733\ldots$

Notice that $E(V)$ is not equal to 0.56. This means that V, the sample variance, is a biased estimator of the population variance.

It is possible, however, to modify the sample statistic V in order to obtain an unbiased estimator.

As a start, check that in the example above $E(V) = \frac{2}{3} \times 0.56$. This is an instance of a general rule.

If V is the sample variance of a sample of size n taken from a population with an unknown variance σ^2, then

$$E(V) = \frac{n-1}{n} \times \sigma^2.$$

Given this general rule and with a little thought about the meaning of expectation you should be able to see that

$$E\left(\frac{nV}{n-1}\right) = \sigma^2.$$

This means that

$$V = \left(\frac{X_1^2 + X_2^2 + \cdots + X_n^2}{n}\right) - \overline{X}^2$$

is a biased estimator of σ^2, but that

$$\frac{nV}{n-1} = \frac{n}{n-1}\left(\left(\frac{X_1^2 + X_2^2 + \cdots + X_n^2}{n}\right) - \overline{X}^2\right)$$

is an unbiased estimator of σ^2.

The expression $\dfrac{n}{n-1}\left(\left(\dfrac{X_1^2 + X_2^2 + \cdots + X_n^2}{n}\right) - \overline{X}^2\right)$ is usually denoted by S^2, or by $\hat{\sigma}^2$.

The expression for S^2 can be written in $\sum$-notation as

$$S^2 = \frac{n}{n-1}\left(\sum\frac{X^2}{n} - \overline{X}^2\right).$$

Recall that in S1 Section 3.7 you saw that

$$\sum\frac{X^2}{n} - \overline{X}^2 = \frac{1}{n}\sum(X - \overline{X})^2.$$

You can therefore define S^2 alternatively as

$$S^2 = \frac{n}{n-1}\left(\frac{1}{n}\sum(X - \overline{X})^2\right) = \frac{1}{n-1}\sum(X - \overline{X})^2.$$

Here is a summary of the methods for obtaining unbiased estimates of the mean and variance of a population from sample values $x_1, x_2, \ldots, x_n$.

> If you take a sample with values $x_1, x_2, \ldots, x_n$ from a population,
>
> - an unbiased estimate of the mean, μ, of the population is the sample mean,
> - an unbiased estimate of the variance, σ^2, of the population is
>
> $$s^2 = \frac{n}{n-1}\left(\sum\frac{x^2}{n} - \overline{x}^2\right) = \frac{1}{n-1}\sum(x - \overline{x})^2.$$

Notice that the upper-case letters $X_1, X_2, \ldots, X_n$ and S have been replaced here by lower-case letters $x_1, x_2, \ldots, x_n$ and s because the definition refers to a set of sample values which you have actually obtained.

You now know two different formulae for variance: the formula that you met in S1 Chapter 3,

$$\sum\frac{x^2}{n} - \overline{x}^2 \qquad \text{or its equivalent} \qquad \frac{1}{n}\sum(x - \overline{x})^2,$$

and the formula that was just derived,

$$s^2 = \frac{n}{n-1}\left(\sum\frac{x^2}{n} - \overline{x}^2\right) = \frac{1}{n-1}\sum(x - \overline{x})^2.$$

You do not have a choice, however, about which formula to use in a given situation. The context of your calculation will determine which formula you must use.

If the values $x_1, x_2, \ldots, x_n$ represent the whole population, that is, all the values of interest, and you wish to calculate the variance of these values, then use

$$\sum \frac{x^2}{n} - \bar{x}^2 \text{ or its equivalent } \frac{1}{n}\sum(x - \bar{x})^2.$$

If, on the other hand, you are trying to estimate the variance of a larger population from which the values $x_1, x_2, \ldots, x_n$ are a sample, then use

$$s^2 = \frac{n}{n-1}\left(\sum \frac{x^2}{n} - \bar{x}^2\right) \text{ or its equivalent } \frac{1}{n-1}\sum(x - \bar{x})^2.$$

Most calculators have separate keys for these two different variances.

Example 4.7.3

(a) Nine CDs were played and the playing time of each CD was recorded. The times, in minutes, are given below.

    49 56 55 68 61 57 61 52 63

Find the mean playing time of the nine CDs and the variance of the playing times.

(b) A student was doing a project on the playing times of CDs. She wished to estimate the mean playing time for CDs sold in the UK and she wished also to estimate the variance of playing times of CDs sold in the UK. She took a sample of nine CDs and recorded their playing times. The results are given below.

    49 56 55 68 61 57 61 52 63

 (i) Use the student's data to estimate the mean playing time for CDs sold in the UK.

(ii) Use the student's data to estimate the variance of the playing times of CDs sold in the UK.

Notice that the two parts, (a) and (b) look very similar. However in part (a) you are only interested in the playing times of the nine CDs which have been selected.

In part (b) you wish to make estimates of population parameters from the sample data that you have been given.

(a) $\bar{x} = \frac{1}{9}(49 + 56 + \cdots + 63) = 58$, so the mean is 58 minutes.

$$\begin{aligned}
\text{Variance} &= \sum \frac{x^2}{n} - \bar{x}^2 \\
&= \tfrac{1}{9}(49^2 + 56^2 + \cdots + 63^2) - 58^2 \\
&= 30.4\ldots,
\end{aligned}$$

so the variance is 30.4 min^2, correct to 3 significant figures.

(b) In this part you are estimating the mean and variance of the population.

(i) Recall that the unbiased estimator of the population mean, μ, is the mean of the sample $\bar{x}$, so the estimate of μ will be 58 minutes.

(ii) To obtain an unbiased estimate of σ^2, you need to use $s^2 = \dfrac{n}{n-1}\left(\sum \dfrac{x^2}{n} - \bar{x}^2\right)$.

As $\sum \dfrac{x^2}{n} - \bar{x}^2$ has already been calculated, to find S^2 all that needs to be done is to multiply $\sum \dfrac{x^2}{n} - \bar{x}^2$ by $\dfrac{n}{n-1}$, which in this case is $\frac{9}{8}$.

Therefore s^2, the unbiased estimate of σ^2, is $\frac{9}{8} \times 30.4\ldots = 34.25 = 34.3$, correct to 3 significant figures.

Example 4.7.4

A fishing crew recorded the masses in pounds (lb) of 200 fish of a particular species that were caught on their trawler. The results are summarised in the table below. The weights given are mid-class values.

Weight of fish (lb)	0.5	1.25	1.75	2.25	2.75	3.5	4.5	5.5	7.0	10.5
Number of fish in class	21	32	33	24	18	21	16	12	11	12

Assuming that these fish are a random sample from the population of this species, estimate

(a) the mean mass, in pounds, of a fish of this species,

(b) the variance of masses of fish of this species.

(a) First compile a frequency table to calculate totals for xf and x^2f.

Weight of fish, x (lb) (mid-class value)	Number of fish in class, f	xf	x^2f
0.5	21	10.5	5.25
1.25	32	40	50
1.75	33	57.75	101.0...
2.25	24	54	121.5
2.75	18	49.5	136.1...
3.5	21	73.5	257.2...
4.5	16	72	324
5.5	12	66	363
7.0	11	77	539
10.5	12	126	1323
Total	200	626.25	3220.1875

To find the mean of the sample use the formula

$$\bar{X} = \frac{\sum xf}{\sum f} = \frac{626.25}{200} = 3.13125, \text{ so the sample mean is } 3.131\,25 \text{ lb.}$$

Since the sample mean is an unbiased estimator of the population mean, you can take this value as the estimate of the mean mass of all fish of this species.

Therefore the estimate of the mean mass of fish of this species is 3.131 25 lb.

(a) The variance of the sample is given by

$$\text{variance} = \frac{\sum x^2 f}{\sum f} - \bar{x}^2 = \frac{3220.1875}{200} - 3.131\,25^2 = 6.296\ldots$$

To obtain the unbiased estimate of the population variance, multiply the variance of the sample by $\frac{n}{n-1}$, which in this case is $\frac{200}{199}$.

$$s^2 = \frac{200}{199}\left(\frac{\sum x^2 f}{\sum f} - \bar{x}^2\right) = \tfrac{200}{199} \times 6.296\ldots$$

$$= 6.33, \text{ correct to 3 significant figures.}$$

Exercise 4C

1 A random sample of 10 people working for a certain company with 4000 employees are asked, at the end of a day, how much they had spent on lunch that day. The results in £ are as follows.

   1.98   1.84   1.75   1.94   1.56   1.88   1.05   2.10   1.85   2.35

   Calculate unbiased estimates of the mean and variance of the amounts spent on lunch that day by all workers employed by the company.

2 Fifty boxes of matches were selected at random from a large carton of such boxes. The number of matches in each box was counted. The results are summarised by $\sum x = 2400$, $\sum x^2 = 115\,212$. Calculate

   (a) the mean and variance of the number of matches in a box for the sample of 50 boxes,

   (b) unbiased estimates of the mean and variance of the number of matches in a box for all the boxes in the carton.

3 The diameters of 20 randomly chosen plastic doorknobs of a certain make were measured. The results, x cm, are summarised by $\sum(x - 5) = 2.3$ and $\sum(x - 5)^2 = 0.54$. Find

   (a) the variance of the diameters in the sample,

   (b) an unbiased estimate of the variance of the diameters of all knobs produced.

4 The number of vehicle accidents occurring along a long stretch of a particular motorway each day was monitored for a period of 100 randomly chosen days. The results are summarised in the following table.

Number of accidents	0	1	2	3	4	5	6
Number of days	8	12	27	35	13	4	1

   (a) Find unbiased estimates of the mean and variance of the daily number of accidents.

(b) Estimate the probability that the mean number of accidents per day over a period of a month of 30 days is greater than 2.7.

Give a reason why your estimate in part (b) may be considerably in error.

5 A random sample of 150 pebbles was collected from a part of Brighton beach. The masses of the pebbles, correct to the nearest gram, are summarised in the following grouped frequency table.

Mass (g)	10–19	20–29	30–39	40–49	50–59	60–69	70–79	80–89
Frequency	1	4	22	40	49	28	4	2

(a) Find, to 3 decimal places, unbiased estimates of the mean and variance of the masses of all the pebbles on this part of the beach.

(b) Estimate the probability that the mean mass of a random sample of 40 pebbles from the same beach is less than 50 g. Give your answer correct to 2 decimal places.

6 Unbiased estimates of the mean and variance of a population, based on a random sample of 24 observations, are 5.5 and 2.42 respectively. Another random observation of 8.0 is obtained. Find new unbiased estimates of the mean and variance with this new information.

Assuming that the sample mean has a normal distribution, estimate the probability that a sample mean based on a sample size of 25 is within 0.01 of the population mean. Explain why your answer is only an estimate.

Miscellaneous exercise 4

1 The makers of a lime drink wish to find out what people think of it and decide to interview a sample of shoppers. Comment briefly on the suitability of each of the following samples.

(a) A sample of shoppers who have just bought the drink.

(b) A sample of shoppers consisting of one person aged 20, one person aged 21, one person aged 22, and so on, up to one person aged 80.

(c) A sample consisting of every 50th shopper.   (OCR)

2 Information about a population can be obtained from a random sample. Explain what you understand by the term random sample.

Comment briefly on the following methods of obtaining a 'random sample' of people from a large town.

(a) Choose random names from the town's telephone directory.

(b) Visit every 10th house in a certain area of the town on a Wednesday morning.

(c) Choose at random people from each postal district in the town in proportion to the population of each district.   (OCR, adapted)

3 The editor of a local newspaper wants to investigate the age distribution of the people who read the paper, and to obtain this information a random sample of the paper's readership is required. For each of the following sampling methods, give one reason why the method may be unsatisfactory.

(a) Reporters from the paper visit various local newsagents and interview a selection of customers in the shops who buy the paper.

(b) A form is printed in one issue of the newspaper, and readers are invited to fill in their details, cut out the form and send it (post free) to the newspaper's office.

(OCR, adapted)

4 Give a reason why the following procedure will not give a random sample of the letters of the alphabet.

Repeatedly choose a page at random from a dictionary and take the initial letter of the first word defined on the page.

Describe a suitable way of obtaining such a sample. (OCR, adapted)

5 Eggs sold in a supermarket are packed in boxes of 12. For each egg, the probability that it is cracked is 0.05, independently of all other eggs. A random sample of n boxes is selected and the variance of the sample mean number of cracked eggs in a box is 0.019. Find the value of n. (OCR, adapted)

6 Thirty apples are chosen at random from a large box of Braeburn apples. Their masses, x grams, are summarised by $\sum x = 3033$ and $\sum x^2 = 306\,676$. Find, to 4 significant figures, unbiased estimates for the mean and variance of the mass of an apple in the box.

The apples are packed in bags of 10 in a shop and the shopkeeper tells customers that most bags weigh more than a kilogram. Show that the shopkeeper's statement is correct, indicating any necessary assumption made in your calculation.

7 The mean of a random sample of n observations drawn from an $N(\mu, \sigma^2)$ distribution is denoted by $\overline{X}$. Given that $P(|\overline{X} - \mu| > 0.5\sigma) < 0.05$

(a) find the smallest value of n,

(b) with this value of n, find $P(\overline{X} < \mu + 0.1\sigma)$.

8 A botanist wishes to estimate the mean μ and standard deviation σ of the depth of the soil in a large rectangular field. Comment on the following methods of obtaining the sample points.

(a) The botanist stands at a point near the centre of the field, facing a particular direction, and throws a stone over her shoulder. The sample point is where the stone lands. This is repeated, changing the direction she faces.

(b) The botanist grids the field into metre squares and uses a table of random numbers to define a sample point at the centre of the square.

Assume that the botanist uses a suitable sampling procedure. She requires the sample mean depth to differ from μ by less than 10% of σ with probability at least $97\frac{1}{2}\%$. Find the smallest sample size that she will have to obtain.

9 The time T hours taken to repair a piece of equipment has a probability density function which may be modelled by

$$f(t) = \begin{cases} \dfrac{24}{7t^4} & 1 \leq t \leq 2, \\ 0 & \text{otherwise.} \end{cases}$$

(a) Find $E(T)$ and $Var(T)$.

(b) $\overline{T}$ denotes the mean of 30 randomly chosen repairs. Assuming that the central limit theorem holds, estimate $P(\overline{T} < 1.2)$.

State, giving a reason, whether your answer has little error or considerable error.

10 A machine is set to produce ball-bearings with mean diameter 1.2 cm. Each day a random sample of 50 ball-bearings is selected and the diameters accurately measured. If the sample mean diameter lies outside the range 1.18 cm to 1.22 cm then it will be taken as evidence that the mean diameter of the ball-bearings produced is not 1.2 cm. The machine will then be stopped and adjustments made to it. Assuming that the diameters have standard deviation 0.075 cm, find the probability that

(a) the machine is stopped unnecessarily,

(b) the machine is not stopped when the mean diameter of the ball-bearings produced is 1.15 cm.

11 The number of night calls to a fire station serving a small town can be modelled by a Poisson distribution with mean 2.7 calls per night.

(a) State the expectation and variance of the mean number of night calls over a period of n nights.

(b) Estimate the probability that during a given year of 365 days the total number of night calls will exceed 1050.

12 It may be assumed that the breaking strength of paving slabs in public areas is normally distributed with mean 50 units and standard deviation 8 units. Random samples of n paving slabs are taken and the mean breaking strength is denoted by $\overline{X}$.

(a) State the distribution of $\overline{X}$, giving its mean and variance.

(b) Find the probability that $\overline{X}$ exceeds 54 in the case $n = 25$.

(c) Find the smallest sample size if the probability that $\overline{X}$ exceeds 54 units is less than 0.01.

If it were not known that the distribution of breaking strengths is normal, what can be said about the form of the distribution of $\overline{X}$ in the case when n is large and also in the case when n is small? (OCR, adapted)

13* The mean of 64 observations of a random variable X, where $E(X) = 9$ and $Var(X) = 4$, is denoted by $\overline{X}$. Find limits symmetrically placed on either side of $E(X)$ within which $\overline{X}$ lies with probability 0.96.

Chebychev's inequality states that if Y has any distribution with mean μ and variance σ^2, then $P(|Y - \mu| < k\sigma) \geq 1 - \dfrac{1}{k^2}$ for $k \geq 1$.

Find the value of k for which $1 - \dfrac{1}{k^2} = 0.96$. Hence use Chebychev's inequality to find another pair of limits for $\overline{X}$. Comment on these limits in relation to those already found.

5 Hypothesis testing: continuous variables

Part of the purpose of statistics is to help you to make informed decisions based on data. This chapter is the first of a series of chapters about decision making, which in statistics is called 'hypothesis testing'. When you have completed it you should

- understand the nature of a hypothesis test
- understand the difference between a one-tail and a two-tail test
- be able to formulate a null hypothesis and an alternative hypothesis
- understand the terms 'significance level', 'rejection region', 'acceptance region' and 'test statistic'
- be able to carry out a hypothesis test of a population mean for a sample drawn from a normal distribution of known variance, and also for a large sample.

5.1 An introductory example

Over a number of years a primary school has recorded the reading ages of children at the beginning and end of each academic year. The teachers have found that during Year 3 the increase in reading age is normally distributed with mean 1.14 years and standard deviation 0.16 years. This year they are going to trial a new reading scheme: other schools have tried this scheme and found that it led to a greater increase in reading age. At the end of the year the teachers will use the mean increase in reading age, $\bar{x}$, of the 40 children in Year 3 to help them answer the question: 'Does the new reading scheme give better results than the old one in our school?'

The difficulty in answering this question lies in the fact each child progresses at a different rate so that different values of $\bar{x}$ will be obtained for different groups of children. It is easy to check whether $\bar{x}$ is greater than 1.14 years. It is not easy to know whether a value of $\bar{x}$ greater than 1.14 years reflects the effectiveness of the new scheme or is just due to random variation between children.

This chapter describes a statistical method for arriving at a decision. The following sections break down the process into several stages.

5.2 Null and alternative hypotheses

There are two theories about how the new reading scheme performs in this particular school. The first is that using the new scheme makes no difference. This theory is called a **null hypothesis**. It is denoted by the symbol H_0. In this example, where the mean of the past increases in reading age is 1.14 years, the null hypothesis can be expressed by $H_0 : \mu = 1.14$. Note that H_0 proposes a single value for the population mean, μ, which is based on past experience.

A 'hypothesis' is a theory which is assumed to be true unless evidence is obtained which indicates otherwise. 'Null' means 'nothing' and the term 'null hypothesis' means a 'theory of no change', that is 'no change' from what would be expected from past experience.

The other theory is that the new reading scheme is more effective than the old one; that is, that the population mean will increase. This is called the **alternative hypothesis** and is given the symbol H_1. So the alternative hypothesis in this case is $H_1 : \mu > 1.14$. The alternative hypothesis proposes the way in which μ will have changed if the new reading scheme is more effective than the old one.

The procedure which is used to decide between these two opposing theories is called a **hypothesis test** or sometimes a **significance test**. In this example the test will be **one-tail** because the alternative hypothesis proposes a change in the mean in only one direction, in this case an increase. It is also possible to have a one-tail test in which the alternative hypothesis proposes a decrease in the mean. Tests in which the alternative hypothesis suggests a difference in the mean in either direction are called **two-tail**.

Example 5.2.1
For the following situations give null and alternative hypotheses and say whether a hypothesis test would be one-tail or two-tail.

(a) In the past an athlete has run 100 metres in 10.3 seconds on average. He has been following a new training programme which he hopes will decrease the time he takes to run 100 metres. He is going to time himself on his next six runs.

(b) The bags of sugar coming off a production line have masses which vary slightly but which should have a mean value of 1.01 kg. A sample is to be taken in order to test whether there has been any change in the mean.

(c) The mean volume of liquid in bottles of lemonade should be at least 2 litres. A sample of bottles is taken in order to test whether the mean volume has fallen below 2 litres.

(a) The null hypothesis proposes a single value for μ, $H_0 : \mu = 10.3$ based on the athlete's past performance. The alternative hypothesis proposes how μ might have changed, $H_1 : \mu < 10.3$. This is a one-tail test.

(b) The null hypothesis proposes a single value for μ, $H_0 : \mu = 1.01$ based on the mass which the bags should have. The alternative hypothesis proposes how μ might have changed, $H_1 : \mu \neq 1.01$. This is a two-tail test.

(c) The null hypothesis proposes that μ should be at least 2, that is $\mu \geq 2$. However, you will see later in the chapter that a single value of μ is needed in order to carry out the calculation in a hypothesis test. So, in this example, the null hypothesis $H_0 : \mu = 2$ is taken. This null hypothesis satisfies the criterion that μ is at least 2. A sample is taken in order to test whether the mean has fallen below 2, so the alternative hypothesis is $H_1 : \mu < 2$. This is a one-tail test.

For a hypothesis test on the population mean, μ, the null hypothesis, H_0, proposes a value, μ_0, for μ,

$$H_0 : \mu = \mu_0.$$

The alternative hypothesis, H_1, suggests the way in which μ might differ from μ_0. H_1 can take three forms:

$H_1 : \mu < \mu_0$, a one-tail test for a decrease;
$H_1 : \mu > \mu_0$, a one-tail test for an increase;
$H_1 : \mu \neq \mu_0$, a two-tail test for a difference.

Exercise 5A

In the following situations, state suitable null and alternative hypotheses involving a population with mean μ. You will need some of your answers in Exercise 5B.

1 Bars of Choco are claimed by the manufacturer to have a mean mass of 102.5 grams. A test is carried out to see whether the mean mass of Choco bars is less than 102.5 grams.

2 The mean factory assembly time for a particular electronic component is 84 s. It is required to test whether the introduction of a new procedure results in a different assembly time.

3 In a report it was stated that the average age of all hospital patients was 53 years. A newspaper believes that this figure is an underestimate.

4 The manufacturer of a certain battery claims that it has a mean life of 30 hours. A suspicious customer wishes to test the claim.

5 A large batch of capacitors is judged to be satisfactory by an electronics factory if the mean capacitance is at least 5 microfarads. A test is carried out on a batch to determine whether it is satisfactory.

5.3   Critical values

Once you have decided on your null and alternative hypotheses the next step is to devise a rule for choosing between them. Look again at the reading scheme example. The rule will be based on the sample mean, $\bar{x}$. The teachers are only interested in the new scheme if it improves the average increase in reading age and so only values of $\bar{x}$ greater than 1.14 might lead them to drop the old scheme in favour of the new one. Initially, you might think that *any* value of $\bar{x}$ which is greater than 1.14, years would show that the new scheme is more effective. A little more thought shows that is too simple a rule.

It is possible to obtain a sample mean $\bar{x}$ that is greater than 1.14 even if the new reading scheme is not effective at all. To see this suppose that there is no difference between the new reading scheme and the old one. Then both μ and σ will be the same under the two schemes and X will be distributed as $N(1.14, 0.16^2)$.

You should recall from Section 4.6 that if $X \sim N(\mu, \sigma^2)$, then $\overline{X} \sim N\left(\mu, \dfrac{\sigma^2}{n}\right)$; so for samples consisting of 40 children, the mean, $\overline{X}$, will be distributed as $N\left(1.14, \dfrac{0.16^2}{40}\right)$.

Fig. 5.1 shows the distribution of $\overline{X}$.

You can see from this diagram that there is a probability of $\frac{1}{2}$ that the sample mean will be greater than 1.14, even though you assumed that there is no change in the population mean.

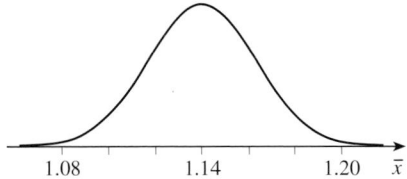

Fig. 5.1. Distribution of mean increase in reading age for the children in Section 5.1 if the new scheme is ineffective.

How big does the sample mean have to be before you can conclude that the population mean is likely to have increased from 1.14? Most people would agree that if a sample mean of 2.00 is obtained then it is unlikely that the population mean is still 1.14, but what about a sample mean of 1.19? One way of tackling this problem is to divide the possible outcomes into two regions: the **rejection** (or **critical**) **region** and the **acceptance region**.

The rejection region will contain values at the top end of the distribution in Fig. 5.1.

If the sample mean is in the rejection region, you reject H_0 in favour of H_1: you conclude that the population mean has increased. If the sample mean is in the acceptance region, you do not reject H_0: there is insufficient evidence to say that the new reading scheme is more effective.

The rejection region is chosen so that it is 'unlikely' for the sample mean to fall in the rejection region when H_0 is true. It is a matter of opinion what you mean by 'unlikely' but the usual convention among statisticians is that an event which has a probability of 0.05, that is 1 in 20, or less, is 'unlikely'.

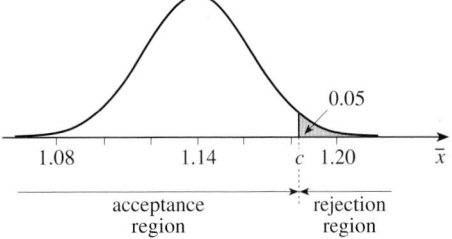

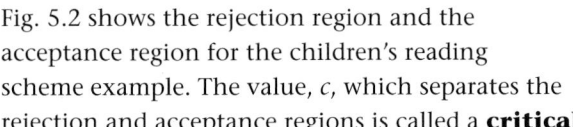

Fig. 5.2. Acceptance and rejection regions for the children's reading age example.

Fig. 5.2 shows the rejection region and the acceptance region for the children's reading scheme example. The value, c, which separates the rejection and acceptance regions is called a **critical value**. It can be calculated (using the tables on pages 178–9) as follows.

Since $\Phi(z) = 0.95$, the value of the standardised normal variable, z, corresponding to c, is $z = 1.645$.

The values of the standardised and original variables are related by $z = \dfrac{\overline{x} - \mu}{\sqrt{\dfrac{\sigma^2}{n}}}$, where $Z \sim N(0, 1)$.

Substituting in this equation gives $1.645 = \dfrac{c - 1.14}{\sqrt{\dfrac{0.16^2}{40}}}$.

Rearranging gives $c = 1.645 \sqrt{\dfrac{0.16^2}{40}} + 1.14 = 1.18$, correct to 3 significant figures.

The rejection region is given by $\overline{X} \geqslant 1.18$ years.

At the end of the year the observed value for the sample mean was $\overline{x} = 1.19$ years. Since this value is in the rejection region, you can conclude that the observed result is unlikely to be explained by random variation: it is more likely to be due to an increase in the population mean. This suggests that the new reading scheme does give better results than the old one.

In this example a decision is made by considering the value of the sample mean. The sample mean, $\overline{X}$, is called the **test statistic** for this hypothesis test. The rejection region was defined so that the probability of the test statistic falling in it, *if* H_0 *is true*, is at most 0.05, or 5%. This probability is called the **significance level** of the test. It gives the probability of rejecting H_0 when it is in fact true. In this example it gives the probability of concluding that the new reading scheme is better even when it is not. You might feel that this is too high a risk of being wrong and choose instead to use a significance level of, say, 0.01, or 1%.

Example 5.3.1

Find the rejection region for a test at the 1% significance level for the children's reading scheme example.

Now $\Phi(z) = 0.99$ giving $z = 2.326$. Substituting into $z = \dfrac{\overline{x} - \mu}{\sqrt{\dfrac{\sigma^2}{n}}}$ gives

$$2.326 = \frac{c - 1.14}{\sqrt{\dfrac{0.16^2}{40}}}.$$

Rearranging gives $c = 1.20$, correct to 3 significant figures.

The rejection region is $\overline{X} \geqslant 1.20$.

The observed value of 1.19 years is no longer in the rejection region and so H_0 is not rejected at the 1% significance level.

You may feel that it is unsatisfactory that the result of a hypothesis test should depend on the significance level chosen. This point is discussed in more detail in Chapter 7.

In a two-tail test the rejection region has two parts, because both high and low values of $\overline{X}$ are unlikely if the null hypothesis is true. Example 5.3.2 illustrates this situation.

Example 5.3.2

In the past a machine has produced rope which has a breaking load which is normally distributed with mean 1000 N and standard deviation 21 N. A new process has been introduced. In order to test whether the mean breaking load has changed a sample of 50 pieces of rope is taken, the breaking strain of each piece measured and the mean calculated.

(a) Define suitable null and alternative hypotheses for testing whether the breaking load has changed.

(b) Taking the sample mean as the test statistic, find the rejection region for $\overline{X}$ for a hypothesis test at the 5% significance level.

(c) The sample mean for the 50 pieces of rope was 1003 N. What can you deduce?

> (a) The null hypothesis states the value which the mean breaking load should take, $H_0 : \mu = 1000$.
>
> The alternative hypothesis states how μ might have changed, $H_1 : \mu \neq 1000$.
>
> (b) If H_0 is true, then the sample mean, $\overline{X} \sim N\left(1000, \dfrac{21^2}{50}\right)$.
>
> Fig. 5.3 shows the distribution of $\overline{X}$ with the rejection and acceptance regions. There are two critical values labelled c_1 and c_2.

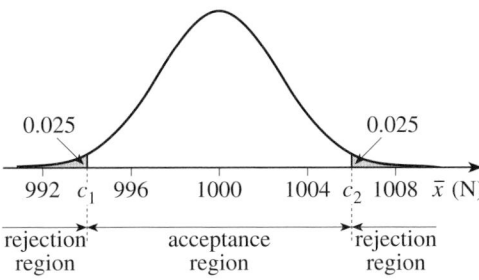

Fig. 5.3. Acceptance and rejection regions for Example 5.3.2.

> To find the upper critical value, use $\Phi(z) = 0.975$, since the 0.05 probability is split equally between the two 'tails' of the distribution. The required value of z is 1.960.
>
> Substituting into $z = \dfrac{\overline{x} - \mu}{\sqrt{\dfrac{\sigma^2}{n}}}$ gives $1.960 = \dfrac{c_2 - 1000}{\sqrt{\dfrac{21^2}{50}}}$.
>
> Rearranging gives $c_2 = 1006$, to the nearest integer.
>
> By symmetry, $c_1 = 994$.
>
> So the rejection region is $\overline{X} \leqslant 994$ and $\overline{X} \geqslant 1006$.

> (c) The observed sample mean of $\overline{x} = 1003$ is not in the rejection region. There is not enough evidence to say that the mean has changed and it can be concluded that the new process is satisfactory.

Note that the conclusion to a hypothesis test should always be given in context.

Here is a summary of the terms introduced in this section, followed by a list of the steps involved in carrying out a hypothesis test.

> The **test statistic** is calculated from the sample. Its value is used to decide whether the null hypothesis, H_0, should be rejected.
>
> The **rejection** (or **critical**) **region** gives the values of the test statistic for which the null hypothesis, H_0, is rejected.
>
> The **acceptance region** gives the values of the test statistic for which the null hypothesis, H_0, is not rejected.
>
> The boundary value(s) of the rejection region is (are) called the **critical value(s)**.
>
> The **significance level** of a test gives the probability of the test statistic falling in the rejection region when H_0 is true.

> If H_0 is rejected, then H_1 is automatically accepted.

> To carry out a hypothesis test:
>
> **Step 1**   Define the null and alternative hypotheses.
>
> **Step 2**   Decide on a significance level.
>
> **Step 3**   Determine the critical value(s).
>
> **Step 4**   Calculate the test statistic.
>
> **Step 5**   Decide on the outcome of the test depending on whether the value of the test statistic is in the rejection or the acceptance region.
>
> **Step 6**   State the conclusion in words.

Exercise 5B

In the following questions, the rejection (critical) regions should be found in terms of the sample mean, $\overline{X}$.

1   The random variable X has a normal distribution, $N(\mu, 4)$. A test of the null hypothesis $\mu = 10$ against the alternative hypothesis $\mu > 10$ is carried out, at the 5% significance level, using a random sample of 9 observations of X. The rejection region is found to be $\overline{X} \geqslant 11.10$. State the conclusion of the test in the following cases.

   (a) $\overline{X} = 12.3$ (b) $\overline{X} = 8.6$

2 The random variable Y has a normal distribution, $N(\mu, 9)$. A test of the null hypothesis $\mu = 15$ against the alternative hypothesis $\mu < 15$ is carried out at the 10% significance level, using a random sample of 16 observations. Show that the rejection region is $\overline{Y} < 14.04$.

State the conclusion of the test in the following cases.

(a) $\overline{Y} = 15.5$　　　(b) $\overline{Y} = 12.7$

3 The random variable X has a normal distribution, $N(\mu, 25)$. A test of the null hypothesis $\mu = 20$ against the alternative hypothesis $\mu \neq 20$ is carried out at the 5% significance level, using a random sample of 4 observations. Show that the rejection region is $\overline{X} < 15.1$ and $\overline{X} > 24.9$

State the conclusion of the test in the following cases.

(a) $\overline{X} = 17$　　　(b) $\overline{X} = 13$　　　(c) $\overline{X} = 30$

4 For the situation in Exercise 5A Question 1, a random sample of 12 bars had a mean mass of 101.4 g. Test, at the 5% significance level, whether the mean mass of all Choco bars is less than 102.5 g, assuming that the mass of a Choco bar is normally distributed with standard deviation 1.7 g.

5 For the situation in Exercise 5A Question 2, a random sample of 40 components had mean assembly time 81.2 s. Assuming that the assembly time of a component has a normal distribution with standard deviation 6.1 s, carry out a test at the 5% significance level of whether the mean for all components differs from 84.0 s.

6 Referring to Exercise 5A Question 5, a random sample of 6 capacitors was selected from the batch. Their capacitances were measured in microfarads with the following results.

　　5.12　4.81　4.79　4.85　5.04　4.61

Assuming that the capacitances have a normal distribution with standard deviation 0.35 microfarads, test, at the 2% significance level, whether the batch is satisfactory.

7 The blood pressure of a group of hospital patients with a certain type of heart disease has mean 85.6. A random sample of 25 of these patients volunteered to be treated with a new drug and a week later their mean blood pressure was found to be 70.4. Assuming a normal distribution with standard deviation 15.5 for blood pressures, and using a 1% significance level, test whether the mean blood pressure for all patients treated with the new drug is less than 85.6.

8 Two-litre bottles of a brand of spring water are advertised as containing 6.8 mg of magnesium. In a random sample of 10 of these bottles the mean amount of magnesium was found to be 6.92 mg. Assuming that the amounts of magnesium are normally distributed with standard deviation 0.18 mg, test whether the mean amount of magnesium in all similar bottles differs significantly from 6.8 mg. Use a 5% significance level.

9 The lives of a certain make of battery have a normal distribution with mean 30 h and variance 2.54 h². When a large consignment of these batteries is delivered to a store the quality control manager tests the lives of 8 randomly chosen batteries. The mean life was 28.8 h. Test whether there is cause for complaint. Use a 3% significance level.

10 The birth weights of babies born in a certain large hospital maternity unit during the year 2003 had a normal distribution with mean 3.21 kg and standard deviation 0.73 kg. During the first week of August, there were 24 babies born with a mean weight of 3.17 kg. Using a 5% significance level, test whether the sample is likely to differ from a sample chosen at random from the year's births at the hospital.

5.4   Standardising the test statistic

In the previous exercise the rejection region for each question was different and you had to find it before you could obtain the result of the hypothesis test. You may have spotted that the calculation could be shortened by standardising the value of $\overline{X}$ using

$$Z = \frac{\overline{X} - \mu}{\sqrt{\dfrac{\sigma^2}{n}}} = \frac{\overline{X} - \mu}{\dfrac{\sigma}{\sqrt{n}}}$$

and taking Z as the test statistic. For a given type of test, one-tail or two-tail, at a given significance level the rejection region for Z will always be the same.

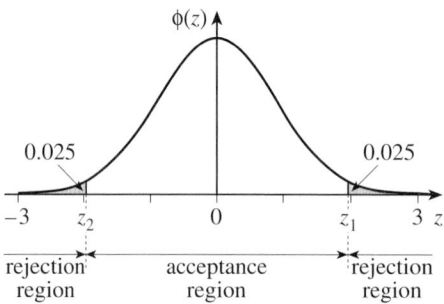

Fig. 5.4. Acceptance and rejection regions for Z for a two-tail test at the 5% significance level.

For example, Fig. 5.4 illustrates the rejection region of Z for a two-tail test at the 5% significance level. The upper critical value is obtained from $\Phi(z_1) = 0.975$, giving $z_1 = 1.960$ and, by symmetry, the lower critical value, $z_2 = -1.960$. Thus the rejection region is $Z \geqslant 1.960$ and $Z \leqslant -1.960$, which you can write more compactly as $|Z| \geqslant 1.960$. The following examples illustrate this approach.

Example 5.4.1

A test of mental ability has been constructed so that, for adults in the UK, the test score is normally distributed with mean 100 and standard deviation 15. A doctor wishes to test whether sufferers from a particular disease differ in mean from the general population in their performance on this test. She chooses a random sample of 10 sufferers. Their scores on the test are

119   131   95   107   125   90   123   89   103   103.

Carry out a test at the 5% significance level to test whether sufferers from the disease differ from the general population in the way in which they perform at this test.   (OCR, adapted)

The null and alternative hypotheses are $H_0 : \mu = 100$ and $H_1 : \mu \neq 100$ respectively, where μ is the mean score in a test of mental ability.

This is a two-tail test at the 5% significance level. As explained above, the rejection region for the test statistic, Z, is $|Z| \geq 1.960$.

Under H_0, $\overline{X} \sim N\left(100, \dfrac{15^2}{10}\right).$

'Under H_0' is another way of saying 'If H_0 is true'.

For this sample,

$$\overline{x} = \tfrac{1}{10}(119 + 131 + 95 + 107 + 125 + 90 + 123 + 89 + 103 + 103) = 108.5.$$

When $\overline{x} = 108.5$, $z = \dfrac{\overline{x} - \mu}{\sqrt{\dfrac{\sigma^2}{n}}} = \dfrac{(108.5 - 100)}{\sqrt{\dfrac{15^2}{10}}} = 1.792$, correct to 3 decimal places.

The observed value of Z is not in the rejection region so H_0 is not rejected. There is insufficient evidence, at the 5% significance level, to suggest that sufferers from this disease differ from the general population in their performance on the test.

Example 5.4.2
A manufacturer claims that its light bulbs have a lifetime which is normally distributed with mean 1500 hours and standard deviation 30 hours. A shopkeeper suspects that the bulbs do not last as long as is claimed because he has had a number of complaints from customers. He tests a random sample of six bulbs and finds that their lifetimes are 1472, 1486, 1401, 1350, 1511, 1591 hours. Is there evidence, at the 1% significance level, that the bulbs last a shorter time than the manufacturer claims?

The null and alternative hypotheses are $H_0 : \mu = 1500$ and $H_1 : \mu < 1500$ respectively, where μ is the mean lifetime of a light bulb in hours.

This is a one-tail test for a decrease at the 1% level. Fig. 5.5 shows the rejection region

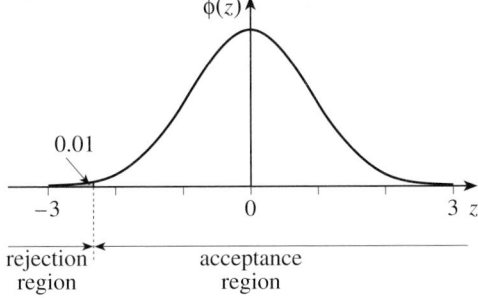

Fig. 5.5. Acceptance and rejection regions for Example 5.4.2.

for Z. The critical value is obtained from $\Phi(z) = 0.01$, giving $z = -2.326$, and the rejection region is $Z \leqslant -2.326$.

Under H$_0$, $\overline{X} \sim \mathrm{N}\left(1500, \dfrac{30^2}{6}\right)$.

For this sample,

$$\overline{x} = \tfrac{1}{6}(1472 + 1486 + 1401 + 1350 + 1511 + 1591) = 1468.5.$$

When $\overline{x} = 1468.5$, $z = \dfrac{\overline{x} - \mu}{\sqrt{\dfrac{\sigma^2}{n}}} = \dfrac{1468.5 - 1500}{\sqrt{\dfrac{30^2}{6}}} = -2.572$, correct to 3 decimal places.

The observed value of Z is in the rejection region. There is evidence, at the 1% significance level, that the manufacturer's bulbs do not last as long as claimed.

You can generalise this method as follows.

> The test statistic Z can be used to test a hypothesis about a population mean, H$_0 : \mu = \mu_0$, for samples drawn from a normal distribution of known variance σ^2. For a sample of size n, the value of Z is given by
>
> $$z = \frac{\overline{x} - \mu}{\sqrt{\dfrac{\sigma^2}{n}}} = \frac{\overline{x} - \mu}{\dfrac{\sigma}{\sqrt{n}}}. \qquad (5.1)$$
>
> The rejection region for Z depends on H$_1$ and the significance level used. The critical values for some commonly used rejection regions are given below.
>
> | | Two-tail | One-tail | One-tail |
> |---|---|---|---|
> | Significance level | H$_1 : \mu \neq \mu_0$ | H$_1 : \mu > \mu_0$ | H$_1 : \mu < \mu_0$ |
> | 10% | ± 1.645 | 1.282 | -1.282 |
> | 5% | ± 1.960 | 1.645 | -1.645 |
> | 2% | ± 2.326 | 2.054 | -2.054 |
> | 1% | ± 2.576 | 2.326 | -2.326 |
>
> Values for a one-tail test for an increase in the population mean can be found from the table on page 179. The probabilities given refer to the acceptance region.

Exercise 5C

1 Cans of lemonade are filled by a machine which is set to dispense an amount which is normally distributed with mean 330 ml and standard deviation 2.4 ml. A quality control manager suspects that the machine is over-dispensing and tests a random sample of 8 cans. The volumes of the contents, in ml, are as follows.

$$329 \quad 327 \quad 331 \quad 326 \quad 334 \quad 343 \quad 328 \quad 339$$

Test, at the $2\tfrac{1}{2}$% significance level, whether the manager's suspicion is justified.

2 The masses of loaves from a certain bakery have a normal distribution with mean μ grams and standard deviation σ grams. When the baking procedure is under control, $\mu = 508$ and $\sigma = 18$. A random sample of 25 loaves from a day's output had a total mass of 12 554 grams. Does this provide evidence at the 10% significance level that the process is not under control?

3 A machine produces elastic bands with breaking tension T newtons, where $T \sim N(45.1, 19.0)$. On a certain day, a random sample of 50 bands was tested and found to have a mean breaking tension of 43.4 newtons. Test, at the 4% significance level, whether this indicates a change in the mean breaking tension.

4 The cholesterol level of healthy males under the age of 21 is normally distributed with mean 160 and standard deviation 10. A random sample of 200 university students, all under age 21, had a mean cholesterol level of 161.8. Test, at the 1% significance level, whether all male university students under age 21 have a mean cholesterol level greater than 160.

5 The mean and standard deviation of the number of copies of *The Daily Courier* sold by a newsagent were 276.4 and 12.2 respectively. During 24 days following an advertising campaign, the total number of copies of *The Daily Courier* sold by the newsagent was 6713. Stating your assumptions, test at the 5% significance level whether the data indicate that the campaign was successful.

6 The average time that I have to wait for the 8.15 bus is 4.3 minutes. A new operator takes over the service, with the same timetable, and my average waiting time for 10 randomly chosen days under the new operator is 3.4 minutes. Assuming that the waiting time has a normal distribution with standard deviation 1.8 minutes, test whether the average waiting time under the new operator has decreased. Use a 10% significance level.

7 The marks of all candidates in an A-Level Statistics examination are normally distributed with mean 42.3 and standard deviation 11.2. The 15 candidates entered from Erehwon High School have a mean mark of 49.8. Test, at the 1% significance level, whether Erehwon High School has unusually good results for this examination.

5.5 Large samples

In the examples considered so far you have assumed that the samples were drawn from a normal distribution and that the variance of this distribution is known. In practice, there are many cases where you cannot be sure that the population distribution is normal and you may or may not have accurate information about its variance. However, the method of hypothesis testing which has been described in this chapter can still be applied provided that the sample is large. Consider first the distribution from which the sample is taken. Although this may not be normal, the central limit theorem (see Section 4.4) tells you that the sample mean, $\overline{X}$, is normally distributed provided that the sample is large. Next, consider the population variance. An unbiased estimate of this can be calculated from the sample using the equation on page 97.

$$s^2 = \frac{n}{n-1} \left(\sum \frac{x_i^2}{n} - \overline{x}^2 \right).$$

If the sample is large, this estimate is sufficiently accurate to replace σ^2 in Equation 5.1. The term 'large' is not very precise. A rule of thumb would be that 'large' means a sample size of 30 or more.

> The test statistic Z can be used to test a hypothesis about a population mean, $H_0 : \mu = \mu_0$, for large samples drawn from any population.
>
> For a sample of size n, the value of Z is given by Equation 5.1. If the population variance, σ^2, is unknown, it can be replaced by its estimate, s^2 and the value of the test statistic is $z = \dfrac{\bar{x} - \mu}{\sqrt{\dfrac{s^2}{n}}}$.
>
> A 'large' sample is one for which $n \geqslant 30$.

Example 5.5.1

A new surgical technique has been developed in an attempt to reduce the time that patients have to spend in hospital after a particular operation. In the past, the mean time spent in hospital was 5.3 days. For the first 50 patients on whom the new technique was tried, the mean time spent in hospital was 5.0 days with an estimated population variance of 0.4^2 days^2. Is there evidence at the 2% significance level that the new technique has reduced the time spent in hospital?

The null and alternative hypotheses are $H_0 : \mu = 5.3$ and $H_1 : \mu < 5.3$ respectively, where μ is the mean time spent in hospital in days.

The population distribution is not given, but, since the sample is large, the test statistic Z can still be used. This is a one-tail test for a decrease at the 2% significance level so the rejection region is $Z \leqslant -2.054$.

$$z = \frac{\bar{x} - \mu}{\sqrt{\dfrac{s^2}{n}}} = \frac{5.0 - 5.3}{\sqrt{\dfrac{0.4^2}{50}}} = -5.303, \text{ correct to 3 decimal places.}$$

The calculated value of z is in the rejection region, so H_0 is rejected: there is evidence at the 2% significance level that the time in hospital has been reduced by the new technique.

Example 5.5.2

An inspector of items from a production line takes, on average, 21.75 seconds to check each item. After the installation of a new lighting system the times, t seconds, to check each of 50 randomly chosen items from the production line are summarised by $\sum t = 1107$ and $\sum t^2 = 24\,592.35$.

(a) Calculate an unbiased estimate of the population variance of the time to check an item under the new lighting system.

(b) Test at the 5% significance level whether there is evidence that the population mean time has changed from 21.75 seconds.

(OCR, adapted)

(a) An unbiased estimate of population variance is given by

$$s^2 = \frac{n}{n-1}\left(\frac{\sum t_i^2}{n} - \bar{t}^2\right) = \frac{50}{49}\left(\frac{24\,592.35}{50} - \left(\frac{1107}{50}\right)^2\right) = 1.701\ldots$$

(b) The null and alternative hypotheses are $H_0 : \mu = 21.75$ and $H_1 : \mu \neq 21.75$ respectively, where μ is the mean time in seconds to check an item from the production line.

The population distribution and variance are not given, but, since the sample is large, the test statistic Z can still be used. For a two-tail test at the 5% significance level the rejection region for the test statistic Z is $|Z| \geqslant 1.960$.

For the given sample, $\bar{x} = \dfrac{1107}{50} = 22.14$.

$$z = \frac{\bar{x} - \mu}{\sqrt{\dfrac{s^2}{n}}} = \frac{22.14 - 21.75}{\sqrt{\dfrac{1.701\ldots}{50}}} = 2.114, \text{ correct to 3 decimal places.}$$

This value is in the rejection region. There is evidence at the 5% significance level that the population mean has changed.

Exercise 5D

1 The continuous random variable X has mean μ. A test of the hypothesis $\mu = 23$ is to be carried out at the 2% significance level. A random sample of 50 observations of X gave a sample mean $\bar{x} = 21.8$ with an estimated population variance $s^2 = 12.94$. Carry out a two-tail test.

2 A machine set to produce metal discs of diameter 11.90 cm has an annual service. After the service a random sample of 36 discs is measured and found to have a mean diameter of 11.930 cm and gives an estimated population variance of 0.072 cm^2. Test, at the 1% significance level, whether the machine is now producing discs of mean diameter greater than 11.90 cm.

3 In Lanzarote the mean daily number of hours of sunshine during April is reported to be $5\frac{1}{4}$ hours. During a particular year, during April, the daily amounts of sunshine, x hours, were recorded and the results are summarised by $\sum x = 162.3$ and $\sum x^2 = 950.6$. Test, at the 5% significance level, whether April of that year had an unusual amount of sunshine.

4 Boxes of the breakfast cereal Crispo indicate that they contain 375 grams. After receiving several complaints that the boxes contain less than the stated amount, a supermarket manager weighs the contents of a random sample of 40 boxes from a large consignment. The masses, x grams, of the contents are summarised by $\sum(x - 375) = -46$ and $\sum(x - 375)^2 = 616$. Test, at the 5% significance level, whether the mean mass of the contents of all boxes in the consignment is less than 375 grams.

5 The Galia melons produced by a fruit grower under usual conditions have a mean mass of 0.584 kg. The fruit grower decides to produce a crop organically and a random sample of

75 melons, ready for market, had masses, x kg, summarised by $\sum x = 45.39$ and $\sum x^2 = 29.03$. Test, at the 10% significance level, whether the melons grown organically are heavier, on average, than those grown under the usual conditions.

6 The diameters of a random sample of 60 cans of a certain brand of tomato were measured. The results, x cm, are summarised by $\sum(x - 6) = 48.9$ and $\sum(x - 6)^2 = 40.07$. The mean diameter of all the cans produced is denoted by μ cm. Test, at the $2\frac{1}{2}$% significance level, the following hypotheses.

(a) $\mu \neq 6.8$ (b) $\mu > 6.8$ (c) $\mu < 6.8$

5.6   An alternative method of carrying out a hypothesis test

Another way of carrying out a hypothesis test is to calculate the probability that the test statistic takes the observed value (or a more extreme value) and to compare this probability with the significance level. If the probability is less than the significance level then the null hypothesis is rejected. The result is said to be 'significant' at the given significance level. Fig. 5.6 shows that this method will always give the same result as the previous method.

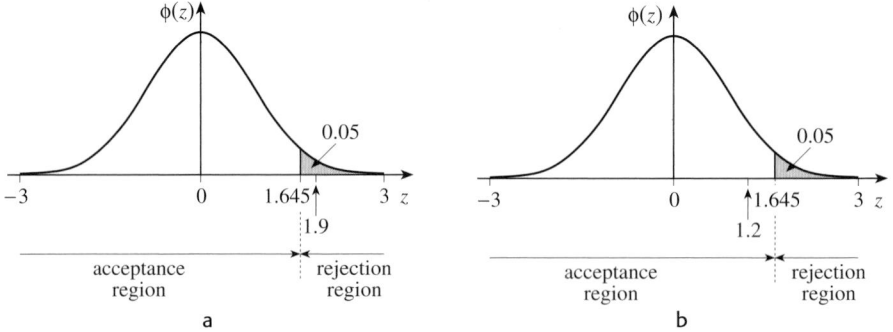

Fig. 5.6. Diagrams showing the relation between probabilities and significance levels.

Fig. 5.6a shows the rejection region for Z for a one-tail test for an increase at the 5% significance level. If Z takes a value in the rejection region, for example 1.9, then you can see from this figure that $P(Z \geqslant 1.9)$ is less than 0.05, which would also lead to the rejection of H_0. If Z takes a value in the acceptance region, for example 1.2, as shown in Fig. 5.6b, then $P(Z \geqslant 1.2)$ is greater than 0.05 and H_0 would not be rejected. To illustrate this idea, look again at Example 5.5.1. In this example, the test statistic took the value -5.30 (correct to 3 significant figures). Low values of Z were of interest so a 'more extreme value' here means a value less than -5.30. The probability that Z took this value or a more extreme value is

$$P(Z \leqslant -5.30) = 1 - \Phi(5.30) \approx 0.$$

Since this probability is less than 2%, the result is significant at the 2% level and so the null hypothesis is rejected. As you would expect this is the same as the conclusion which was reached before. However, this way of quoting the result conveys more information: it shows that the result was significant not only at the 2% level but at a much lower significance level.

Giving a probability (sometimes called a **p-value**) rather than using critical values requires a little more work. However, the use of microcomputers means that it is now easy to give a probability and most statistical programs give the result of a hypothesis test in this form.

The following example illustrates this approach in a two-tail test.

Example 5.6.1

A machine is designed to produce rods 2 cm long with a standard deviation of 0.02 cm. The lengths may be taken as normally distributed. The machine is moved to a new position in the factory, and in order to check whether the setting for the mean length has altered, the lengths of the first ten rods are measured. The standard deviation may be considered to be unchanged. If these lengths, in cm, are as given below, test at the 5% significance level whether the setting has altered or not.

2.04   1.97   1.99   2.03   2.04   2.10   2.01   1.98   1.97   2.02   (OCR, adapted)

This is a two-tail test with the null hypothesis assuming that the mean is unaltered.

The null and alternative hypotheses are $H_0 : \mu = 2$ and $H_1 : \mu \neq 2$ respectively, where μ is the mean length in centimetres of a rod.

Sample mean $= \frac{1}{10}(2.04 + 1.97 + 1.99 + 2.03 + 2.04 + 2.10 + 2.01 + 1.98 + 1.97 + 2.02)$

$$= 2.015.$$

Since the population is normally distributed, $\overline{X}$ is also normally distributed.

Under H_0, $\overline{X} \sim N\left(2, \frac{0.02^2}{10}\right)$.

$$\text{Thus } P(\overline{X} \geqslant 2.015) = P\left(Z \geqslant \frac{2.015 - 2}{\frac{0.02}{\sqrt{10}}}\right) = P(Z \geqslant 2.372)$$

$$= 1 - \Phi(2.372) = 1 - 0.9912 = 0.0088 = 0.88\%.$$

Since this is a two-tail test, this probability should be compared with half of the value specified in the significance level, that is $2\frac{1}{2}\%$, as shown in Fig. 5.7.

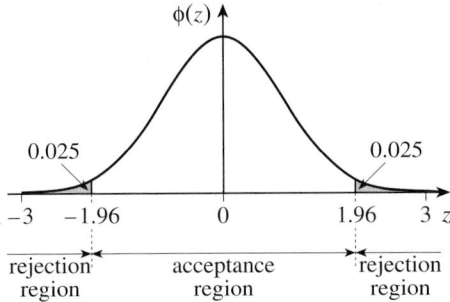

Fig. 5.7. Acceptance and rejection regions for a two-tail test at the 5% significance level.

Since 0.88% is less than $2\frac{1}{2}$%, the result is significant at the 5% level. It can be assumed that the mean length of the rods produced by the machine has been affected by the move.

Either method of carrying out a hypothesis test, using critical values or using probabilities, is satisfactory and usually you should use the method which you find easier. However, in the next chapter you will meet situations where the probability approach is simpler. For this reason, it is suggested that you carry out Exercise 5E using the probability method.

5.7 Practical activities

1 Just a minute! (*You may already have data available for this activity from S1.*) Do people tend to over- or underestimate time intervals? Ask as large a sample of people as possible to estimate a time interval of one minute. You will need to decide on a standard procedure for doing this. Record the value of the estimates to the nearest second. Use your sample to test the null hypothesis $H_0 : \mu = 60$. You could carry out this experiment for more than one distinct group, for example children in a certain age range and adults.

2 Investigating an optical illusion Each person in the sample is presented with a diagram similar to that shown in Fig. 5.8 and asked to mark the centre of the horizontal line by eye. Ask as many people as possible.

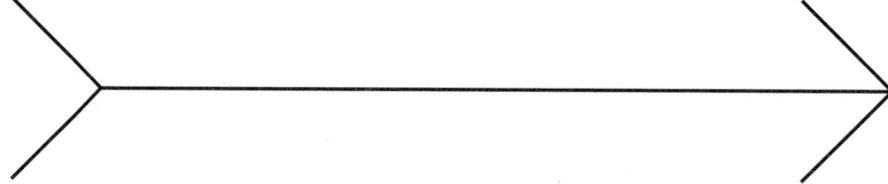

Fig. 5.8

Another sample is asked to mark the centre of a line of the same length as before but without the arrows on the ends.

Analyse the results as follows. Measure the deviation of each mark from the centre of the line, taking deviations to the right as positive and those to the left as negative. For each sample test whether the mean deviation differs significantly from zero. Comment on your results.

Exercise 5E

Carry out the hypothesis tests in this exercise by calculating probabilities.

1 The random variable X has a normal distribution with mean μ and variance 25. A random sample of 20 observations of X is taken and the sample mean is denoted by $\overline{X}$. This is used to test the null hypothesis $\mu = 30$ against the alternative hypothesis $\mu < 30$.

(a) Calculate $P(\overline{X} \leqslant 28.4)$.

(b) If the sample mean is, in fact, 28.4, state whether the null hypothesis is rejected at the

(i) 5% significance level, (ii) 10% significance level.

2 A charity has a large number of collection boxes in a variety of locations. They are emptied on a regular basis and during 2003 the mean amount collected per box (on emptying) was £8.54. Early in 2004, a random sample of 50 boxes was emptied and the contents, £x, are summarised by $\sum(x - 8) = 38.4$ and $\sum(x - 8)^2 = 240.41$. Carry out a test at the 5% significance level of whether the data provide evidence that the mean is now different from £8.54.

3 The alkalinity of soil is measured by its pH value. It has been found from many previous measurements that the pH values in a particular area have mean 8.42 and standard deviation 0.74. After an unusually hot summer the pH values were measured at 36 randomly chosen locations in the area and the sample mean value was found to be 8.63. Calculate $P(\overline{X} > 8.63)$ when $\mu = 8.42$.

What can be concluded

(a) at the 5% significance level, (b) at the 1% significance level?

4 Longbrite candles are supposed to burn for at least 7 hours. To check this, a random sample was tested; 30 Longbrite candles were lit, and the times, t hours, before they went out were recorded. The results are summarised by $\sum(t - 7) = -2.40$ and $\sum(t - 7)^2 = 2.95$. Carry out a test at the 10% significance level of whether the Longbrite candles burn, on average, for at least 7 hours.

5 The percentage salinity of the water in a stretch of sea was measured at 45 randomly chosen places during the summer of 2003. The sample mean percentage was 31.18 and an unbiased estimate of population variance was 0.579^2. Carry out a test at the 5% significance level of whether the mean salinity of the sea in that area is greater than 31%.

6 A teacher wrote an examination paper which she thought the average student should take 80 minutes to complete. She gave the paper to 35 randomly chosen students. The sample mean was 81.4 minutes and an unbiased estimate of population variance was 2.9^2 min^2. Find the smallest significance level at which it would be accepted that the mean time for all students taking the paper would differ from 80 minutes.

Miscellaneous exercise 5

1 Metal struts used in a building are specified to have a mean length of 2.855 m. The lengths have a normal distribution with standard deviation 0.0352 m. A batch of 15 struts is sent to a building site and the lengths are measured. The sample mean length is 2.841 m.

A test is to be carried out, at the 5% significance level, to decide whether the batch is from the specified population.

(a) Stating your hypotheses, find the rejection region in terms of Z.

(b) State the conclusion of the test.

2 A random variable, X, has a normal distribution with unknown mean but known variance of 12.4. The mean of a random sample of 10 observations of X is denoted by $\overline{X}$. The acceptance region of a test of the null hypothesis $\mu = 25$ is $\overline{X} > 22.41$.

(a) State the alternative hypothesis.   (b) Find the significance level of the test.

(c) If the hypothesised value of μ were greater than 25 would the significance level corresponding to the same acceptance region be larger or smaller than that found in part (b)? Give a reason for your answer.

3 The contents of a brand of Greek yoghurt can be assumed to have masses which are normally distributed with standard deviation 2.58 grams. A new machine for filling the cartons is purchased and a random sample of 20 cartons filled by this machine is used to test the null hypothesis that the mean mass of the contents is μ_0 grams. Using the standard deviation of 2.58 grams, the rejection region of the test is $\overline{X} \leqslant 208.81$ or $\overline{X} \geqslant 211.19$.

(a) Find the value of μ_0.   (b) Find the significance level of the test.

4 Sarah, who has diabetes, has to monitor her blood glucose levels, which vary throughout the day. The results from a sample of 75 readings, x, taken at random times over a week, are summarised by $\sum x = 511.5$ and $\sum x^2 = 4027.89$.

(a) Assuming a normal distribution, test at the 5% significance level whether Sarah's mean blood glucose level, μ, is greater than 6.0.

(b) Find the set of values of μ_0 for which it would be accepted that $\mu > \mu_0$ at the 10% significance level.

(c) State, giving a reason, whether the conclusion of the test in part (a) would be valid

(i) if it could no longer be assumed that blood glucose level has a normal distribution,

(ii) if the 75 readings were all taken at weekends.

5 A total crop weight, x kg, of each of 64 bean plants is measured by a horticulturalist and the results are summarised by $\sum x = 303.4$ and $\sum x^2 = 1615.96$. Find unbiased estimates of the population mean and variance.

The horticulturalist wishes to test the hypothesis that the mean crop weight per plant is 5 kg against the alternative hypothesis that the mean crop weight is less than 5 kg. Carry out the test at the 10% significance level.

Find the smallest significance level at which the test would result in rejection of the null hypothesis.   (OCR)

6 An athletics coach has the use of a gymnasium which he sets out for circuit training. The time taken for a new athlete to complete the circuit on each of a large number of occasions is noted. The mean value of these times is 100 seconds and the standard deviation is 3 seconds. The distribution of the times may be assumed to be normal. Three months later, after the athlete has been training daily, his times, in seconds, to complete the circuit on 10 occasions are as follows.

96.8   101.2   98.2   99.6   98.0   95.6   98.0   100.0   95.2   97.4

Verify that these values show, at the 5% significance level, that the athlete's performance in circuit training has improved.

Calculations based on a large number of further trials show that at this stage the mean value of the time taken by the athlete is 98 seconds and the standard deviation is 3 seconds. What would be the maximum total time for 10 circuits at some later stage which would provide evidence, at the 5% significance level, of further improvement?   (OCR)

7 An ambulance station serves an area which includes more than 10 000 houses. It has been decided that if the mean distance of the houses from the ambulance station is greater than 10 miles then a new ambulance station will be necessary. The distance, x miles, from the station of each of a random sample of 200 houses was measured, the results being summarised by $\sum x = 2092.0$ and $\sum x^2 = 24\,994.5$.

(a) Calculate, to 4 significant figures, unbiased estimates of

   (i) the population mean distance, μ miles, of houses from the station,

   (ii) the population variance of the distance of the houses from the station.

   State what you understand by 'unbiased estimate'.

(b) A test of the null hypothesis $\mu = 10$ against the alternative hypothesis $\mu > 10$ is carried out at the α% significance level, using a random sample of size 200. The rejection region for this test is $\overline{X} \geqslant 10.65$, where $\overline{X}$ denotes the sample mean.

   (i) Calculate the value of α.

   (ii) State the conclusion of the test using the sample data.

(c) Suppose that it could not be assumed that the distances are normally distributed. State whether the answers to part (a) and part (b) would still hold.   (OCR, adapted)

6 Hypothesis testing: discrete variables

This chapter takes further the idea of hypothesis testing introduced in the previous chapter. When you have completed it you should

- be able to formulate hypotheses and carry out a hypothesis test of a population proportion either by evaluation of binomial probabilities or by the use of the normal approximation
- be able to formulate hypotheses and carry out a test of a population mean using a single observation drawn from a Poisson distribution
- understand the difference between a nominal and an actual significance level.

6.1 Testing a population proportion

You have probably seen advertisements for dairy spreads which claim that the spread cannot be distinguished from butter. How could you set about testing this claim? One way would be to take pairs of biscuits and put butter on one biscuit in each pair and the dairy spread on the other. The pairs of biscuits would be given to a number of tasters who would be asked to identify the biscuit with butter on it. Half the tasters would be given the 'butter' biscuit first, and the other half the 'butter' biscuit second.

Suppose you decided to use 10 tasters. How would you set about drawing a conclusion from your results? The method of hypothesis testing described in the last chapter can be adapted to this situation. First it is necessary to formulate a null hypothesis and an alternative hypothesis. It is usual to start from a position of doubt: you assume that the tasters cannot identify the butter and that they are guessing. In this situation the probability that a taster chosen at random will get the correct result is $\frac{1}{2}$. This can be expressed by the null hypothesis $H_0 : p = \frac{1}{2}$. If some of the tasters can actually identify the butter then $p > \frac{1}{2}$. This can be expressed as an alternative hypothesis, $H_1 : p > \frac{1}{2}$.

> Can you see why it is difficult to take any other null hypothesis?

If H_0 is true, the number, X, of tasters who identify the buttered biscuit correctly is a random variable with distribution $B(10, \frac{1}{2})$. Fig. 6.1 shows this distribution.

High values of X would suggest that H_0 should be rejected in favour of H_1. The most straightforward method of carrying out a hypothesis test for a discrete variable is to use the approach of Section 5.6 and calculate the probability that X takes the observed or a more extreme value, assuming that H_0 is true, and compare this probability with the specified

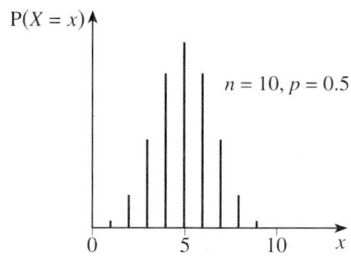

Fig. 6.1. Distribution $B(10, \frac{1}{2})$.

significance level. Suppose that 9 out of the 10 people had identified the butter and you chose a significance level of 5%. Using cumulative binomial probability tables (pages 168–173) gives

$$P(X \geqslant 9) = 1 - P(X \leqslant 8) = 1 - 0.9893 = 0.0107 = 1.07\%.$$

This probability is less than 5% so the result is significant at the 5% level. H_0 is rejected and there is evidence, at the 5% significance level, that the proportion of people who can distinguish the butter is greater than $\frac{1}{2}$.

As in the previous chapter the possible values of X can be divided into an acceptance region and a rejection region. However the situation here is complicated by the fact that X is a discrete variable. Table 6.2 shows the probability distribution of X.

x	$P(X = x)$
0	0.0010
1	0.0098
2	0.0439
3	0.1172
4	0.2051
5	0.2461
6	0.2051
7	0.1172
8	0.0439
9	0.0098
10	0.0010

Table 6.2. Probability distribution for B(10, $\frac{1}{2}$).

For a nominal significance level of, say, 5%, you will find that there is no rejection region which exactly corresponds to this probability. For example, for a rejection region of $X \geqslant 8$, the probability of a result in the rejection region is $0.0439 + 0.0098 + 0.0010 = 0.0547$ and so the actual significance level of the test is 5.47%; for $X \geqslant 9$, the actual significance level is 1.08%. This point will be considered in more detail in Section 7.3.

The following examples show further tests of this type.

Example 6.1.1
A national opinion poll claims that 40% of the electorate would vote for party R if there were an election tomorrow. A student at a large college suspects that the proportion of young people who would vote for them is lower. She asks 16 fellow students, chosen at random from the college roll, which party they would vote for. Three choose party R. Show, at the 10% significance level, that this indicates that the reported figure is too high for the young people at the student's college.

The null and alternative hypotheses are $H_0 : p = 0.4$ and $H_1 : p < 0.4$ respectively.

Let X be the number of students who choose party R. Under H_0, $X \sim B(16, 0.4)$.

Using cumulative binomial probability tables, $P(X \leqslant 3) = 0.0651 = 6.51\% < 10\%$.

The result is significant at the 10% level. This indicates that the reported figure is too high for young people at the student's college.

Example 6.1.2

In order to test a coin for bias it is tossed 20 times. The result is 14 heads and 6 tails. Test, at the 10% significance level, whether the coin is biased.

This is a two-tail test since, before the coin is tossed, there is no indication in which direction, if any, it might be biased. If the coin is unbiased, the probability of a head (or a tail) is $p = \frac{1}{2}$.

The null and alternative hypotheses are $H_0 : p = \frac{1}{2}$ and $H_1 : p \neq \frac{1}{2}$ respectively.

Let X be the number of heads resulting from 20 tosses. Under H_0, $X \sim B(20, 0.5)$. On average you would expect 10 heads. The observed value of 14 is on the high side so, using cumulative binomial probability tables,

$$P(X \geqslant 14) = 1 - P(X \leqslant 13) = 1 - 0.9423 = 0.0577 = 5.77\%.$$

Since this is a two-tail test at the 10% significance level, this probability must be compared with 5%. Since 5.77% > 5% the result is not significant and the null hypothesis is not rejected: there is insufficient evidence, at the 10% level, to say that the coin is biased.

To carry out a hypothesis test on a discrete variable, calculate the probability of the observed or a more extreme value and compare this probability with the significance level. For a one-tail test, reject the null hypothesis if this probability is less than the significance level; for a two-tail test use the side that produces a probability of less than 50% and reject the null hypothesis if this probability is less than half of the significance level.

Exercise 6A

1   The random variable X is distributed $B(10, p)$. A single observation of X has the value 1. Test the null hypothesis $H_0 : p = 0.6$ against the alternative hypothesis $H_1 : p < 0.6$ at the 10% significance level.

2   The random variable Y is distributed $B(20, p)$. A single observation of Y has the value 15. Test the null hypothesis $H_0 : p = 0.5$ against the alternative hypothesis $H_1 : p \neq 0.5$ at the 5% significance level.

3   A large housing estate contains a children's playground, and on one particular evening 12 boys and 6 girls were playing there. Assuming these children are a random sample of all children living on the estate, test, at the 10% significance level, whether there are equal numbers of boys and girls on the estate.

4 An advertisement in a newspaper inserted by a car dealer claimed, 'At least 95% of our customers are satisfied with our services.'

In order to check this statement a random sample of 25 of the dealer's customers were contacted and 22 agreed that they were satisfied with the dealer's services. Carry out a test, at the 5% significance level, of whether the data support the claim.

5 The lengths of nails produced by a machine have a normal distribution with mean 2.5 cm. A random sample of 16 nails is selected from a drum containing a large number of these nails. The nails are measured and 13 are found to have length greater than 2.5 cm. Test, at the $2\frac{1}{2}$% significance level, whether the mean length of the nails in the drum is greater than 2.5 cm. State where in the test the information that the nails have a normal distribution is used.

6 A test of 'telepathy' is devised using cards with faces coloured either red, green, blue or yellow, in equal numbers. When a card is placed face down on a table, at random, Ilesh believes he can forecast the colour of the face correctly. The cards are thoroughly mixed, one is selected and placed face down on the table and Ilesh forecasts the colour of the face. This procedure was repeated 20 times.

(a) It is given that Ilesh was correct on 8 occasions. Test, at the 5% significance level, whether Ilesh's results were better than could have been achieved by chance.

(b) How many correct forecasts would Ilesh have had to make to be significant at the 1% level?

7 A dice is suspected of being loaded to give more sixes when thrown than would be expected from a fair dice. In order to test this suspicion, the dice is thrown 30 times. Ten sixes are obtained. Carry out a test at the 5% significance level to test this suspicion.

8 A magazine article reported that 80% of computer owners use the internet regularly. Lisa believed that the true figure was different and she consulted 12 of her friends who owned computers. Six said that they were regular users of the internet.

(a) Test Lisa's belief at the 10% significance level.

(b) Comment on the reliability of the test in the light of Lisa's sample.

6.2 Testing a population proportion for large samples

When the sample is large, you can calculate probabilities by using the fact that the binomial distribution can be approximated by the normal distribution with a continuity correction. The following examples illustrate the method.

Example 6.2.1
In a multiple choice paper a candidate has to select one of four possible answers to each question. On a paper with 100 questions a student gets 34 correct answers. Test, at the 5% significance level, the null hypothesis that the student is guessing the answers.

> If the student is guessing the answers then the probability that any one answer is correct is $\frac{1}{4}$. If the student is not guessing then the proportion of correct answers should be greater than this.

The null and alternative hypotheses are $H_0 : p = \frac{1}{4}$ and $H_1 : p > \frac{1}{4}$ respectively.

Let X be the number of correct answers. Under H_0, $X \sim B\left(100, \frac{1}{4}\right)$.

The probability of the observed or a more extreme value is $P(X \geqslant 34)$. In order to find this probability, $X \sim B\left(100, \frac{1}{4}\right)$ is approximated by a normal distribution with

$$\mu = np = 100 \times \tfrac{1}{4} = 25,$$
$$\sigma^2 = npq = 100 \times \tfrac{1}{4} \times \tfrac{3}{4} = 18.75.$$

So $X \sim B\left(100, \frac{1}{4}\right)$ is approximated by $V \sim N(25, 18.75)$.

$$P(X \geqslant 34) \approx P(V \geqslant 33.5) \qquad \text{(using a continuity correction, Section 2.8)}$$
$$= P\left(Z \geqslant \frac{33.5 - 25}{\sqrt{18.75}}\right)$$
$$= P(Z \geqslant 1.963)$$
$$= 1 - \Phi(1.963)$$
$$= 1 - 0.9752$$
$$= 0.0248$$
$$= 2.48\%$$
$$< 5\%.$$

The null hypothesis can be rejected: there is evidence, at the 5% significance level, that the student is not guessing.

If you like there is no need to carry the calculation beyond the point where the value of $Z (= 1.963)$ is obtained. Instead you can use the idea of a rejection region, which was developed in Section 5.3. For a one-tail test at the 5% significance level, the rejection region for the test statistic Z is $Z \geqslant 1.645$. The observed value of Z is in the rejection region and H_0 is rejected, as before. You can use whichever method you prefer.

The following is an example of a two-tail test.

Example 6.2.2
If births are equally likely on any day of the week then the proportion of babies born at the weekend should be $\frac{2}{7}$. Out of a random sample of 490 children it was found that 132 were born at the weekend. Does this provide evidence, at the 5% significance level, that the proportion of babies born at the weekend differs from $\frac{2}{7}$?

The null and alternative hypotheses are $H_0 : p = \frac{2}{7}$ and $H_1 : p \neq \frac{2}{7}$ respectively.

Let X be the number of babies born at the weekend. Under H_0, $X \sim B\left(490, \frac{2}{7}\right)$.

Approximate X by $V \sim N\left(490 \times \frac{2}{7}, \ 490 \times \frac{2}{7} \times \frac{5}{7}\right) = N(140, 100)$.

Since 132 is lower than 140, the mean under H_0, find

$$P(X \leqslant 132) \approx P(V \leqslant 132.5)$$
$$= P\left(Z \leqslant \frac{132.5 - 140}{\sqrt{100}}\right)$$
$$= P(Z \leqslant -0.75).$$

For a two-tail test at the 5% significance level the rejection region is $|Z| \geqslant 1.96$. The calculated value of $|Z|$ is 0.75, which does not lie in the rejection region. The value of $\frac{2}{7}$ for the proportion of babies born at the weekend is accepted.

If you wish to work with probabilities, you would continue the calculation to find $P(Z \leqslant -0.75) = 0.2266 = 22.66\%$. Since $22.66\% > 2\frac{1}{2}\%$ (remember that this is a two-tail test) the null hypothesis is not rejected.

Exercise 6B

1 A jar contains a large number of coloured beads, some of which are red. A random sample of 80 of these beads is selected and 19 are found to be red. Test, at the 10% significance level, whether 30% of the beads in the jar are red.

2 A new cold relief drug is tested for effectiveness on 150 volunteers, and 124 of them found the drug beneficial. The manufacturers believe that more than 75% of people suffering from a cold will find the drug beneficial. Test the manufacturers' belief at the $2\frac{1}{2}\%$ significance level.

3 A selling price of £22,000 has been proposed for a new model of car manufactured by a large company. The price will be adopted if more than 40% of potential customers are willing to pay that price. A sample of 50 potential customers was supplied with the car's specification and 29 agreed to pay the proposed price. Carry out a test, at the 1% significance level, to decide whether the company should adopt the price of £22,000.

4 A parcel delivery service claims that at least 80% of their parcels are delivered within 48 hours of posting. A check on 200 parcels found that 152 were delivered within 48 hours of posting. Test the delivery service's claim at the 5% significance level.

5 In Western Europe, 8% of males are colour-blind. A random sample of 500 males was selected from a town in France and 53 men were found to be colour-blind. Carry out a test of whether the town contains a different proportion of colour-blind males than in Western Europe as a whole, at a significance level of

   (a) 5%,   (b) 2%.

6 The drop-out rate of students enrolled at a certain university is reported to be 13.2%. The Dean of Students suspects that the drop-out rate for science students is greater than 13.2%, and she examines the records of a random sample of 95 of these students. The number of drop-outs was found to be 20. Test the Dean's suspicion at the 2% significance level.

6.3 Testing a population mean for a Poisson distribution

The ideas developed in this and the previous chapter can also be applied when the Poisson distribution is a suitable model for the population from which the sample is drawn. The approach used for this discrete variable is similar to that used in the two previous sections.

Example 6.3.1

The random variable X has a Poisson distribution with mean λ. A single observation of X has the value 12. Test, at the 5% significance level, the null hypothesis $H_0 : \lambda = 7$ against the alternative hypothesis $H_1 : \lambda > 7$.

$$P(X \geqslant 12) = 1 - P(X \leqslant 11)$$
$$= 1 - 0.9467 \qquad \text{(from cumulative Poisson probability tables)}$$
$$= 0.0533$$
$$= 5.3\%$$
$$> 5\%.$$

The null hypothesis is not rejected: there is insufficient evidence to say that the mean is greater than 7.

Example 6.3.2

In the past an office photocopier has failed, on average, once every three weeks. A new, more expensive, photocopier is on trial which the manufacturers claim is more reliable. In the first 27 weeks of use this new photocopier fails four times. Assuming that the failures of the photocopier occur independently and at random, test, at the 5% significance level, whether there is evidence that the new photocopier is more reliable than the old one.

If the failures of the photocopier occur independently and at random then the number of failures in a given time interval can be modelled by a Poisson distribution. The null hypothesis will be a theory of 'no change'; that is, the new photocopier fails once every three weeks. So λ, the mean number of failures per week, is equal to $\frac{1}{3}$.

The null and alternative hypotheses are $H_0 : \lambda = \frac{1}{3}$ and $H_1 : \lambda < \frac{1}{3}$ respectively.

Let X be the number of failures in 27 weeks. Under H_0, $X \sim Po(27 \times \frac{1}{3}) = Po(9)$.

The observed value of X is 4. Using cumulative Poisson probability tables,

$$P(X \leqslant 4) = 0.055 = 5.5\% > 5\%.$$

The result is not significant: at the 5% significance level there is insufficient evidence to say that the new photocopier is better than the old one.

Although the initial test of the photocopier did not give a significantly better result at the 5% level, the fact that $P(X \leqslant 4)$ was close to 5% encouraged the office to continue using the photocopier for a longer trial period. The results are analysed in the following example.

Example 6.3.3

In the next 27 weeks the photocopier in Example 6.3.2 failed four more times. Using the results for the whole of the 54-week trial period, test, at the 5% significance level, whether there is evidence that the new photocopier is more reliable than the old one.

The null and alternative hypotheses are $H_0 : \lambda = \frac{1}{3}$ and $H_1 : \lambda < \frac{1}{3}$ respectively, as before, where λ is the mean number of failures per week.

Let X be the number of failures in 54 weeks. Under H_0, $X \sim Po\left(54 \times \frac{1}{3}\right) \sim Po(18)$.

The observed value of X is $4 + 4$, which is 8.

$$P(X \leqslant 8) = 0.0071 = 0.71\% < 5\%.$$

Now the result is significant and the null hypothesis is rejected. There is evidence, at the 5% significance level, that the new photocopier is more reliable than the old one.

This result is interesting because it shows how extra information can lead to a more informed decision. Each of the 27-week periods taken separately would not have given a significant result, but when the information was pooled the result was significant not only at the 5% level but also at the 1% level.

6.4 Practical activities

1 A matter of taste   Can people distinguish between different varieties of cola-flavoured drink? Choose two brands. Present each person in your sample with two glasses of one brand and one of the other and explain that you are going to ask them to pick the odd one out. You should toss a coin in order to decide which brand is presented twice. The glasses should be given in a random order and it would be helpful to give each person a glass of water to clear their palate if necessary. Allow people to retaste the drinks if they wish. If there are noticeable differences in colour between the two brands then you could use a mixture of differently coloured plastic beakers in order to conceal this. Ask as large a sample of people as possible and record whether or not they pick out the odd drink correctly.

What is the probability that a person will correctly pick out the odd drink if there is no detectable difference in flavour? Carry out a hypothesis test taking as your null hypothesis that p has this value.

2 Crossed arms   Most people have a very marked preference for the way in which they cross their arms. Try this out for yourself. Cross your arms and note which forearm is on top. Now try to cross your arms with the other forearm on top. You will probably find that this requires a bit of thought! Is a person chosen at random equally likely to prefer left over right as right over left? Ask a number of people to cross their arms and note which forearm is on top. Collect results from as large a sample as possible and test $H_0 : p = \frac{1}{2}$, $H_1 : p \neq \frac{1}{2}$, where p is the probability that a person crosses their arms right over left.

3 A test of 'telepathy'   Carry out an experiment on the lines of that described in Question 6 of Exercise 6A. There is no need to limit yourself to 20 trials.

Exercise 6C

1 The random variable Y is distributed $Po(\lambda)$. A single observation of Y has the value 3. Test the null hypothesis $H_0 : \lambda = 6$ against the alternative hypothesis $H_1 : \lambda < 6$ at the 10% significance level.

2 The random variable X has a Poisson distribution with mean λ. A single observation of X has the value 8. Test the null hypothesis $\lambda = 3.4$ against the alternative hypothesis $\lambda > 3.4$ at the 5% significance level.

3 The number of car accidents that occur along a certain stretch of road may be assumed to have a Poisson distribution with mean 4 per week. In the first two weeks after a new warning sign had been erected, 3 accidents occurred on the road. Test, at the 5% significance level, whether this indicates a reduction in the mean accident rate.

During the third week 4 accidents occurred on the road. Does this extra information alter the conclusion of the test?

4 A company manufactures 5 amp fuses and, under normal conditions, 7% of the fuses are faulty. They are packed in boxes of 60.
   (a) Explain why the number of faulty fuses in a randomly chosen box has an approximate Poisson distribution.
   (b) A box randomly chosen from a day's production has 9 faulty fuses. Test, at the 5% significance level, whether the percentage of faulty fuses on that day is different from 7%.

5 The number of errors in a page of manuscript word-processed by my secretary has a Poisson distribution with mean 1.4. I received a manuscript on a particular day and counted 4 errors on a randomly chosen page. Test, at the 10% significance level, whether this indicates that the manuscript was not word-processed by my secretary.

6 During winter months, the number of emergency calls received by a power company occur randomly at a uniform rate of 6 per day. During three days in August 2004 the power company received a total of 9 emergency calls. Test at the 5% significance level whether the mean number of emergency calls per day, at this time of the year, is less than 6.

Miscellaneous exercise 6

Part A contains questions on this chapter only. Part B contains questions on the contents of both Chapters 5 and 6.

Part A
1 A leading newspaper reported that 2 out of every 3 female football club fans were able to explain the offside rule correctly. Derby County supporters believed that more of their female fans could explain the rule correctly. To prove their point a random sample of 20 female Derby County fans was questioned outside Pride Park after a match, and 17 were able to explain the offside rule correctly.

(a) Carry out a test, at the 10% significance level, of the hypothesis that the proportion of female Derby County fans that can explain the offside rule correctly is more than $\frac{2}{3}$.

(b) Have the supporters 'proved their point'?

2 The probability of a drawing pin landing point up when dropped onto a horizontal floor from a height of one metre is denoted by p. When the drawing pin is dropped 25 times it lands point up 5 times.

(a) Test the null hypothesis $p = 0.4$ against the alternative hypothesis $p < 0.4$ at the $2\frac{1}{2}$% significance level.

(b) Find, from the table of cumulative binomial probabilities, a set of values of p_0 for which it would be accepted that $p < p_0$ at the $2\frac{1}{2}$% significance level.

3 It is suggested that one-third of all mathematicians are left-handed. In a survey, 51 out of 174 mathematicians were found to be left-handed. Assuming that the sample was random, carry out a test, at the 5% significance level, of whether or not the sample confirms the suggestion.   (OCR, adapted)

4 In the promotion of Doggo, a new animal food, it was asserted that more dogs prefer the new food to the current brand leader. In a test of this assertion, 40 dogs were given a choice of Doggo and the current brand leader.

(a) Find the smallest number of dogs that would have to prefer Doggo for the promoter's assertion to be accepted at the 5% significance level.

(b) What then is the actual significance level of the test?

5 A supermarket buys a large batch of plastic bags from a manufacturer to be used in the store. In previous batches 7% of the bags were defective. A quality control manager wishes to test whether the batch has a higher defective rate than 7%, in which case the batch will be returned to the manufacturer. He examines 125 randomly selected bags and finds that 14 are defective. Using a distributional approximation, carry out the manager's test at the 3% significance level and state whether he should return the batch.

6 During the period from May 1997 to April 2000, 17 lap-top computers were lost by employees at the Ministry of Agriculture, Fisheries and Food. After a rigorous enquiry it was hoped that the rate of loss would drop.

(a) State what must be assumed for the number of lap-top computers lost during a fixed period of time to have a Poisson distribution.

(b) Find the greatest number of lap-top computers that can be lost during the next three years in order to be significant, at the $2\frac{1}{2}$% significance level, of a drop in the loss rate.

7 A machine that weaves a carpet of width 2 m produces slight flaws in the carpet at a rate of 1.8 per metre length.

(a) State what must be assumed for the number of flaws in a given length of carpet to have a Poisson distribution.

(b) After the machine is given an overhaul a random sample of 3 m length of the carpet is examined and found to have 2 flaws. Test, at the 5% significance level, whether the rate of incidence of the flaws has decreased.   *continued* . . .

(c) A further 1 m length of the carpet is found to have no flaw. Pooling the two results, determine whether the conclusion of the above test changes.

8 Wild flowers of a certain species grow randomly in a forest area and at a uniform rate of 7.6 per $10\,000\,\text{m}^2$.

(a) Suggest a suitable probability distribution of the number of the flowers that grow in an area of 2500 m^2 of the forest.

(b) After an unusually fine summer month, when the forest was visited by a large number of tourists, the forest managers wished to investigate whether the number of flowers of the species had decreased. In a pilot test a randomly chosen 2500 m^2 area of the forest was studied and found to contain no flower of this species. Test whether this indicates, at the 5% significance level, that the number of flowers of the species has decreased.

(c) In a further study, the managers examined 50 randomly selected areas of 2500 m^2 of forest. In 13 of the areas no flower of the species was found. Using a significance level of 5%, test whether this indicates that the number of flowers of the species has decreased.

Part B

9 The mass of Vitamin E in a capsule made by a drug company is normally distributed with mean μ mg and standard deviation 0.058 mg. A random sample of 16 capsules was analysed and the mean mass of Vitamin E was 4.97 mg. Test, at the 2% significance level, the null hypothesis $\mu = 5.00$ against the alternative hypothesis $\mu < 5.00$.

10 The proportion of patients who suffer an allergic reaction to a drug used to treat a particular medical condition is assumed to be 0.036. When 500 patients were treated with the drug, 28 suffered an allergic reaction. Test, at the 5% significance level, whether the quoted figure of 0.036 is an underestimate. (OCR, adapted)

11 Students using a college canteen for lunch paid an average of £2.04 during 2003. A new catering company was appointed in 2004 and after the company had provided food for one month a random sample of 60 students was asked to state the amount spent daily on lunch. The results, £x, were summarised by $\sum x = 136.80$ and $\sum x^2 = 348.49$. Test, at the 3% significance level, whether the average amount paid by students for lunch had increased.

The person who carried out the above test included in his report the following incorrect statement. Give a corrected version. 'It is not necessary for the population to have a normal distribution since the sample size is large and the Central Limit Theorem states that any sufficiently large sample is normal.' (OCR, adapted)

12 A firm manufactures glass vases and the proportion of defective vases is 0.2. The quality control department wants to reduce the proportion of defective vases and makes changes to the manufacturing procedure. A random sample of 25 vases is then examined and 2 are found to be defective. Test at the 10% significance level whether the proportion of defective vases has been reduced.

13 The age, x years, of each of the women giving birth at a maternity hospital in the year 2003 was recorded correct to 1 decimal place. In a random sample of 120 cases it was found that $\sum x = 3468$ and $\sum x^2 = 110\,151$. The ages of all women giving birth in the hospital has mean μ years and standard deviation σ years.

(a) Calculate unbiased estimates of μ and σ^2.

(b) Carry out a significance test, at the 5% significance level, in which the null hypothesis $\mu = 30.0$ is tested against the alternative hypothesis $\mu < 30.0$.

(c) It was subsequently found that an error had been made in recording the value of $\sum x^2$ for the sample. Find the greatest actual value of $\sum x^2$ for the sample which would give rise to a different conclusion in part (b).   (OCR, adapted)

14 On average, 4 out of 5 new television sets of a particular brand are fault-free during the first year of purchase. A new design is marketed and a random sample of 20 sets is monitored by the manufacturer over a period of a year. The number of fault-free sets during this period is 19.

(a) Test, at the 5% significance level, whether the proportion of fault-free sets of this new design is greater than 4 out of 5.

(b) What is the smallest significance level at which it would be accepted that the proportion of fault-free sets is greater than 4 out of 5?

(c) Find a set of values of p_0 for which it would be accepted, at the 5% significance level, that $p > p_0$.

15 The lifetime of a Brightray battery has a normal distribution with mean μ hours and standard deviation $4\frac{3}{4}$ hours. A random sample of 36 batteries is selected and the sum of the lifetimes is found to be 585 hours.

(a) Show that the null hypothesis $\mu = 15\frac{1}{2}$ cannot be rejected, at any significance level, in favour of the alternative hypothesis $\mu < 15\frac{1}{2}$.

(b) Find the p-value of the test of the null hypothesis $\mu = 15\frac{1}{2}$ against the alternative hypothesis $\mu > 15\frac{1}{2}$.

What is the conclusion of the test at the 5% significance level?

16 The average number of telephone calls received each day by a Sight Help Line in Derby was 2.5. After a publicity campaign in the press and on radio, it was found that the total number of calls to the Line, over a period of 2 days, was 9.

(a) State a suitable probability distribution to use in a test of whether the daily average number of calls to the Line has increased.

What must be assumed for the validity of the chosen probability distribution?

(b) Carry out the test at the 5% significance level.

17 Scientists are at present unable to predict the occurrence of major earthquakes, and so these may be considered as random events. The current incidence is at a rate of 1 every 2 years. During a particular year there were 3 major earthquakes. At what significance level can it be accepted that the mean number of earthquakes for that period was greater than 1 in 2 years?   (OCR, adapted)

18 A student answers a test consisting of 12 multiple choice questions, in each of which the correct response has to be selected from four possible given answers. The student only gets 2 of the questions correct and the teacher claims that 'this shows that the student did worse than anyone would just do by guessing'. Denoting the probability of the student answering a question correctly by p, carry out a suitable test to investigate the teacher's claim at the 10% significance level.

Hence state with a reason whether you agree with the teacher's claim.   (OCR, adapted)

19 Metal washers are produced in a factory in batches of 10 000. In the production process occasional faults occur at random, resulting in defective washers being produced. On average, the proportion of defective washers is 0.03%. Explain why you would expect a Poisson distribution to provide a suitable model for the number of defective washers in a batch.

Using a Poisson distribution, show that approximately 5% of batches contain no defective washers.

Following a change in the manufacturing procedure it is suspected that the proportion of batches containing no defective washers is now greater that 5%. It is desired to test whether this is the case. State appropriate hypotheses for a significance test.

Carry out the test, at the 10% significance level, given that in a random sample of 10 batches there were 2 containing no defective washers.   (OCR, adapted)

20 Cartons of milk are tested by a consumer association both for quantity and for ease of opening. A random sample of 100 cartons is examined and the quantity, x litres, of milk in each carton is determined. The results are summarised by $\sum(x - 1) = 1.21$ and $\sum(x - 1)^2 = 0.5377$. Test, at the 5% significance level, whether the mean quantity of milk in a carton is 1.005 litres against the alternative hypothesis that it is greater than 1.005 litres.

A cheaper design of carton is introduced and the consumer association decides to carry out a new test. A random sample of 100 cartons is tested and 53 are found easy to open. Test, at the 5% significance level, whether the proportion of cartons that are easy to open is less than 65%.   (OCR, adapted)

21 A store discovers that its credit card machine rejects, on average, one card in every 890 transactions. Let X denote the number of rejections in a randomly chosen 2136 transactions.

(a) Explain why the distribution of X may be approximated by a Poisson distribution.

(b) On a particular day when there were 2136 transactions the number of rejected cards was 6. Test, at the 5% significance level, whether there is evidence that the average number of rejected cards has increased.

22 The manufacturers of a certain type of laser printer state that when used under 'typical business conditions' the toner cartridge in the printer should last for 'approximately 3000 pages'. A survey involving 150 randomly chosen printers used in business was carried out and the number of pages, x, printed before a new toner cartridge had to be replaced is

summarised by $\sum x = 4.731 \times 10^5$ and $\sum x^2 = 1.620 \times 10^9$, each correct to 4 significant figures. Carry out a test, at the $2\frac{1}{2}\%$ significance level, that the mean number of pages that can be printed is 3000 against the alternative hypothesis that it is greater than 3000.

The printer manufacturers consider that their printer produces noticeably higher quality print than other, comparable machines. Of a random sample of 150 users who were asked their opinions about this, 51 agreed with the manufacturers and the remainder either disagreed or had no opinion. Test, at the 5% significance level, the null hypothesis that the proportion of users agreeing with the printer manufacturers about the print quality is 40% against the alternative hypothesis that it is not 40%.   (OCR, adapted)

7 Errors in hypothesis testing

This chapter investigates the situation where the wrong conclusion is drawn from a hypothesis test. When you have completed it you should

- know what Type I and Type II errors are
- be able to calculate Type I and Type II errors in the context of the normal, binomial and Poisson distributions.

7.1 Type I and Type II errors

When you carry out a hypothesis test your final step is to reject or to accept the null hypothesis. For example, in the situation described in Section 6.3, where a new photocopier was being tested, the users of the photocopier had to choose between the conclusions

(a) the new photocopier is better than the old one or

(b) the new photocopier is not better than the old one.

The result of the hypothesis test will help the users to decide on their next action. If they came to conclusion (a) they would probably decide to keep the new photocopier; if they came to conclusion (b) they would probably keep the old photocopier. Similarly, the teachers described in Section 5.1, who were trying out a new reading scheme, had to choose between

(c) the new reading scheme is better than the old one or

(d) the new reading scheme is not better than the old one.

If they came to conclusion (c) they would probably introduce the new scheme; if they came to conclusion (d) they would probably stick to their current reading scheme.

When such a decision is made after carrying out a hypothesis test, it may be either correct or incorrect. You can never be absolutely certain that you have made the right decision because you have to rely on a limited amount of evidence. For example, the photocopier can only be tested for a limited period; the reading scheme can only be tested on a sample of children. The situation is similar to that in a trial where the defendant is found either guilty or not guilty on the basis of the evidence brought forward. In this case there are four possible situations (which are mutually exclusive).

The defendant is innocent and is found not guilty: in this case the decision is correct.
The defendant is innocent but is found guilty: in this case the decision is incorrect.
The defendant is guilty but is found not guilty: in this case the decision is incorrect.
The defendant is guilty and is found guilty: in this case the decision is correct.

Suppose that in a criminal court of law a defendant is assumed innocent unless found guilty 'beyond reasonable doubt'. The initial assumption of innocence is equivalent to the null hypothesis and the theory that the defendant is guilty is equivalent to the alternative hypothesis. Deciding what constitutes 'beyond reasonable doubt' is equivalent to setting a significance level. Similarly in a hypothesis test there are four possible situations, again mutually exclusive.

H_0 is true and H_0 is accepted: in this case the decision is correct.
H_0 is true but H_0 is rejected: in this case the decision is incorrect.
H_0 is not true but H_0 is accepted: in this case the decision is incorrect.
H_0 is not true and H_0 is rejected: in this case the decision is correct.

You can see that there are two different ways in which an incorrect decision could be made. In order to distinguish between them they are called Type I and Type II errors.

> A **Type I error** is made when a true null hypothesis is rejected.
> A **Type II error** is made when a false null hypothesis is accepted.

Making an incorrect decision can be costly in various ways. For example, suppose that a fire alarm was tested to see whether it was still functioning correctly after a power cut. You might take as the null and alternative hypotheses

H_0: the alarm is functioning correctly,
H_1: the alarm is not functioning correctly.

A Type II error in this situation would mean that you assumed that the alarm was functioning correctly when in fact it was not. This could result in injury, loss of life or damage to property. A Type I error would mean that you thought the alarm was not working correctly when in fact it was. This could mean expenditure on unnecessary repairs or replacement.

> Try to analyse in a similar way the 'costs' of making Type I and Type II errors for
>
> (a) the photocopier example
>
> (b) the reading scheme example.

The examples given in this chapter should make you appreciate that it is important to assess the risk of making errors when carrying out a hypothesis test. In order to do this you have to calculate

$$P(\text{Type I error}) = P(\text{rejecting } H_0 \mid H_0 \text{ true})$$
and $$P(\text{Type II error}) = P(\text{accepting } H_0 \mid H_0 \text{ false}).$$

The following sections show you how these probabilities are calculated for the different types of test which you have met in Chapters 5 and 6.

7.2   Type I and Type II errors for tests involving the normal distribution

If you look back to Section 5.3, which considered continuous variables, you will see that the probability of the test statistic falling in the rejection region, when H_0 is true, is equal to the significance level of the test. If the test statistic falls in the rejection region then H_0 will be rejected when it is in fact true; that is, a Type I error will be made.

> When the distribution of the test statistic is continuous, P(Type I error) is equal to the significance level of the test.

The choice of significance level for a hypothesis test is thus related to the value of P(Type I error) which you are prepared to accept. The choice of a significance level should depend in the first instance on how serious the consequences of a Type I error are. The more serious the consequences, the lower the value of the significance level which should be used. For example, if the consequences of a Type I error were not serious, you might use a significance level of 10%; if the consequences were very serious you might use a significance level of 0.1%.

Consider the reading scheme example. A Type I error in this case would mean that the new scheme was adopted even though it did not produce better results. As a result money would be wasted on a new scheme which was no better than the old one. If the new scheme is not any better and the teachers use a 5% significance level then there is a 1 in 20 chance that the money will be wasted. If the new material is very costly then the teachers might feel that such a risk is unacceptable and choose a significance level of 1% or even less depending on the resources of their school. If on the other hand the new scheme is not very expensive, or they need to replace their reading material anyway, then they might take a significance level of 10% or even 20%.

A Type II error involves accepting a false null hypothesis, which means that you fail to detect a difference in μ. You would expect the probability of this happening to depend on how much μ has changed: if there is a small difference in μ it could easily go undetected but if there is a big difference in μ then you would expect to detect it. This is why the alternative hypothesis has to be defined more exactly before P(Type II error) can be calculated.

The following example illustrates the method.

Example 7.2.1
A machine fills 'one' litre squash bottles. When the machine is working correctly the contents of the bottles are normally distributed with mean 1.002 litres and standard deviation 0.002 litre. The performance of the machine is tested at regular intervals by taking a sample of 9 bottles and calculating their mean content. If this mean content falls below a certain value, it is assumed that the machine is not performing correctly and it is stopped.

(a) Set up null and alternative hypotheses for a test of whether the machine is working correctly.

(b) For a test at the 5% significance level, find the rejection region taking the sample mean as the test statistic.

(c) Give the value for the probability of a Type I error.

(d) Find P(Type II error) if the mean content of the bottles has fallen to the nominal value of 1.000 litre.

(e) Find the range of values of μ for which the probability of making a Type II error is less than 0.001.

   (a) $H_0 : \mu = 1.002$ (the machine is working correctly);
       $H_1 : \mu < 1.002$ (the mean contents has fallen).

   (b) Under H_0, $\overline{X} \sim N\left(1.002, \dfrac{0.002^2}{9}\right)$.

For a one-tail test for a decrease at the 5% level, the rejection region for the test statistic Z is $Z \leqslant -1.645$. Since $Z = \dfrac{\overline{X} - \mu}{\sqrt{\dfrac{\sigma^2}{n}}}$ this means that $\dfrac{\overline{X} - 1.002}{\sqrt{\dfrac{0.002^2}{9}}} \leqslant -1.645$.

Rearranging gives the rejection region for the sample mean as $\overline{X} \leqslant 1.0009\ldots$, or $\overline{X} \leqslant 1.00$, correct to 3 significant figures.

In Fig. 7.1, the broken curve shows the distribution of $\overline{X}$ if H_0 is true and the hatched area shows the P(Type I error).

   (c) For a continuous test statistic, P(Type I error) = significance level = 0.05.

   (d) P(Type II error) = P(accepting H_0 | H_0 false)
                 = P($\overline{X} > 1.0009\ldots$ | $\mu = 1.000$),

that is P($\overline{X}$ is in acceptance region | μ is no longer 1.002 but 1.000).
This probability is shown by the solid shaded area in Fig. 7.1, where the solid curve shows the distribution of $\overline{X}$ if H_1 is true.

$$P(\overline{X} > 1.0009\ldots \mid \mu = 1.000) = P\left(Z > \dfrac{1.0009\ldots - 1.000}{\sqrt{\dfrac{0.002^2}{9}}}\right)$$
$$= P(Z > 1.355)$$
$$= 1 - \Phi(1.355)$$
$$= 1 - 0.9123$$
$$= 0.0877.$$

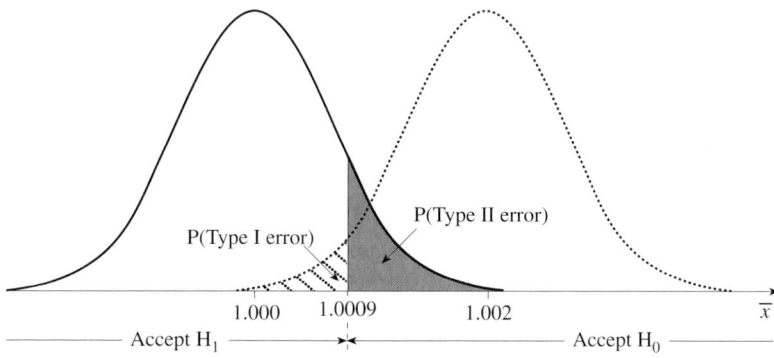

Fig. 7.1. Type I and Type II errors.

(e) First find the value of z for which the probability of making a Type II error is 0.001. Looking back to part (d) this would require $\Phi(z) = 0.999$ and hence $z = 3.090$.

The value of μ which gives this value can be obtained from

$$z = 3.090 = \frac{1.0009\ldots - \mu}{\sqrt{\dfrac{0.002^2}{9}}}.$$

Solving gives $\mu = 0.9988$.

So for $\mu < 0.9988$ the probability of making a Type II error is less than 0.001.

In Example 7.2.1 the consequence of setting the significance level at 5% is that there is a probability of 5% of stopping the machine unnecessarily when it is working correctly. With this significance level the probability of failing to detect that the mean contents of the bottles has fallen to the nominal value of 1.000 litre is 8.77%. It is interesting to see what happens to the P(Type II error) when a lower significance level is used. This is done in the next example.

Example 7.2.2
Repeat Example 7.2.1 parts (b) to (d) with a significance level of 1%.

(b) For a one-tail test for a decrease at the 1% level, the rejection region for the test statistic Z is $Z \leqslant -2.326$ so

$$\frac{\overline{X} - 1.002}{\sqrt{\dfrac{0.002^2}{9}}} \leqslant -2.326.$$

Rearranging gives the rejection region for the sample mean as $\overline{X} \leqslant 1.000\,45$.

(c) P(Type I error) = significance level = 0.01.

(d) P(Type II error) = P(accepting H_0 | H_0 false)
$$= P(\overline{X} > 1.000\,45 \mid \mu = 1.000),$$

that is P($\overline{X}$ is in acceptance region | μ is no longer 1.002 but 1.000).

$$P(\overline{X} > 1.000\,45 \mid \mu = 1.000) = P\left(Z > \frac{1.000\,45 - 1.000}{\sqrt{\dfrac{0.002^2}{9}}}\right)$$

$$= P(Z > 0.674)$$
$$= 1 - \Phi(0.674) = 1 - 0.7499 = 0.2501.$$

For this second calculation, at the 1% significance level, the value of P(Type I error) has been reduced but the value of P(Type II error) has increased. You would expect this result from looking at Fig. 7.1. If the critical value is altered so that one type of error increases, the other will decrease. This means that in setting a significance level it may be necessary to assess the risks involved in committing both types of error and balance one against the other. The only way in which both types of error can be reduced at the same time is by taking a larger sample, so that the overlap of the distributions in Fig. 7.1 is reduced.

The following example shows how to calculate P(Type II error) for a two-tail test.

Example 7.2.3

Boxes of a certain breakfast cereal have contents whose masses are normally distributed with mean μ and standard deviation 15 grams. A test of the null hypothesis $\mu = 375$ against the alternative hypothesis $\mu \neq 375$ is carried out at the 5% significance level using a random sample of 16 boxes.

(a) For what values of the sample mean is the alternative hypothesis accepted?

(b) Given that the actual value of μ is 380, find the probability of making a Type II error.

(OCR, adapted)

(a) Under H_0, $\overline{X} \sim N\left(375, \dfrac{15^2}{16}\right)$.

For a two-tail test at the 5% significance level, the rejection region is $|Z| \geq 1.96$.

Now $Z = \dfrac{\overline{X} - 375}{\sqrt{\dfrac{15^2}{16}}}$.

You can check that when $Z = 1.96$, $\overline{X} = 382.35$, and when $Z = -1.96$, $\overline{X} = 367.65$. Thus the alternative hypothesis is accepted when $\overline{X} \geq 382.35$ or $\overline{X} \leq 367.65$.

(b) P(Type II error)

$= P\left(382.35 > \overline{X} > 367.65 \mid \mu = 380\right)$

$= P\left(\dfrac{382.35 - 380}{\sqrt{\dfrac{15^2}{16}}} > Z > \dfrac{367.65 - 380}{\sqrt{\dfrac{15^2}{16}}}\right)$

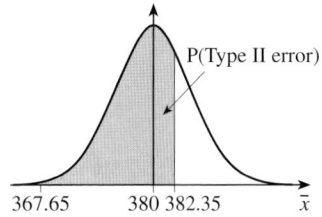

$= P(0.627 > Z > -3.293)$

$= \Phi(0.627) - (1 - \Phi(3.293))$

$= 0.7347 - (1 - 0.9995)$

$= 0.734$, correct to 3 decimal places.

Exercise 7A

1   The random variable X has a normal distribution with mean μ and variance 12.8. A test, at the 5% significance level, of the null hypothesis $\mu = 5$ against the alternative hypothesis $\mu > 5$ is carried out using a random sample of 20 observations of X.

(a) Give the rejection region of the test, in terms of the sample mean, $\overline{X}$.

(b) Find the probability of a Type II error in the test when the true value of μ is 7.

2   In a test of the quality of Luxiglow paint, which is intended to cover an area of at least 10 m² per litre can, a random sample of 15 cans is tested. The mean area per can covered by the 15 cans is denoted by $\overline{X}$ m². It may be assumed that the area covered by a can has a normal distribution with standard deviation 0.51 m².

(a) Find, in terms of $\overline{X}$, the rejection region of a test, at the $2\frac{1}{2}$% significance level, that the mean area covered by all litre cans of the paint is at least 10 m².

(b) For a particular sample, $\overline{X} = 10.3$. State the type of error that could not occur.

continued ...

(c) Given that the mean cover per can of paint is actually 9.6 m², calculate the probability of making a Type II error in the test.

3 In a quality control check 5 randomly selected packs of butter are weighed. The masses of all packs of butter may be assumed to have a normal distribution with mean μ grams and standard deviation 2.7 grams. A test of the null hypothesis $\mu = 247$ against the alternative hypothesis $\mu \neq 247$ is carried out at the $\alpha\%$ significance level. It is decided to accept the null hypothesis if the sample mean lies between 245 grams and 249 grams.

(a) Find the value of α.

(b) Given that the actual value of μ is 250, find the probability of making a Type II error in the test.

(c) What can be said about the probability of making a Type II error when the value of μ is greater than 250?

4 The number of daily absences by employees of a large company has mean 1.94 and standard deviation 0.22. A new system of working is introduced in the hope that this will reduce the number of absences, and it is found that there were 68 absences during the first 40 days of the new system. Treating the 40 days as a random sample

(a) test, at the 5% significance level, whether the new system had the desired effect,

(b) calculate the probability of making a Type II error in the test in part (a) when the mean number of absences is actually 1.8,

(c) state, in the context of the question, what is meant by a Type II error.

5 Studies have shown that the time taken for adults to memorise a list of 12 words has mean 3.8 minutes and standard deviation 1.8 minutes. Taking a course in mnemonics is believed to reduce the mean. To investigate this belief a test, at the 5% significance level, is proposed based on a random sample of 36 people who took the course. Each was given the same list of 12 words to memorise.

(a) Find the rejection region of the test in terms of the sample mean time. Assume that the standard deviation remains at 1.8 minutes.

(b) Given that the actual mean time for the 12 words is 2.9 minutes after taking the course, find the probability of making a Type II error in the test.

Suppose now that the test is based on a random sample of 40 people.

(c) Show that the probability of making a Type II error (when the actual mean time is 2.9 minutes) is smaller than that found in part (b).

6* The breaking strength of lengths of wire required in the manufacture of a certain piece of machinery has a normal distribution with mean 30 N and standard deviation 0.38 N. A random sample of 9 lengths of the wire is tested to determine whether the population mean breaking strength is less than 30 N. A Type I error for the test has probability 0.04.

(a) Find the set of values of the sample's mean breaking strength for which it would be accepted that the mean breaking strength is not less than 30 N.

(b) Given that the probability of making a Type II error in the test is to be less than 0.025, find the set of possible values of the actual mean breaking strength.

7.3   Type I and Type II errors for tests involving the binomial distribution

In Section 6.1 you met the idea that, for a discrete distribution, it is not usually possible to find a rejection region which corresponds exactly to the specified significance level. You may find it helpful to look back at Section 6.1 before going on to the following example.

Example 7.3.1

An experiment on telepathy is carried out by two people. One person, A, chooses a card at random from a standard pack and concentrates on it. The other person, B, who cannot see the card, has to write down the suit of the card. This is done for 18 cards in all and X, the number of cards whose suit is correctly identified, is counted.

(a) State suitable hypotheses, involving a probability, for a hypothesis test which could indicate whether person B is able to name the correct suit more often than would be expected by chance.

(b) What would be the rejection region for the test statistic X for a test at the 10% significance level?

(c) The nominal significance level of this test is 10%. What is the actual significance level?

(a) If person B is guessing, the probability of being correct is $\frac{1}{4}$; if person B has telepathic powers the probability of being correct will be greater than this, so take $H_0 : p = \frac{1}{4}$ and $H_1 : p > \frac{1}{4}$.

(b) Under H_0, $X \sim B(18, 0.25)$. If you inspect the cumulative binomial probability tables and 'work backwards' you will see that, if H_0 is true,

$$P(X \geqslant 7 \mid p = 0.25) = 1 - P(X \leqslant 6 \mid p = 0.25)$$
$$= 1 - 0.8610$$
$$= 0.1390$$
$$= 13.9\% > 10\%,$$

so H_0 is accepted.

$$P(X \geqslant 8 \mid p = 0.25) = 1 - P(X \leqslant 7 \mid p = 0.25)$$
$$= 1 - 0.9431$$
$$= 0.0569$$
$$= 5.69\% < 10\%,$$

so H_0 is rejected.

Thus, the rejection region is $X \geqslant 8$.

(c) The actual significance level of the test is $P(X \geqslant 8 \mid p = 0.25) = 5.69\%$. This is equal to $P(\text{Type I error})$.

This is not very close to the desired significance level (10% in this example) and this will often be the case in tests involving discrete variables.

For a hypothesis test involving a discrete variable, for example a variable which has a binomial or a Poisson distribution, the rejection region is defined so that

P(test statistic falls in rejection region | H_0 true)
   $\leqslant$ nominal significance of the test.

Actual significance level of the test

   = P(test statistic falls in rejection region | H_0 true)

and this is also the probability of a Type I error.

The following example shows how to calculate P(Type II error).

Example 7.3.2
A supplier of primrose seeds claims that their germination rate is 0.95. A purchaser of the seeds suspects that the germination rate is lower than this. In order to test this claim the purchaser plants 20 seeds in similar conditions, counts the number, X, which germinate and carries out a hypothesis test at the 5% significance level.

(a) Formulate suitable null and alternative hypotheses to test the seed supplier's claim.

(b) For what values of X would the null hypothesis be rejected?

(c) The nominal significance level of this test is 5%. What is the actual significance level?

(d) What is the probability of a Type I error using this test?

(e) Calculate P(Type II error) if the probability that a seed germinates is in fact 0.80.

   (a) $H_0 : p = 0.95$, $H_1 : p < 0.95$.

   (b) Low values of X will lead to the null hypothesis being rejected and so the rejection region takes the form $X \leqslant c$. Under H_0, $X \sim B(20, 0.95)$. Inspection of the cumulative binomial probability tables shows that

      $P(X \leqslant 16 \mid p = 0.95) = 0.0159 = 1.59\% < 5\%$, so H_0 is rejected;

      $P(X \leqslant 17 \mid p = 0.95) = 0.0755 = 7.55\% > 5\%$, so H_0 is accepted.

      So H_0 is rejected if $X \leqslant 16$, and the rejection region for the test is $X \leqslant 16$.

   (c) The actual significance level = P(test statistic falls in rejection region | H_0 is true)
          $= 0.0159 = 1.59\%$.

   (d) P(Type I error) $= P(X \leqslant 16 \mid p = 0.95) = 0.0159$.

   (e) P(Type II error) $= P(X > 16 \mid p = 0.8)$
          $= 1 - P(X \leqslant 16 \mid p = 0.8)$
          $= 1 - 0.5886 = 0.4114$.

The value of P(Type II error) in Example 7.3.2 indicates that there is a fairly high probability that the hypothesis test will fail to detect a fall in the germination rate from 0.95 to 0.80.

The following example illustrates a two-tail test.

Example 7.3.3

The dice used in a board game is rolled 30 times and the number, X, of sixes is counted.

(a) Set up suitable null and alternative hypotheses for testing whether the dice is biased either towards or away from six.

(b) What would be the result of a test at the 10% significance level if $X = 9$?

(c) What is the rejection region for X for a test at the 10% significance level?

(d) What is P(Type I error) for this test?

(e) Find P(Type II error) if the dice is in fact biased so that the probability of getting a six is 0.5.

   (a) $H_0 : p = \frac{1}{6}$, $H_1 : p \neq \frac{1}{6}$.

   (b) Under H_0, $X \sim B\left(30, \frac{1}{6}\right)$. The value $X = 9$ is on the high side since, on average, you would expect 5 sixes in 30 throws. From the cumulative binomial probability tables

$$P\left(X \geq 9 \mid p = \frac{1}{6}\right) = 1 - P\left(X \leq 8 \mid p = \frac{1}{6}\right)$$
$$= 1 - 0.9494 = 0.0506 = 5.06\% > 5\%$$

so H_0 is not rejected.

The probability is compared with $\frac{1}{2} \times 10\% = 5\%$ since a two-tail test is being carried out.

There is no evidence, at the 10% significance level, that the dice is biased.

   (c) The null hypothesis could be rejected for either high or low values of X (since a two-tail test is being carried out) and so there are two parts to the rejection region. Firstly you need to find a value c such that $P\left(X \leq c \mid p = \frac{1}{6}\right) \leq 0.05$. Inspection of the cumulative binomial probability tables shows that

$$P\left(X \leq 2 \mid p = \frac{1}{6}\right) = 0.1020 \geq 0.05, \text{ so accept } H_0,$$

and $P\left(X \leq 1 \mid p = \frac{1}{6}\right) = 0.0295 \leq 0.05$, so reject H_0,

so the lower part of the rejection region is $X \leq 1$.

Secondly you need a value d such that $P\left(X \geq d \mid p = \frac{1}{6}\right) \leq 0.05$.

$$P\left(X \geq 9 \mid p = \frac{1}{6}\right) = 1 - P\left(X \leq 8 \mid p = \frac{1}{6}\right)$$
$$= 1 - 0.9494 = 0.0506 \geq 0.05, \text{ so accept } H_0,$$

and $P\left(X \geq 10 \mid p = \frac{1}{6}\right) = 1 - P\left(X \leq 9 \mid p = \frac{1}{6}\right)$

$$= 1 - 0.9803 = 0.0197 \leq 0.05, \text{ so reject } H_0,$$

so the upper part of the rejection region is $X \geq 10$.

The null hypothesis is rejected when $X \leq 1$ or $X \geq 10$.

(d) $P(\text{Type I error}) = P(X \leqslant 1 \text{ or } X \geqslant 10 \mid p = \frac{1}{6})$

$\qquad\qquad\qquad\quad = 0.0295 + (1 - 0.9803) = 0.0492 = 4.92\%.$

This is well below the desired significance level of 10%. It would be possible to get a significance level closer to this value by taking the rejection region as $X \leqslant 1$ and $X \geqslant 9$, which gives a significance level of 8.01%. However, it is usual practice if a two-tail test is required to calculate the rejection region as in part (c) unless you are asked to find a rejection region such that $P(\text{Type I error})$ is as close as possible to the nominal significance level.

(e) Taking the rejection region found in part (c) gives

$\qquad P(\text{Type II error}) = P(1 < X < 10 \mid p = 0.5)$

$\qquad\qquad\qquad\qquad = P(X \leqslant 9 \mid p = 0.5) - P(X \leqslant 1 \mid p = 0.5)$

$\qquad\qquad\qquad\qquad = 0.0214 - 0.0000 = 0.0214.$

In Example 7.3.3. the low value of $P(\text{Type II error})$ indicates that the hypothesis test would be effective in detecting a dice biased so that the probability of getting a six is 0.5.

For large samples it becomes easier to find a rejection region which gives $P(\text{Type I error})$ close to the required significance level. As you saw in Section 6.2, testing a population proportion for a large sample is done using the normal approximation to the binomial distribution. The following example shows how to calculate $P(\text{Type I error})$ and $P(\text{Type II error})$ in this situation.

Example 7.3.4

It is suspected that a gaming club is running an unfair roulette wheel. The wheel is given 3700 trial spins and X, the number of times that zero (on which the club wins) turns up is counted. There are 37 possible scores on a trial spin, labelled 0 to 36, and these should have equal probability.

(a) For what values of X would you conclude that the wheel was biased in favour of zero if a hypothesis test was carried out at the 5% significance level?

(b) For this test calculate $P(\text{Type II error})$ if the probability of getting zero is in fact $\frac{3}{37}$.

$\qquad\qquad\qquad\qquad\qquad\qquad\qquad\qquad\qquad\qquad\qquad\qquad\qquad\qquad$ (OCR, adapted)

(a) If the wheel is fair then the probability of getting zero is $\frac{1}{37}$. If the wheel is unfair it will favour the club so the probability of getting zero is greater than this.

The null and alternative hypotheses are $H_0 : p = \frac{1}{37}$ and $H_1 : p > \frac{1}{37}$ respectively. Under H_0, $X \sim B(3700, \frac{1}{37})$.

Using the normal approximation,

$\qquad \mu = np = 3700 \times \frac{1}{37} = 100$, and $\sigma^2 = npq = 3700 \times \frac{1}{37} \times \frac{36}{37} = \frac{3600}{37}$, so

$\qquad X \sim B(3700, \frac{1}{37})$ is approximated by $V \sim N(100, \frac{3600}{37})$.

For a one-tail test for an increase at the 5% significance level, H_0 is rejected if $Z \geqslant 1.645$. The corresponding rejection region for V is given by

$$\frac{V - 100}{\sqrt{\dfrac{3600}{37}}} \geqslant 1.645 \quad \text{giving} \quad V \geqslant 116.2$$

Allowing for the continuity correction, this corresponds to

$$X \geqslant 116.2 + 0.5 = 116.7.$$

The rejection region is taken as $X \geqslant 117$, by rounding up to the nearest integer.

(b) If $p = \frac{3}{37}$, then the distribution of X can be approximated by

$$V \sim N\left(3700 \times \tfrac{3}{37},\ 3700 \times \tfrac{3}{37} \times \tfrac{34}{37}\right) = N\left(300, \tfrac{10\,200}{37}\right).$$

$$
\begin{aligned}
\text{P(Type II error)} &= \text{P}(X \leqslant 116) \\
&\approx \text{P}(V \leqslant 116.5) \quad \text{(including the continuity correction)}
\end{aligned}
$$

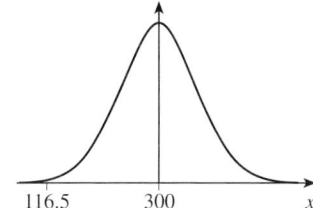

$$
= \text{P}\left(Z < \frac{116.5 - 300}{\sqrt{\dfrac{10\,200}{37}}} \right)
$$

$$= \text{P}(Z < -11.05)$$

$$\approx 0.$$

The hypothesis test described in Example 7.3.4 would be extremely effective at detecting a degree of bias such that the probability of getting zero is $\frac{3}{37}$.

Exercise 7B

1 A newspaper reported that 55% of households own more than two television sets. Each of a random sample of 30 households in Melchester is contacted and the number of households owning more than two television sets is denoted by N. A test of whether the proportion p of households in Melchester owning more than two television sets is different from 55% is carried out at a nominal 5% significance level.

   (a) Obtain the rejection region of the test in terms of N.

   (b) Calculate P(Type I error).

   (c) State the conclusion of the test when $N = 20$.

   (d) Calculate P(Type II error) when the actual value of p is 60%.

2 An election to the presidency of a society of 8000 members is shortly to take place. After a pre-election speech by Mrs Robinson (a candidate), a random sample of 25 people who listened to the speech was asked about their voting intentions. The number who say that they will vote for Mrs Robinson is denoted by R. A test is carried out at a nominal 5%

significance level of whether Mrs Robinson will be elected, which will happen if she gets more than 50% of the votes cast.

(a) Find the rejection region of the test in terms of R and state the conclusion of the test when $R = 19$.

(b) What is the actual significance level of the test?

(c) Given that 65% of all members will vote for Mrs Robinson, find the probability of making a Type II error in the test.

3 A drug for treating phlebitis has proved effective in 75% of cases when it has been used. A new drug has been developed which, it is believed, will be more successful and it is used on a sample of 16 patients with phlebitis. A test is carried out to determine whether the new drug has a greater success rate than 75% and the test statistic is X, the number of patients cured by the new drug. It is decided to accept that the new drug is more effective if $X > 14$.

(a) Find α, the probability of making a Type I error.

(b) Find β, the probability of making a Type II error when the actual success rate is 80%.

What can be said about the values of α and β if, with the same decision procedure $(X > 14)$, the sample size were larger than 16?

4 Of a certain make of electric toaster, 10% have to be returned for service within three months of purchase. A modification to the toaster is made in the hope that it will be more reliable. Out of 24 modified toasters sold in a store none was returned for service within three months of purchase. The proportion of all the modified toasters that are returned for service within three months of purchase is denoted by p.

(a) State, in terms of p, suitable hypotheses for a test.

(b) Test whether there is evidence, at a nominal 10% significance level, that the modified toaster is more reliable than the previous model in that it requires less service.

(c) What is the probability of making a Type I error in the test?

(d) Find the set of values of p for which P(Type II error) < 0.25.

5 A bus company has agreed to supply a new service to a country area if more than 70% of the people in the area will use the service. A random sample of 120 people living in the area is questioned. Let the number who say they will use the service be denoted by S. The bus company carries out a test at a nominal 2% significance level to decide whether they should run the service. They assume that the responses are truthful.

(a) Find, in terms of S, the rejection region of the test.

(b) Estimate the true significance level of the test.

(c) Let the proportion of all the people in the area who will use the service be denoted by p. Find the approximate value of p_0 such that, for $p > p_0$, P(Type II error) $< \frac{1}{2}$.

6 It is known that many crimes are committed by people with backgrounds of drug abuse. A proportion of 60% has been suggested and, to investigate this, a researcher undertakes a study of 100 criminals and will carry out a test at a nominal 10% significance level. The null hypothesis is that the proportion of such criminals is 60% and the alternative hypothesis is that the proportion differs from 60%.

(a) Find the rejection region of the test.

(b) Find P(Type I error) for the test.

(c) What is the conclusion of the test if 62 of the 100 criminals have backgrounds of drug abuse?

(d) Find P(Type II error) for the test when the actual proportion is 40%.

7* In the population as a whole, about 8% of females have red hair. A statistics student living in Birmingham wishes to test whether the percentage in Birmingham differs from 8%. He plans a test at a nominal 1% significance level and observes a random sample of 500 females in several areas of the city.

(a) Find the actual significance level α of the test.

(b) Find the probability β of making a Type II error in the test when the actual proportion of red-haired females in Birmingham is 4%.

(c) Find the value of β if the sample size were 1000. What general result does this indicate?

7.4 Type I and Type II errors for tests involving the Poisson distribution

Examples involving the Poisson distribution are handled in a similar way to those involving the binomial distribution, both being discrete variables.

Example 7.4.1
In an intensive survey of dune land it was found that the average number of plants of a particular species was 16 per m^2. After a hard winter it is suspected that these plants have tended to be killed off. In order to test this hypothesis a randomly chosen area of 1 m^2 is selected and the number of these plants, X, growing in it is counted. You may assume that the distribution of X can be modelled by a Poisson distribution.

(a) State suitable null and alternative hypotheses.

(b) Taking X as the test statistic, find the rejection region for a test at the 10% significance level.

(c) What is P(Type I error)?

(d) Calculate P(Type II error) if the mean number of plants per square metre has changed to
    (i) 12   (ii) 6.

Do you think that the assumption of a Poisson model is likely to be justified in this situation?

      (a) $H_0 : \lambda = 16, \quad H_1 : \lambda < 16$.

      (b) $P(X \leqslant 10 \mid \lambda = 16) = 0.0774 = 7.74\% < 10\%$, so reject H_0.
          $P(X \leqslant 11 \mid \lambda = 16) = 0.1270 = 12.7\% > 10\%$, so accept H_0.

          The rejection region is $X \leqslant 10$.

      (c) P(Type I error) $= 0.0774$.

(d)   (i) P(Type II error) $= P(X > 10 \mid \lambda = 12)$
$$= 1 - P(X \leqslant 10 \mid \lambda = 12)$$
$$= 1 - 0.3472 = 0.6528.$$

(ii) P(Type II error) $= P(X > 10 \mid \lambda = 6)$
$$= 1 - P(X \leqslant 10 \mid \lambda = 6)$$
$$= 1 - 0.9574 = 0.0426.$$

As you would expect, P(Type II error) decreases as λ gets lower.

If the plants are distributed at random then the Poisson distribution should be a good model. If the plants propagate by seeds which are distributed by the wind then they are likely to be randomly distributed. If, however, they spread by underground roots then the plants might occur in groups.

Example 7.4.2
The average number of flaws per 100 metre length of yarn produced by a machine has been found to be 7. After the machine has been serviced, the number, X, of flaws in the first 100 metres of yarn produced by the machine is 11.

(a) Carry out a two-tail hypothesis test at the 10% level to test whether the average number of flaws produced by the machine has changed.

(b) For what values of X would the null hypothesis be rejected?

(c) What is the actual significance level of the test?

(d) What is P(Type I error)?

(e) Calculate P(Type II error) if the average number of flaws has changed to 10.

(a) Assuming that the flaws are produced independently and at random, a suitable model for X would be the Poisson distribution.

$$H_0 : \lambda = 7, \qquad H_1 : \lambda \neq 7.$$

Under H_0, $X \sim Po(7)$.

From the cumulative Poisson probability tables,

$$P(X \geqslant 11 \mid \lambda = 7) = 1 - P(X \leqslant 10 \mid \lambda = 7)$$
$$= 1 - 0.9015 = 0.0985 = 9.85\% > 5\%, \text{ so accept } H_0.$$

The probability is compared with $\frac{1}{2} \times 10\% = 5\%$ since a two-tail test is being carried out.

There is insufficient evidence to say that the average number of flaws has changed.

(b) The null hypothesis could be rejected for either high or low values of X (since a two-tail test is being carried out) and so there are two parts to the rejection region. Firstly you need to find a value c such that $P(X \leq c \mid \lambda = 7) \leq 0.05$. Inspection of the cumulative Poisson probability tables shows that

$$P(X \leq 3 \mid \lambda = 7) = 0.0818 = 8.18\% > 5\%, \text{ so accept } H_0.$$
$$P(X \leq 2 \mid \lambda = 7) = 0.0296 = 2.96\% < 5\%, \text{ so reject } H_0.$$

The lower part of the rejection region is $X \leq 2$.

Secondly you need a value d such that $P(X \geq d \mid \lambda = 7) \leq 0.05$.

$$P(X \geq 12 \mid \lambda = 7) = 1 - P(X \leq 11 \mid \lambda = 7)$$
$$= 1 - 0.9467 = 0.0533 > 0.05, \text{ so accept } H_0.$$
$$P(X \geq 13 \mid \lambda = 7) = 1 - P(X \leq 12 \mid \lambda = 7)$$
$$= 1 - 0.9730 = 0.0270 < 0.05, \text{ so reject } H_0.$$

The upper part of the rejection region is $X \geq 13$.

The null hypothesis is rejected when $X \leq 2$ or $X \geq 13$.

(c) The actual significance level of the test is

$$P(X \leq 2 \text{ or } X \geq 13 \mid \lambda = 7) = 0.0296 + (1 - 0.9730) = 0.0566.$$

(d) P(Type I error) = actual significance level
$$= 0.0566$$
$$= 5.66\%.$$

(e) P(Type II error) $= P(2 < X < 13 \mid \lambda = 10)$
$$= P(X \leq 12 \mid \lambda = 10) - P(X \leq 2 \mid \lambda = 10)$$
$$= 0.7916 - 0.0028 = 0.7888.$$

Exercise 7C

1 The random variable X has a Poisson distribution with mean 6.5. A single observation of X is made and a test at a nominal significance level of 10% is carried out of whether the mean has decreased. Find

(a) the critical region of the test in terms of X,

(b) the probability of making a Type I error in the test,

(c) the probability of making a Type II error when the mean is actually 5.5.

Given that the observed value of X was 4, state the conclusion of the test and the type of error that was made.

2 The number of vehicle accidents at a crossroads controlled by traffic lights may be modelled by a Poisson distribution with mean 1.5 per week. After a change in timing of the lights there were 6 accidents during the next 8 weeks. Is this evidence, at a nominal 5% significance level, of a reduction in the weekly mean number of accidents?

What type of error might have been made in the test?

3 The number of times that a printing machine stops for attention during a given week has a Poisson distribution with mean 4. The machine undergoes some intensive adjustment and a two-tail test is carried out, based on the total number of stoppages, X, that occur over a period of 3 weeks. The test is of whether the mean number of stoppages per week has changed. The nominal significance level of the test is 5%.

(a) Find, in terms of X, the rejection region of the test.

(b) Find the actual significance level of the test.

(c) State the conclusion of the test for the case $X = 9$.

(d) Calculate the probability of making a Type II error when the actual mean number of weekly stoppages (after the adjustments) is 2.0.

4 The number of insurance sales made by Julie, a telephone sales operative, averages 0.8 per day. State what must be assumed for the number of sales made on a randomly chosen day to have a Poisson distribution.

Julie is given some extra training and her total sales over a period of 20 days after the training are denoted by T. It may be assumed that T has a Poisson distribution.

A test of whether the daily mean has increased is carried out at a significance level as close as possible to 5%.

(a) Find the rejection region of the test.

(b) What is the true significance level of the test?

(c) Find the probability of making a Type II error in the test when the mean number of daily sales is actually 0.9. Comment on its value.

5 The proportion of all patients given laser surgery to treat astigmatism and short-sightedness and who suffer complications is reported to be, on average, 1 in 20. A newly formed company who give this treatment in a shopping mall in an American city has given concern to a monitoring agency because the number of reported complications appears to be high. Records of the first 90 patients treated by the company are obtained and the agency will carry out a test, at a nominal 10% significance level, of whether the true proportion of patients suffering complications is $\frac{1}{20}$. The number of patients who suffer complications is denoted by N.

(a) Explain why the distribution of N can be approximated by a Poisson distribution.

(b) State, giving a reason, whether the agency should carry out a one-tail test or a two-tail test.

(c) Find the rejection region of the test in terms of N.

(d) State the type of error that might be made in the cases

(i) $N = 5$, (ii) $N = 10$.

(e) Estimate the probability of making a Type II error in the test when the actual proportion of complications attributed to the company is $\frac{1}{10}$.

6 The number of red cells in a small standard volume of blood of a healthy person may be modelled by a Poisson distribution with mean 12. Ranjana is suspected by her doctor of having an abnormally high red cell count and is given a blood test. The number of red cells in a standard volume of her blood is denoted by R. A statistical test of whether the doctor's suspicion is confirmed is carried out at a nominal 5% significance level.

(a) Find the acceptance region of the test in terms of R.

(b) What is the probability of making a Type I error in the test?

(c) Find the probability of making a Type II error in the test when the mean is actually 19.

Miscellaneous exercise 7

1 In a significance test of a population mean μ, the null hypothesis $\mu = 0.3$ is tested against the alternative hypothesis $\mu \neq 0.3$ at the 10% significance level.

(a) State, if possible, the probability of making a Type I error. If it is not possible then give a reason.

(b) State, giving a reason, whether it is possible for both a Type I error and a Type II error to occur in the test.

(c) State the type of error that might occur in the test given that the null hypothesis is rejected.

2 The number of misprints in mathematics books of about 300 pages published by a certain press (not this one, we hope!) has a distribution which can be modelled by a Poisson distribution with mean 4.8. A new director of publishing was appointed and in the first month of the director's appointment 5 mathematics books of about 300 pages were published. One of these was selected at random and a careful check found m misprints.

(a) Find the rejection region of a test, at a nominal 5% significance level, of whether there is evidence of a reduction in the mean number of misprints per book.

(b) For the case $m = 1$, state the conclusion of the test.

(c) Given that the mean number of misprints had actually fallen from 4.8 to 0.5, find the probability of making a Type II error in the test.

3 A certain fly spray is known to kill at least 90% of flies on which it is used. A modification is made to the spray which a researcher believes will kill fewer than 90%. The actual proportion of flies killed by the modified spray is denoted by p. The spray is applied to 200 flies and kills k of them.

(a) Use a suitable approximation (which should be justified) to find the set of values of k for which it would be accepted that $p < 0.9$ at a nominal $2\frac{1}{2}$% significance level.

(b) Explain why the significance level cannot be exactly $2\frac{1}{2}$% and estimate the true significance level of the test.

(c) The null hypothesis was accepted when the modified spray actually killed 85% of all flies on which it was used. State the type of error that occurred and calculate the probability of making that type of error.

4 An employee is accused by his employer of being late for work too often. The employee claims that, on average, he is late on no more than one day in ten. The employer finds that, over a random sample of 20 days, the employee is late on r days. The employer carries out a significance test, at the 5% level, to decide whether, on average, the employee is late on more than one day in ten.

(a) State suitable null and alternative hypotheses for the test.

(b) Find the set of values of r for which the null hypothesis would be rejected, and state the conclusion of the test in the case $r = 4$.

(c) Given that, in fact, the probability that the employee is late for work on a randomly chosen day is 0.2, find the probability of making a Type II error in the test.   (OCR)

5 The mass of a chocolate bar of a particular brand has a normal distribution with mean μ grams and standard deviation 0.946 grams. The null hypothesis $\mu = 100$ is tested against the alternative hypothesis $\mu \neq 100$ using a random sample of 4 of the bars. The sample mean has mass denoted by $\overline{X}$ grams and the acceptance region of the test is $|\overline{X} - 100| < 1.10$.

(a) Find the significance level of the test.

(b) The test is carried out independently with different random samples of 4 bars until the null hypothesis is rejected. Find the expectation of the number of tests that will have to be carried out.

(c) Find the probability that a single test on 4 bars detects a change in μ from 100 to 101. State how this probability is related to a Type II error.   (OCR, adapted)

6 A factory manufactures plastic cups. The probability of a randomly chosen cup being defective is 0.02.

Cups are sold in packs of 20. A quality controller monitors the production process by recording the total number of defective cups in a random sample of 10 packs.

(a) Explain why the total number of defective cups in 10 packs can be modelled by a Poisson distribution, and state the value of its parameter.

(b) In a particular sample of 10 packs the total number of defective cups observed was 8. Test, at a nominal 5% significance level, whether the proportion of defective cups produced has increased. You should state your hypotheses and your conclusion clearly.

(c) Find the probability of making a Type I error in the test in part (b).

(d) For the case when the proportion of defective cups has increased to 0.03, find the probability of making a Type II error in a test based on the number of defective cups in a sample of 10 packs.   (OCR, adapted)

7 The lengths of a component used in the construction of a model aeroplane are being checked. Each of a random sample of 200 of the components, selected from a large batch, is measured and the lengths, x mm, are summarised by $\sum x = 1484.2$ and $\sum x^2 = 11\,098.19$.

(a) Calculate an unbiased estimate of the variance of the lengths of all components in the batch.

(b) State what is meant by 'an unbiased estimate'.

The components are produced in large batches and it is required that the mean length, μ mm, of the components in a batch should be at most 7.40 mm. Batches which do not meet this standard are rejected. The decision whether or not to reject a batch is based on a random sample of 200 components drawn from the batch. The mean length is denoted by $\overline{X}$.

(c) Find the rejection region of a test, at the 5% significance level, of whether or not a batch should be rejected.

(d) Find an approximation to the probability of making a Type II error when carrying out the test for the case when $\mu = 7.50$.

(e) Explain why (even without consideration of rounding errors) the answers to part (c) and part (d) are approximate.

8 For a statistics project Emma decides to investigate the possible existence of telepathy between her mother and herself. An experiment is set up using five differently coloured cards. One of these cards is chosen at random and shown to Emma's mother who concentrates on it for 20 seconds. At the same time, Emma concentrates and then names what she thinks is the colour of the chosen card. This is carried out 20 times altogether and on 7 occasions Emma names the correct colour.

(a) State suitable hypotheses, involving a probability, for a significance test that could indicate whether Emma is able to name the correct colour more often than would be expected by chance.

(b) Carry out the test at a nominal 5% significance level.

(c) State the type of error that might have been made in the conclusion of the test. Under what circumstances would this error not have been made? (OCR, adapted)

9 Water used in a cooling tower is discharged into a river. Regulations require that the mean temperature of the discharged water should be no higher than 75 °C in order not to affect adversely the river's ecosystem. Samples of water are taken close to the cooling tower at random times over a period of a month and the temperatures recorded. The mean temperature of the water over this period is denoted by μ °C.

(a) State suitable hypotheses which can be used in a test of whether the regulations are observed.

(b) Describe, in the context of the question, the two types of error that might be made in the test.

(c) State, giving a reason, which type of error an environmentalist would consider to be less serious.

(d) For a particular sample of 30 readings the sample mean temperature was 76.16 °C with sample standard deviation 2.62 °C. Carry out the test at the 10% significance level.

10 Factory-made dolls are assembled manually and the assembly times have a normal distribution with mean μ seconds and standard deviation 2.8 seconds. The usual method of assembly has $\mu = 12.4$ and in order to reduce this figure a supervisor has suggested a new method of assembly. A random sample of 10 workers will use the new method to assemble 5 dolls. If the sample mean time for assembling the 50 dolls is less than 11.4 seconds then the supervisor will decide to adopt the new method.

(a) State suitable hypotheses for the test implied by the supervisor's decision, and calculate the significance level of this test. It may be assumed that the standard deviation is 2.8 seconds.

(b) Calculate the probability of making a Type II error in the test when, in fact, $\mu = 10.0$.

(c) Find the smallest sample size that would have to be used so that, with the same decision procedure, the probability β of making a Type II error is smaller than 0.1. Find the value of β in this case.

11* A random variable X has a normal distribution with mean μ and variance 25. The null hypothesis $\mu = 20$ is tested against the alternative hypothesis $\mu < 20$ at the 10% significance level, using the mean $\overline{X}$ of a random sample of n observations of X.

(a) Find, in terms of $\overline{X}$ and n, the rejection region of the test.

(b) Show that the probability β of making a Type II error in the test, when the actual value of μ is 19, is given by $\beta = 1 - \Phi\left(\frac{1}{5}\left(\sqrt{n} - 6.41\right)\right)$.

(c) Evaluate β when $n = 225$.

(d) What happens to the value of β as n increases?

(e) Find the value of n for which β is as close as possible to 0.01.

Revision exercise

1 A random variable X has probability density function $f(x)$ given by

$$f(x) = \begin{cases} kx(1-x) & \text{for } 0 \leqslant x \leqslant 1, \\ 0 & \text{otherwise.} \end{cases}$$

Show that the mean and variance of X are 0.5 and 0.05 respectively.

Find the probability that an observation chosen at random from this distribution is more than two standard deviations from the mean. (OCR)

2 State the conditions under which you might reasonably expect a random variable to follow a Poisson distribution. Illustrate your answer with reference to experiments you may have carried out.

Calculate the probability that a variable with a Poisson distribution with parameter 5 has the value 10.

'Divorce proceedings on the increase' was the headline in a local newspaper. The article revealed that in the past five working days ten petitions for divorce had been filed in the local court. This compares with an average of one per working day over the past year.

Would a one- or two-tail test be appropriate in testing the claim of the headline? State the null and alternative hypotheses you would use in conducting such a test. Carefully explaining the steps you take, carry out the test at the 2% significance level. Does it agree with the claim of the headline? Justify the probability distribution you employ.

What conclusion would you have reached had you conducted the test at the 5% level? Explain, using illustrative examples to support your explanation, how changing a significance level may have a bearing on the outcome of a test. (OCR)

3 State the conditions required for a random variable to be modelled by a binomial distribution.

(a) Just prior to the last general election, eight randomly selected people were asked which of two colours, blue or red, they favoured. Two chose blue. Conduct an appropriate test, using the binomial distribution, to judge whether there is sufficient evidence to suggest that red is the favoured colour in the general population.

(b) On the same day a market research organisation interviewed 2000 randomly selected people and asked them the same question. Of these, 932 opted for blue. Conduct an appropriate test, at the 5% level of significance, to determine if there is sufficient evidence to support the view that blue is not the people's favourite.

(c) What is meant by the phrase 'at the 5% level of significance'? (OCR)

4 The lengths in millimetres of nine screws selected at random from a large consignment are found to be 7.99, 8.01, 8.00, 8.02, 8.03, 7.99, 8.00, 8.01, 8.01.

(a) Calculate unbiased estimates of the population mean and variance.

(b) Assuming a normal distribution with variance 0.0001, test, at the 5% level, the hypothesis that the population mean is 8.00 against the alternative hypothesis that the population mean is not 8.00. (OCR)

5   What do you understand by the phrase 'an unbiased estimate of population variance'?

(a) An infinite population consists of the numbers 1, 2, 3 in equal proportion. Write down the population mean, and hence calculate the population variance.

(b) Random samples of size 2 are obtained from the population. Write down all possible samples of size 2. Hence write down the probability distribution of the means of samples of size 2. Obtain the expected value of the mean and determine if the 'sample mean' is unbiased in this case.

(c) Obtain the distribution of sample variance and find the expected value of sample variance. Demonstrate that the sample variance is not an unbiased estimator of population variance in this case. Show also that

$$\frac{n}{n-1} \times (\text{sample variance})$$

is an unbiased estimator in this case, where n is the sample size. (OCR)

6   Under what circumstances would you reasonably expect to be able to use the binomial distribution to model a probability distribution? When may a binomial distribution be approximated by a normal distribution?

Recent astronomical observations indicate that, of the 16 stars closest to our Sun, about half are accompanied by an orbiting planet at least the size of Jupiter.

(a) Assume that the proportion of such stars in the Galaxy is 50%. Using standard cumulative probability tables, write down the probability that, in a group of 16 stars,

(i) exactly 8,   (ii) at least 8

have such a planetary system.

(b) The Pleiades are a cluster of some 500 stars. Use an appropriate approximation to determine the probability that there are between 230 and 270 (inclusive) stars in the Pleiades with accompanying planets at least the size of Jupiter. (OCR, adapted)

7   A computer was programmed to provide 14 random digits in the range 0 to 9 inclusive.

(a) Calculate the probability that 7 of the digits it produced were less than 3.

(b) Using appropriate tables calculate the probability that it produced fewer than 7 or more than 10 digits which were less than 3.

(c) Later, the computer produced 150 random digits in the range 0 to 9 inclusive. Calculate the approximate probability that at least half the digits were more than 5.

(d) Four hundred pairs of random digits were also generated. Calculate, using an appropriate approximation, the probability that there were exactly three pairs of double zeros among them. (OCR)

8   Describe an experiment that you may have conducted to illustrate the normal distribution. Justify, with reference to features of this distribution, its use in the experiment.

The quantity of juice, in ml, that can be extracted from different sizes of oranges follows a normal distribution as given in the table.

	Mean	Variance
Small	70	49
Medium	90	σ^2

(a) What is the probability that more than 80 ml of juice can be extracted from one small orange?

(b) It is known that 5% of medium oranges produce more than 105 ml of juice. Calculate the value of σ.

(c) If I buy 5 small oranges, find the probability that at least 4 of them will produce over 80 ml of juice. (OCR, adapted)

9 A continuous random variable X has a probability density function given by

$$f(x) = \begin{cases} a - \frac{1}{2}(x-1)^2 & \text{for } 0 \leq x \leq 2, \\ 0 & \text{otherwise.} \end{cases}$$

Calculate

(a) the value of a, (b) μ, the mean of the distribution,

(c) σ^2, the variance of the distribution. (OCR, adapted)

10 A servicing engineer finds that the number of jobs he completes in a working session has a Poisson distribution with mean 4. If the sessions are independent, what is the distribution of the number of jobs he completes in n sessions, and how may this be approximated when n is large?

If he has 100 jobs to do, how many sessions should he allow in order to be 95% sure that he will be able to complete them all? (OCR)

11 From past experience, it is known that the time a customer took to be served in a Post Office was a normal variable with mean 6.2 minutes and standard deviation 2.1 minutes.

A new queuing system was introduced by the manager and after this a survey of 20 customers was carried out to see whether there was a decrease in the time it took for a customer to be served. Let T be the time in minutes for a randomly chosen customer to be served after the new queuing system has been introduced and let $t_1, t_2, \ldots, t_{20}$ be the random sample of 20 observations of T. The results may be summarised as

$$\sum t = 108.4.$$

The standard deviation of T is assumed to be 2.1 minutes.

(a) Test, at the 5% level, the hypothesis that the mean time for a customer to be served has reduced after the introduction of the new queuing system.

(b) For the test given in part (a) calculate the probability of making a Type II error in the case when the true mean time to be served is 5.8 minutes. (OCR)

12 A random variable X has an $N(15, 9)$ distribution. A random sample of 5 observations of this distribution is to be taken. The mean of the 5 observations is denoted by $\overline{X}$.

(a) State the distribution of $\overline{X}$ and give its mean and variance.

(b) Calculate the probability that $\overline{X}$ is less than 17.

A random variable Y has mean 7 and variance 20. A random sample of 100 observations of this distribution is to be taken. The mean of the 100 observations is denoted by $\overline{Y}$.

(c) Give the mean and variance of $\overline{Y}$.

(d) State the approximate distribution of $\overline{Y}$ and give the name of the theorem which you have used.

(e) Calculate the probability $P(6.9 < \overline{Y} < 7.1)$.

Practice examination 1

Time 1 hour 30 minutes

Answer all the questions.

1 The random variable X has the distribution N(40, 25), and $\overline{X}$ denotes the mean of a random sample of 10 observations of X. Find $P(\overline{X} < 42)$. [5]

2 Statistical investigations may involve random sampling.

(i) Explain briefly what is meant by the term 'random sampling' and state why random sampling is used. [3]

(ii) A random sample of 5 students is to be taken from the 763 students who attend a college. Explain briefly how this could done, using the following extract from a table of random numbers to illustrate your answer. [4]

22097   40581   73381   95189   20034   36948

3 The continuous random variable X has probability density function given by

$$f(x) = \begin{cases} k(3-x)^2 & \text{for } 0 \leqslant x < 3, \\ 0 & \text{otherwise,} \end{cases}$$

where k is a constant.

(i) Show that $k = \frac{1}{9}$. [2]

(ii) Find $P(1 \leqslant X \leqslant 3)$. [2]

(iii) Hence state with a reason whether the median value of X is less than 1 or greater than 1. [1]

(iv) Find $E(X)$. [2]

4 A coffee bean grinding machine produces grains of coffee in one of two sizes, medium and coarse. The diameters of the grains, in suitable units, are normally distributed with parameters as detailed in the table.

Grade of grains	Mean	Standard deviation
Medium	12.5	1.2
Coarse	μ	σ

(i) Calculate the proportion of medium grade grains which are between 12 and 16 (inclusive) in diameter. [3]

(ii) It is known that 30% of the coarse grains have diameters greater than 17 and that 10% have diameters less than 14. Use this information to determine the mean, μ, and the standard deviation, σ, of the coarse grains. [6]

5 A student is investigating the shape of a certain type of shell found on the seashore. She makes several measurements for each shell and combines the results into a single 'shape index', x. The resulting values from a random sample of 208 shells are summarised by
$$\sum x = 633.36, \sum x^2 = 2640.4612.$$

   (i) Calculate unbiased estimates of the population mean and variance for the shape index of shells of this type. [3]

The shells in the student's sample were all collected from exposed seashores. Previous studies of shells of this type found on sheltered shores have shown that the mean value of the shape index is 2.82.

   (ii) Carry out a test, at the 1% significance level, to determine whether there is any difference between the mean shape index for shells found on exposed shores and that for shells found on sheltered shores. You should state your hypotheses and conclusion clearly. [6]

6 It is believed that more baby boys than baby girls are being born.

   (i) State suitable null and alternative hypotheses for a significance test of this belief. [2]

A test at the 5% significance level is to be carried out, based on a random sample of 25 babies.

   (ii) Use tables of cumulative binomial probabilities to determine the critical region for this test. [2]

   (iii) Explain, in the context of this situation, what is meant by a Type I error, and state the probability of a Type I error for this test. [3]

   (iv) If the probability that a baby is a boy is actually 0.55, find the probability of a Type II error for this test. [3]

7 When thin metal wire is being manufactured, occasional defects in the wire occur, making the wire more liable to break at the point where the defect occurs.

   (i) State what needs to be assumed about the occurrence of defects during manufacture if a Poisson distribution is a suitable model for the number of defects that occur in a piece of wire of given length. [2]

For wire produced by manufacturer A, the mean number of defects is 1.6 per 100 m length of wire.

   (ii) Use a Poisson distribution to find the probability that there are between 1 and 4 (inclusive) defects in a randomly chosen 200 m length of wire made by manufacturer A. [3]

   (iii) Use a suitable approximation to find the probability that in a randomly chosen 1000 m length of wire from manufacturer A there will be more than 10 defects. [5]

For wire produced by manufacturer B, the probability of a randomly chosen 50 m length of wire having at least one defect is 0.75, and the distribution of defects may be assumed to follow a Poisson distribution.

   (iv) Calculate the mean number of defects per 100 m length of wire made by manufacturer B. [3]

8 A fair cubical dice is thrown 600 times. Let X represent the number of times that a six appears uppermost.

   (i) Identify the exact distribution of X, and also the distribution which can be used as an approximation. (You should state the values of any parameters for each of these distributions.)   [2]

  (ii) Use the approximating distribution to find the probability that the number of sixes obtained in 600 throws of the dice is at least 120.   [4]

The dice is thrown n times, where n is large enough to ensure that the probability of obtaining at least 50 sixes exceeds 0.99.

 (iii) Form a quadratic inequality in $\sqrt{n}$, and hence find the smallest possible value of n.   [6]

Practice examination 2

Time 1 hour 30 minutes

Answer all the questions.

1 A TV company who screened a football international claims that the match was watched by one third of viewers, while a rival company claims that the proportion of viewers watching was less than this. In a random sample of 200 viewers who were watching TV when the match was on, the number who watched it was 56. Carry out a test, at the 5% significance level, to decide between these claims. State your hypotheses and conclusion clearly. [6]

2 The continuous random variable X has a normal distribution with mean 20 and standard deviation 3. The mean of a random sample of n observations of X is denoted by $\overline{X}$. Given that $P(\overline{X} > 21)$ is between 0.01 and 0.05, find the set of possible values of n. [7]

3 (i) State briefly what you understand by the terms *population* and *sample* in a statistical context. [2]

(ii) Why are samples, rather than complete populations, often used for statistical investigations, and why is it often important for samples to be *random* samples? [2]

(iii) Explain briefly how a random sample of adults living in a certain town might be chosen. [2]

(iv) Give a reason why the sample described in part (iii) might not be ideal as the basis for an investigation into the likely sales of a new range of baby foods in the town's supermarkets. [1]

4 Lessons in a school are supposed to last for 40 minutes. However, a mathematics teacher finds that pupils are usually late for the lessons, and that the actual length of teaching time available can be modelled by a normal distribution with mean 35.5 minutes and standard deviation 1.2 minutes.

(i) Find the probability that the length of teaching time available in a randomly chosen lesson will be between 34.0 and 38.0 minutes. [4]

(ii) The probability that the length of teaching time available in a randomly chosen lesson exceeds m minutes is 0.75. Find m. [3]

5 On the surface of postage stamps there are either one or two phosphor bands. 90% of stamps have two bands and the rest have one band.

(i) Determine, using a normal approximation, the probability that in a random sample of 100 stamps there are between 5 and 15 (inclusive) having one phosphor band. [6]

Of those stamps having only one band, 95% have the band in the centre of the stamp and the remainder have the band on the left edge of the stamp.

(ii) Determine, using a Poisson distribution, the probability that in a random sample of 100 stamps there are fewer than 3 stamps which have only one band, this band being on the left edge of the stamp. [4]

6 A shopkeeper knows that the mean number of DVD players sold per day in his shop is 3.

   (i) Identify a distribution which you might expect to be a reasonable model for the number of DVD players sold by the shopkeeper on a randomly chosen day, giving any parameters of the distribution you have chosen. [1]

   (ii) Find the probability that the shopkeeper sells exactly 5 DVD players on a randomly chosen day. [2]

   (iii) Find the probability that the shopkeeper sells between 4 and 9 DVD players (inclusive) in a randomly chosen two-day period. [2]

   (iv) The shopkeeper opens his shop for six days every week. Use a suitable approximation to determine the number of DVD players which the shopkeeper should have in stock at the beginning of a randomly chosen week to be at least 95% certain of being able to meet demand during that week. [5]

7 A machine produces metal rods, whose lengths are normally distributed with standard deviation 0.1 cm. The machine is set up for the rods to have a mean length of 2 cm. To check whether the setting is accurate, a random sample of 20 rods is taken, and the lengths, x cm, are measured. It is found that $\sum (x - 2) = 0.84$.

   (i) Test, at the 5% significance level, whether the machine has been set up correctly. State your hypotheses and conclusions clearly. [6]

   (ii) Find the probability of making a Type II error in this test if the mean length of rods produced by the machine is in fact 2.05 cm. [6]

8 The amount of petrol, in tens of thousands of litres, sold in a week at a petrol station is modelled by the continuous random variable X, with probability density function given by

$$f(x) = \begin{cases} kx(4 - x^2) & \text{for } 0 < x < 2, \\ 0 & \text{otherwise.} \end{cases}$$

   (i) Find the value of the constant k. [2]

   (ii) Calculate the probability that more than 14 000 litres of petrol is sold in a week. [2]

   (iii) Find the mean and standard deviation of the amount of petrol sold in a week. [5]

   (iv) Show that the median, m, of X satisfies the equation

   $$m^4 - 8m^2 + 8 = 0,$$

   and hence find the median amount of petrol sold in a week. [4]

Cumulative binomial probabilities

The tables give the value of $P(X \leq x)$, where $X \sim B(n, p)$.

n = 5

p	0.05	0.10	0.15	1/6	0.20	0.25	0.30	1/3	0.35	0.40	0.45	0.50	0.55	0.60	0.65	2/3	0.70	0.75	0.80	5/6	0.85	0.90	0.95
x = 0	0.7738	0.5905	0.4437	0.4019	0.3277	0.2373	0.1681	0.1317	0.1160	0.0778	0.0503	0.0313	0.0185	0.0102	0.0053	0.0041	0.0024	0.0010	0.0003	0.0001	0.0001	0.0000	0.0000
1	0.9774	0.9185	0.8352	0.8038	0.7373	0.6328	0.5282	0.4609	0.4284	0.3370	0.2562	0.1875	0.1312	0.0870	0.0540	0.0453	0.0308	0.0156	0.0067	0.0033	0.0022	0.0005	0.0000
2	0.9988	0.9914	0.9734	0.9645	0.9421	0.8965	0.8369	0.7901	0.7648	0.6826	0.5931	0.5000	0.4069	0.3174	0.2352	0.2099	0.1631	0.1035	0.0579	0.0355	0.0266	0.0086	0.0012
3	1.0000	0.9995	0.9978	0.9967	0.9933	0.9844	0.9692	0.9547	0.9460	0.9130	0.8688	0.8125	0.7438	0.6630	0.5716	0.5391	0.4718	0.3672	0.2627	0.1962	0.1648	0.0815	0.0226
4	1.0000	1.0000	0.9999	0.9997	0.9997	0.9990	0.9976	0.9959	0.9947	0.9898	0.9815	0.9688	0.9497	0.9222	0.8840	0.8683	0.8319	0.7627	0.6723	0.5981	0.5563	0.4095	0.2262
5	1.0000	1.0000	1.0000	1.0000	1.0000	1.0000	1.0000	1.0000	1.0000	1.0000	1.0000	1.0000	1.0000	1.0000	1.0000	1.0000	1.0000	1.0000	1.0000	1.0000	1.0000	1.0000	1.0000

n = 6

p	0.05	0.10	0.15	1/6	0.20	0.25	0.30	1/3	0.35	0.40	0.45	0.50	0.55	0.60	0.65	2/3	0.70	0.75	0.80	5/6	0.85	0.90	0.95
x = 0	0.7351	0.5314	0.3771	0.3349	0.2621	0.1780	0.1176	0.0878	0.0754	0.0467	0.0277	0.0156	0.0083	0.0041	0.0018	0.0014	0.0007	0.0002	0.0001	0.0000	0.0000	0.0000	0.0000
1	0.9672	0.8857	0.7765	0.7368	0.6554	0.5339	0.4202	0.3512	0.3191	0.2333	0.1636	0.1094	0.0692	0.0410	0.0223	0.0178	0.0109	0.0046	0.0016	0.0007	0.0004	0.0001	0.0000
2	0.9978	0.9842	0.9527	0.9377	0.9011	0.8306	0.7443	0.6804	0.6471	0.5443	0.4415	0.3438	0.2553	0.1792	0.1174	0.1001	0.0705	0.0376	0.0170	0.0087	0.0059	0.0013	0.0001
3	0.9999	0.9987	0.9941	0.9913	0.9830	0.9624	0.9295	0.8999	0.8826	0.8208	0.7447	0.6563	0.5585	0.4557	0.3529	0.3196	0.2557	0.1694	0.0989	0.0623	0.0473	0.0159	0.0022
4	1.0000	0.9999	0.9996	0.9993	0.9984	0.9954	0.9891	0.9822	0.9777	0.9590	0.9308	0.8906	0.8364	0.7667	0.6809	0.6488	0.5798	0.4661	0.3446	0.2632	0.2235	0.1143	0.0328
5	1.0000	1.0000	1.0000	1.0000	0.9999	0.9998	0.9993	0.9986	0.9982	0.9959	0.9917	0.9844	0.9723	0.9533	0.9246	0.9122	0.8824	0.8220	0.7379	0.6651	0.6229	0.4686	0.2649
6	1.0000	1.0000	1.0000	1.0000	1.0000	1.0000	1.0000	1.0000	1.0000	1.0000	1.0000	1.0000	1.0000	1.0000	1.0000	1.0000	1.0000	1.0000	1.0000	1.0000	1.0000	1.0000	1.0000

n = 7

p	0.05	0.10	0.15	1/6	0.20	0.25	0.30	1/3	0.35	0.40	0.45	0.50	0.55	0.60	0.65	2/3	0.70	0.75	0.80	5/6	0.85	0.90	0.95
x = 0	0.6983	0.4783	0.3206	0.2791	0.2097	0.1335	0.0824	0.0585	0.0490	0.0280	0.0152	0.0078	0.0037	0.0016	0.0006	0.0005	0.0002	0.0001	0.0000	0.0000	0.0000	0.0000	0.0000
1	0.9556	0.8503	0.7166	0.6698	0.5767	0.4449	0.3294	0.2634	0.2338	0.1586	0.1024	0.0625	0.0357	0.0188	0.0090	0.0069	0.0038	0.0013	0.0004	0.0001	0.0001	0.0000	0.0000
2	0.9962	0.9743	0.9262	0.9042	0.8520	0.7564	0.6471	0.5706	0.5323	0.4199	0.3164	0.2266	0.1529	0.0963	0.0556	0.0453	0.0288	0.0129	0.0047	0.0020	0.0012	0.0002	0.0000
3	0.9998	0.9973	0.9879	0.9824	0.9667	0.9294	0.8740	0.8267	0.8002	0.7102	0.6083	0.5000	0.3917	0.2898	0.1998	0.1733	0.1260	0.0706	0.0333	0.0176	0.0121	0.0027	0.0002
4	1.0000	0.9998	0.9988	0.9980	0.9953	0.9871	0.9712	0.9547	0.9444	0.9037	0.8471	0.7734	0.6836	0.5801	0.4677	0.4294	0.3529	0.2436	0.1480	0.0958	0.0738	0.0257	0.0038
5	1.0000	1.0000	0.9999	1.0000	0.9996	0.9987	0.9962	0.9931	0.9910	0.9812	0.9643	0.9375	0.8976	0.8414	0.7662	0.7366	0.6706	0.5551	0.4233	0.3302	0.2834	0.1497	0.0444
6	1.0000	1.0000	1.0000	1.0000	1.0000	0.9999	0.9998	0.9995	0.9994	0.9984	0.9963	0.9922	0.9848	0.9720	0.9510	0.9415	0.9176	0.8665	0.7903	0.7209	0.6794	0.5217	0.3017
7	1.0000	1.0000	1.0000	1.0000	1.0000	1.0000	1.0000	1.0000	1.0000	1.0000	1.0000	1.0000	1.0000	1.0000	1.0000	1.0000	1.0000	1.0000	1.0000	1.0000	1.0000	1.0000	1.0000

n = 8

p	0.05	0.10	0.15	1/6	0.20	0.25	0.30	1/3	0.35	0.40	0.45	0.50	0.55	0.60	0.65	2/3	0.70	0.75	0.80	5/6	0.85	0.90	0.95
x = 0	0.6634	0.4305	0.2725	0.2326	0.1678	0.1001	0.0576	0.0390	0.0319	0.0168	0.0084	0.0039	0.0017	0.0007	0.0002	0.0002	0.0001	0.0000	0.0000	0.0000	0.0000	0.0000	0.0000
1	0.9428	0.8131	0.6572	0.6047	0.5033	0.3671	0.2553	0.1951	0.1691	0.1064	0.0632	0.0352	0.0181	0.0085	0.0036	0.0026	0.0013	0.0004	0.0001	0.0000	0.0000	0.0000	0.0000
2	0.9942	0.9619	0.8948	0.8652	0.7969	0.6785	0.5518	0.4682	0.4278	0.3154	0.2201	0.1445	0.0885	0.0498	0.0253	0.0197	0.0113	0.0042	0.0012	0.0004	0.0002	0.0000	0.0000
3	0.9996	0.9950	0.9786	0.9693	0.9437	0.8862	0.8059	0.7414	0.7064	0.5941	0.4770	0.3633	0.2604	0.1737	0.1061	0.0879	0.0580	0.0273	0.0104	0.0046	0.0029	0.0004	0.0000
4	1.0000	0.9996	0.9971	0.9954	0.9896	0.9727	0.9420	0.9121	0.8939	0.8263	0.7396	0.6367	0.5230	0.4059	0.2936	0.2586	0.1941	0.1138	0.0563	0.0307	0.0214	0.0050	0.0004
5	1.0000	1.0000	0.9998	0.9996	0.9988	0.9958	0.9887	0.9803	0.9747	0.9502	0.9115	0.8555	0.7799	0.6846	0.5722	0.5318	0.4482	0.3215	0.2031	0.1348	0.1052	0.0381	0.0058
6	1.0000	1.0000	1.0000	1.0000	0.9999	0.9996	0.9987	0.9974	0.9964	0.9915	0.9819	0.9648	0.9368	0.8936	0.8309	0.8049	0.7447	0.6329	0.4967	0.3953	0.3428	0.1869	0.0572
7	1.0000	1.0000	1.0000	1.0000	1.0000	1.0000	0.9999	0.9998	0.9998	0.9993	0.9983	0.9961	0.9916	0.9832	0.9681	0.9610	0.9424	0.8999	0.8322	0.7674	0.7275	0.5695	0.3366
8	1.0000	1.0000	1.0000	1.0000	1.0000	1.0000	1.0000	1.0000	1.0000	1.0000	1.0000	1.0000	1.0000	1.0000	1.0000	1.0000	1.0000	1.0000	1.0000	1.0000	1.0000	1.0000	1.0000

n = 9

p	0.05	0.10	0.15	1/6	0.20	0.25	0.30	1/3	0.35	0.40	0.45	0.50	0.55	0.60	0.65	2/3	0.70	0.75	0.80	5/6	0.85	0.90	0.95
x = 0	0.6302	0.3874	0.2316	0.1938	0.1342	0.0751	0.0404	0.0260	0.0207	0.0101	0.0046	0.0020	0.0008	0.0003	0.0001	0.0001	0.0000	0.0000	0.0000	0.0000	0.0000	0.0000	0.0000
1	0.9288	0.7748	0.5995	0.5427	0.4362	0.3003	0.1960	0.1431	0.1211	0.0705	0.0385	0.0195	0.0091	0.0038	0.0014	0.0010	0.0004	0.0001	0.0000	0.0000	0.0000	0.0000	0.0000
2	0.9916	0.9470	0.8591	0.8217	0.7382	0.6007	0.4628	0.3772	0.3373	0.2318	0.1495	0.0898	0.0498	0.0250	0.0112	0.0083	0.0043	0.0013	0.0003	0.0001	0.0000	0.0000	0.0000
3	0.9994	0.9917	0.9661	0.9520	0.9144	0.8343	0.7297	0.6503	0.6089	0.4826	0.3614	0.2539	0.1658	0.0994	0.0536	0.0424	0.0253	0.0100	0.0031	0.0011	0.0006	0.0001	0.0000
4	1.0000	0.9991	0.9944	0.9910	0.9804	0.9511	0.9012	0.8552	0.8283	0.7334	0.6214	0.5000	0.3786	0.2666	0.1717	0.1448	0.0988	0.0489	0.0196	0.0090	0.0056	0.0009	0.0000
5	1.0000	0.9999	0.9994	0.9989	0.9969	0.9900	0.9747	0.9576	0.9464	0.9006	0.8342	0.7461	0.6386	0.5174	0.3911	0.3497	0.2703	0.1657	0.0856	0.0480	0.0339	0.0083	0.0006
6	1.0000	1.0000	1.0000	0.9999	0.9997	0.9987	0.9957	0.9917	0.9888	0.9750	0.9502	0.9102	0.8505	0.7682	0.6627	0.6228	0.5372	0.3993	0.2618	0.1783	0.1409	0.0530	0.0084
7	1.0000	1.0000	1.0000	1.0000	1.0000	0.9999	0.9996	0.9990	0.9986	0.9962	0.9909	0.9805	0.9615	0.9295	0.8789	0.8569	0.8040	0.6997	0.5638	0.4573	0.4005	0.2252	0.0712
8	1.0000	1.0000	1.0000	1.0000	1.0000	1.0000	1.0000	0.9999	0.9999	0.9997	0.9992	0.9980	0.9954	0.9899	0.9793	0.9740	0.9596	0.9249	0.8658	0.8062	0.7684	0.6126	0.3698
9	1.0000	1.0000	1.0000	1.0000	1.0000	1.0000	1.0000	1.0000	1.0000	1.0000	1.0000	1.0000	1.0000	1.0000	1.0000	1.0000	1.0000	1.0000	1.0000	1.0000	1.0000	1.0000	1.0000

n = 10

p	0.05	0.10	0.15	1/6	0.20	0.25	0.30	1/3	0.35	0.40	0.45	0.50	0.55	0.60	0.65	2/3	0.70	0.75	0.80	5/6	0.85	0.90	0.95
x = 0	0.5987	0.3487	0.1969	0.1615	0.1074	0.0563	0.0282	0.0173	0.0135	0.0060	0.0025	0.0010	0.0003	0.0001	0.0000	0.0000	0.0000	0.0000	0.0000	0.0000	0.0000	0.0000	0.0000
1	0.9139	0.7361	0.5443	0.4845	0.3758	0.2440	0.1493	0.1040	0.0860	0.0464	0.0233	0.0107	0.0045	0.0017	0.0005	0.0004	0.0001	0.0000	0.0000	0.0000	0.0000	0.0000	0.0000
2	0.9885	0.9298	0.8202	0.7752	0.6778	0.5256	0.3828	0.2991	0.2616	0.1673	0.0996	0.0547	0.0274	0.0123	0.0048	0.0034	0.0016	0.0004	0.0001	0.0000	0.0000	0.0000	0.0000
3	0.9990	0.9872	0.9500	0.9303	0.8791	0.7759	0.6496	0.5593	0.5138	0.3823	0.2660	0.1719	0.1020	0.0548	0.0260	0.0197	0.0106	0.0035	0.0009	0.0003	0.0001	0.0000	0.0000
4	0.9999	0.9984	0.9901	0.9845	0.9672	0.9219	0.8497	0.7869	0.7515	0.6331	0.5044	0.3770	0.2616	0.1662	0.0949	0.0766	0.0473	0.0197	0.0064	0.0024	0.0014	0.0001	0.0000
5	1.0000	0.9999	0.9986	0.9976	0.9936	0.9803	0.9527	0.9234	0.9051	0.8338	0.7384	0.6230	0.4956	0.3669	0.2485	0.2131	0.1503	0.0781	0.0328	0.0155	0.0099	0.0016	0.0001
6	1.0000	1.0000	0.9999	0.9997	0.9991	0.9965	0.9894	0.9803	0.9740	0.9452	0.8980	0.8281	0.7340	0.6177	0.4862	0.4407	0.3504	0.2241	0.1209	0.0697	0.0500	0.0128	0.0010
7	1.0000	1.0000	1.0000	1.0000	0.9999	0.9996	0.9984	0.9966	0.9952	0.9877	0.9726	0.9453	0.9004	0.8327	0.7384	0.7009	0.6172	0.4744	0.3222	0.2248	0.1798	0.0702	0.0115
8	1.0000	1.0000	1.0000	1.0000	1.0000	1.0000	0.9999	0.9996	0.9995	0.9983	0.9955	0.9893	0.9767	0.9536	0.9140	0.8960	0.8507	0.7560	0.6242	0.5155	0.4557	0.2639	0.0861
9	1.0000	1.0000	1.0000	1.0000	1.0000	1.0000	1.0000	1.0000	1.0000	0.9999	0.9997	0.9990	0.9975	0.9940	0.9865	0.9827	0.9718	0.9437	0.8926	0.8385	0.8031	0.6513	0.4013
10	1.0000	1.0000	1.0000	1.0000	1.0000	1.0000	1.0000	1.0000	1.0000	1.0000	1.0000	1.0000	1.0000	1.0000	1.0000	1.0000	1.0000	1.0000	1.0000	1.0000	1.0000	1.0000	1.0000

n = 12

p	0.05	0.10	0.15	1/6	0.20	0.25	0.30	1/3	0.35	0.40	0.45	0.50	0.55	0.60	0.65	2/3	0.70	0.75	0.80	5/6	0.85	0.90	0.95
x = 0	0.5404	0.2824	0.1422	0.1122	0.0687	0.0317	0.0138	0.0077	0.0057	0.0022	0.0008	0.0002	0.0001	0.0000	0.0000	0.0000	0.0000	0.0000	0.0000	0.0000	0.0000	0.0000	0.0000
1	0.8816	0.6590	0.4435	0.3813	0.2749	0.1584	0.0850	0.0540	0.0424	0.0196	0.0083	0.0032	0.0011	0.0003	0.0001	0.0000	0.0000	0.0000	0.0000	0.0000	0.0000	0.0000	0.0000
2	0.9804	0.8891	0.7358	0.6774	0.5583	0.3907	0.2528	0.1811	0.1513	0.0834	0.0421	0.0193	0.0079	0.0028	0.0008	0.0005	0.0002	0.0000	0.0000	0.0000	0.0000	0.0000	0.0000
3	0.9978	0.9744	0.9078	0.8748	0.7946	0.6488	0.4925	0.3931	0.3467	0.2253	0.1345	0.0730	0.0356	0.0153	0.0056	0.0039	0.0017	0.0004	0.0001	0.0000	0.0000	0.0000	0.0000
4	0.9998	0.9957	0.9761	0.9636	0.9274	0.8424	0.7237	0.6315	0.5833	0.4382	0.3044	0.1938	0.1117	0.0573	0.0255	0.0188	0.0095	0.0028	0.0006	0.0002	0.0001	0.0000	0.0000
5	1.0000	0.9995	0.9954	0.9921	0.9806	0.9456	0.8822	0.8223	0.7873	0.6652	0.5269	0.3872	0.2607	0.1582	0.0846	0.0664	0.0386	0.0143	0.0039	0.0013	0.0007	0.0001	0.0000
6	1.0000	0.9999	0.9993	0.9987	0.9961	0.9857	0.9614	0.9336	0.9154	0.8418	0.7393	0.6128	0.4731	0.3348	0.2127	0.1777	0.1178	0.0544	0.0194	0.0079	0.0046	0.0005	0.0000
7	1.0000	1.0000	0.9999	0.9998	0.9994	0.9972	0.9905	0.9812	0.9745	0.9427	0.8883	0.8062	0.6956	0.5618	0.4167	0.3685	0.2763	0.1576	0.0726	0.0364	0.0239	0.0043	0.0002
8	1.0000	1.0000	1.0000	1.0000	0.9999	0.9996	0.9983	0.9961	0.9944	0.9847	0.9644	0.9270	0.8655	0.7747	0.6533	0.6069	0.5075	0.3512	0.2054	0.1252	0.0922	0.0256	0.0022
9	1.0000	1.0000	1.0000	1.0000	1.0000	1.0000	0.9998	0.9995	0.9992	0.9972	0.9921	0.9807	0.9579	0.9166	0.8487	0.8189	0.7472	0.6093	0.4417	0.3226	0.2642	0.1109	0.0196
10	1.0000	1.0000	1.0000	1.0000	1.0000	1.0000	1.0000	1.0000	0.9999	0.9997	0.9989	0.9968	0.9917	0.9804	0.9576	0.9460	0.9150	0.8416	0.7251	0.6187	0.5565	0.3410	0.1184
11	1.0000	1.0000	1.0000	1.0000	1.0000	1.0000	1.0000	1.0000	1.0000	0.9999	0.9999	0.9998	0.9992	0.9978	0.9943	0.9923	0.9862	0.9683	0.9313	0.8878	0.8578	0.7176	0.4596

Cumulative binomial probabilities

The tables give the value of $P(X \leq x)$, where $X \sim B(n, p)$.

n = 14

p	0.05	0.10	0.15	1/6	0.20	0.25	0.30	1/3	0.35	0.40	0.45	0.50	0.55	0.60	0.65	2/3	0.70	0.75	0.80	5/6	0.85	0.90	0.95
x = 0	0.4877	0.2288	0.1028	0.0779	0.0440	0.0178	0.0068	0.0034	0.0024	0.0008	0.0002	0.0001	0.0000	0.0000	0.0000	0.0000	0.0000	0.0000	0.0000	0.0000	0.0000	0.0000	0.0000
1	0.8470	0.5846	0.3567	0.2960	0.1979	0.1010	0.0475	0.0274	0.0205	0.0081	0.0029	0.0009	0.0003	0.0001	0.0000	0.0000	0.0000	0.0000	0.0000	0.0000	0.0000	0.0000	0.0000
2	0.9699	0.8416	0.6479	0.5795	0.4481	0.2811	0.1608	0.1053	0.0839	0.0398	0.0170	0.0065	0.0022	0.0006	0.0001	0.0001	0.0000	0.0000	0.0000	0.0000	0.0000	0.0000	0.0000
3	0.9958	0.9559	0.8535	0.8063	0.6982	0.5213	0.3552	0.2612	0.2205	0.1243	0.0632	0.0287	0.0114	0.0039	0.0011	0.0007	0.0002	0.0000	0.0000	0.0000	0.0000	0.0000	0.0000
4	0.9996	0.9908	0.9533	0.9310	0.8702	0.7415	0.5842	0.4755	0.4227	0.2793	0.1672	0.0898	0.0426	0.0175	0.0060	0.0040	0.0017	0.0003	0.0000	0.0000	0.0000	0.0000	0.0000
5	1.0000	0.9985	0.9885	0.9809	0.9561	0.8883	0.7805	0.6898	0.6405	0.4859	0.3373	0.2120	0.1189	0.0583	0.0243	0.0174	0.0083	0.0022	0.0004	0.0001	0.0001	0.0000	0.0000
6	1.0000	0.9998	0.9978	0.9959	0.9884	0.9617	0.9067	0.8505	0.8164	0.6925	0.5461	0.3953	0.2586	0.1501	0.0753	0.0576	0.0315	0.0103	0.0024	0.0007	0.0003	0.0000	0.0000
7	1.0000	1.0000	0.9997	0.9993	0.9976	0.9897	0.9685	0.9424	0.9247	0.8499	0.7414	0.6047	0.4539	0.3075	0.1836	0.1495	0.0933	0.0383	0.0116	0.0041	0.0022	0.0002	0.0000
8	1.0000	1.0000	1.0000	0.9999	0.9996	0.9978	0.9917	0.9826	0.9757	0.9417	0.8811	0.7880	0.6627	0.5141	0.3595	0.3102	0.2195	0.1117	0.0439	0.0191	0.0115	0.0015	0.0000
9	1.0000	1.0000	1.0000	1.0000	1.0000	0.9997	0.9983	0.9960	0.9940	0.9825	0.9574	0.9102	0.8328	0.7207	0.5773	0.5245	0.4158	0.2585	0.1298	0.0690	0.0467	0.0092	0.0004
10	1.0000	1.0000	1.0000	1.0000	1.0000	1.0000	0.9998	0.9993	0.9989	0.9961	0.9886	0.9713	0.9368	0.8757	0.7795	0.7388	0.6448	0.4787	0.3018	0.1937	0.1465	0.0441	0.0042
11	1.0000	1.0000	1.0000	1.0000	1.0000	1.0000	1.0000	0.9999	0.9999	0.9994	0.9978	0.9935	0.9830	0.9602	0.9161	0.8947	0.8392	0.7189	0.5519	0.4205	0.3521	0.1584	0.0301
12	1.0000	1.0000	1.0000	1.0000	1.0000	1.0000	1.0000	1.0000	1.0000	0.9999	0.9997	0.9991	0.9971	0.9919	0.9795	0.9726	0.9525	0.8990	0.8021	0.7040	0.6433	0.4154	0.1530
13	1.0000	1.0000	1.0000	1.0000	1.0000	1.0000	1.0000	1.0000	1.0000	1.0000	1.0000	1.0000	0.9999	0.9998	0.9992	0.9966	0.9932	0.9822	0.9560	0.9221	0.8972	0.7712	0.5123
14	1.0000	1.0000	1.0000	1.0000	1.0000	1.0000	1.0000	1.0000	1.0000	1.0000	1.0000	1.0000	1.0000	1.0000	1.0000	1.0000	1.0000	1.0000	1.0000	1.0000	1.0000	1.0000	1.0000

n = 16

p	0.05	0.10	0.15	1/6	0.20	0.25	0.30	1/3	0.35	0.40	0.45	0.50	0.55	0.60	0.65	2/3	0.70	0.75	0.80	5/6	0.85	0.90	0.95
x = 0	0.4401	0.1853	0.0743	0.0541	0.0281	0.0100	0.0033	0.0015	0.0010	0.0003	0.0001	0.0000	0.0000	0.0000	0.0000	0.0000	0.0000	0.0000	0.0000	0.0000	0.0000	0.0000	0.0000
1	0.8108	0.5147	0.2839	0.2272	0.1407	0.0635	0.0261	0.0137	0.0098	0.0033	0.0010	0.0003	0.0001	0.0000	0.0000	0.0000	0.0000	0.0000	0.0000	0.0000	0.0000	0.0000	0.0000
2	0.9571	0.7892	0.5614	0.4868	0.3518	0.1971	0.0994	0.0594	0.0451	0.0183	0.0066	0.0021	0.0006	0.0001	0.0000	0.0000	0.0000	0.0000	0.0000	0.0000	0.0000	0.0000	0.0000
3	0.9930	0.9316	0.7899	0.7291	0.5981	0.4050	0.2459	0.1659	0.1339	0.0651	0.0281	0.0106	0.0035	0.0009	0.0002	0.0001	0.0000	0.0000	0.0000	0.0000	0.0000	0.0000	0.0000
4	0.9991	0.9830	0.9209	0.8866	0.7982	0.6302	0.4499	0.3391	0.2892	0.1666	0.0853	0.0384	0.0149	0.0049	0.0013	0.0008	0.0003	0.0000	0.0000	0.0000	0.0000	0.0000	0.0000
5	0.9999	0.9967	0.9765	0.9622	0.9183	0.8103	0.6598	0.5469	0.4900	0.3288	0.1976	0.1051	0.0486	0.0191	0.0062	0.0040	0.0016	0.0003	0.0000	0.0000	0.0000	0.0000	0.0000
6	1.0000	0.9995	0.9944	0.9899	0.9733	0.9204	0.8247	0.7374	0.6881	0.5272	0.3660	0.2272	0.1241	0.0583	0.0229	0.0159	0.0071	0.0016	0.0002	0.0000	0.0000	0.0000	0.0000
7	1.0000	0.9999	0.9989	0.9979	0.9930	0.9729	0.9256	0.8735	0.8406	0.7161	0.5629	0.4018	0.2559	0.1423	0.0671	0.0500	0.0257	0.0075	0.0015	0.0004	0.0002	0.0000	0.0000
8	1.0000	1.0000	0.9998	0.9996	0.9985	0.9925	0.9743	0.9500	0.9329	0.8577	0.7441	0.5982	0.4371	0.2839	0.1594	0.1265	0.0744	0.0271	0.0070	0.0021	0.0011	0.0001	0.0000
9	1.0000	1.0000	1.0000	1.0000	0.9998	0.9984	0.9929	0.9841	0.9771	0.9417	0.8759	0.7728	0.6340	0.4728	0.3119	0.2626	0.1753	0.0796	0.0267	0.0101	0.0056	0.0005	0.0000
10	1.0000	1.0000	1.0000	1.0000	1.0000	0.9997	0.9984	0.9960	0.9938	0.9809	0.9514	0.8949	0.8024	0.6712	0.5100	0.4531	0.3402	0.1897	0.0817	0.0378	0.0235	0.0033	0.0001
11	1.0000	1.0000	1.0000	1.0000	1.0000	1.0000	0.9997	0.9992	0.9987	0.9951	0.9851	0.9616	0.9147	0.8334	0.7108	0.6609	0.5501	0.3698	0.2018	0.1134	0.0791	0.0170	0.0009
12	1.0000	1.0000	1.0000	1.0000	1.0000	1.0000	1.0000	0.9999	0.9998	0.9991	0.9965	0.9894	0.9719	0.9349	0.8661	0.8341	0.7541	0.5950	0.4019	0.2709	0.2101	0.0684	0.0070
13	1.0000	1.0000	1.0000	1.0000	1.0000	1.0000	1.0000	1.0000	1.0000	0.9999	0.9994	0.9979	0.9934	0.9817	0.9549	0.9406	0.9006	0.8029	0.6482	0.5132	0.4386	0.2108	0.0429
14	1.0000	1.0000	1.0000	1.0000	1.0000	1.0000	1.0000	1.0000	1.0000	1.0000	0.9999	0.9997	0.9990	0.9967	0.9902	0.9863	0.9739	0.9365	0.8593	0.7728	0.7161	0.4853	0.1892
15	1.0000	1.0000	1.0000	1.0000	1.0000	1.0000	1.0000	1.0000	1.0000	1.0000	1.0000	1.0000	0.9999	0.9997	0.9990	0.9985	0.9967	0.9900	0.9719	0.9459	0.9257	0.8147	0.5599
16	1.0000	1.0000	1.0000	1.0000	1.0000	1.0000	1.0000	1.0000	1.0000	1.0000	1.0000	1.0000	1.0000	1.0000	1.0000	1.0000	1.0000	1.0000	1.0000	1.0000	1.0000	1.0000	1.0000

$n = 18$

x	0.05	0.10	0.15	1/6	0.20	0.25	0.30	1/3	0.35	0.40	0.45	0.50	0.55	0.60	0.65	2/3	0.70	0.75	0.80	5/6	0.85	0.90	0.95
0	0.3972	0.1501	0.0536	0.0376	0.0180	0.0056	0.0016	0.0007	0.0004	0.0001	0.0000	0.0000	0.0000	0.0000	0.0000	0.0000	0.0000	0.0000	0.0000	0.0000	0.0000	0.0000	0.0000
1	0.7735	0.4503	0.2241	0.1728	0.0991	0.0395	0.0142	0.0068	0.0046	0.0013	0.0003	0.0001	0.0000	0.0000	0.0000	0.0000	0.0000	0.0000	0.0000	0.0000	0.0000	0.0000	0.0000
2	0.9419	0.7338	0.4797	0.4027	0.2713	0.1353	0.0600	0.0326	0.0236	0.0082	0.0025	0.0007	0.0001	0.0000	0.0000	0.0000	0.0000	0.0000	0.0000	0.0000	0.0000	0.0000	0.0000
3	0.9891	0.9018	0.7202	0.6479	0.5010	0.3057	0.1646	0.1017	0.0783	0.0328	0.0120	0.0038	0.0010	0.0002	0.0000	0.0000	0.0000	0.0000	0.0000	0.0000	0.0000	0.0000	0.0000
4	0.9985	0.9718	0.8794	0.8318	0.7164	0.5187	0.3327	0.2311	0.1886	0.0942	0.0411	0.0154	0.0049	0.0013	0.0003	0.0001	0.0000	0.0000	0.0000	0.0000	0.0000	0.0000	0.0000
5	0.9998	0.9936	0.9581	0.9347	0.8671	0.7175	0.5344	0.4122	0.3550	0.2088	0.1077	0.0481	0.0183	0.0058	0.0014	0.0009	0.0003	0.0000	0.0000	0.0000	0.0000	0.0000	0.0000
6	1.0000	0.9988	0.9882	0.9794	0.9487	0.8610	0.7217	0.6085	0.5491	0.3743	0.2258	0.1189	0.0537	0.0203	0.0062	0.0039	0.0014	0.0002	0.0000	0.0000	0.0000	0.0000	0.0000
7	1.0000	0.9998	0.9973	0.9947	0.9837	0.9431	0.8593	0.7767	0.7283	0.5634	0.3915	0.2403	0.1280	0.0576	0.0212	0.0144	0.0061	0.0012	0.0002	0.0000	0.0000	0.0000	0.0000
8	1.0000	1.0000	0.9995	0.9989	0.9957	0.9807	0.9404	0.8924	0.8609	0.7368	0.5778	0.4073	0.2527	0.1347	0.0597	0.0433	0.0210	0.0054	0.0009	0.0002	0.0001	0.0000	0.0000
9	1.0000	1.0000	0.9999	0.9998	0.9991	0.9946	0.9790	0.9567	0.9403	0.8653	0.7473	0.5927	0.4222	0.2632	0.1391	0.1076	0.0596	0.0193	0.0043	0.0011	0.0005	0.0000	0.0000
10	1.0000	1.0000	1.0000	1.0000	0.9998	0.9988	0.9939	0.9856	0.9788	0.9424	0.8720	0.7597	0.6085	0.4366	0.2717	0.2233	0.1407	0.0569	0.0163	0.0053	0.0027	0.0002	0.0000
11	1.0000	1.0000	1.0000	1.0000	1.0000	0.9998	0.9986	0.9961	0.9938	0.9797	0.9463	0.8811	0.7742	0.6257	0.4509	0.3915	0.2783	0.1390	0.0513	0.0206	0.0118	0.0012	0.0000
12	1.0000	1.0000	1.0000	1.0000	1.0000	1.0000	0.9997	0.9991	0.9986	0.9942	0.9817	0.9519	0.8923	0.7912	0.6450	0.5878	0.4656	0.2825	0.1329	0.0653	0.0419	0.0064	0.0002
13	1.0000	1.0000	1.0000	1.0000	1.0000	1.0000	1.0000	0.9999	0.9997	0.9987	0.9951	0.9846	0.9589	0.9058	0.8114	0.7689	0.6673	0.4813	0.2836	0.1682	0.1206	0.0282	0.0015
14	1.0000	1.0000	1.0000	1.0000	1.0000	1.0000	1.0000	1.0000	1.0000	0.9998	0.9990	0.9962	0.9880	0.9672	0.9217	0.8983	0.8354	0.6943	0.4990	0.3521	0.2798	0.0982	0.0109
15	1.0000	1.0000	1.0000	1.0000	1.0000	1.0000	1.0000	1.0000	1.0000	1.0000	0.9999	0.9993	0.9975	0.9918	0.9764	0.9674	0.9400	0.8647	0.7287	0.5973	0.5203	0.2662	0.0581
16	1.0000	1.0000	1.0000	1.0000	1.0000	1.0000	1.0000	1.0000	1.0000	1.0000	1.0000	0.9999	0.9997	0.9987	0.9954	0.9932	0.9858	0.9605	0.9009	0.8272	0.7759	0.5497	0.2265
17	1.0000	1.0000	1.0000	1.0000	1.0000	1.0000	1.0000	1.0000	1.0000	1.0000	1.0000	1.0000	1.0000	0.9999	0.9996	0.9993	0.9984	0.9944	0.9820	0.9624	0.9464	0.8499	0.6028
18	1.0000	1.0000	1.0000	1.0000	1.0000	1.0000	1.0000	1.0000	1.0000	1.0000	1.0000	1.0000	1.0000	1.0000	1.0000	1.0000	1.0000	1.0000	1.0000	1.0000	1.0000	1.0000	1.0000

$n = 20$

x	0.05	0.10	0.15	1/6	0.20	0.25	0.30	1/3	0.35	0.40	0.45	0.50	0.55	0.60	0.65	2/3	0.70	0.75	0.80	5/6	0.85	0.90	0.95
0	0.3585	0.1216	0.0388	0.0261	0.0115	0.0032	0.0008	0.0003	0.0002	0.0000	0.0000	0.0000	0.0000	0.0000	0.0000	0.0000	0.0000	0.0000	0.0000	0.0000	0.0000	0.0000	0.0000
1	0.7358	0.3917	0.1756	0.1304	0.0692	0.0243	0.0076	0.0033	0.0021	0.0005	0.0001	0.0000	0.0000	0.0000	0.0000	0.0000	0.0000	0.0000	0.0000	0.0000	0.0000	0.0000	0.0000
2	0.9245	0.6769	0.4049	0.3287	0.2061	0.0913	0.0355	0.0176	0.0121	0.0036	0.0009	0.0002	0.0000	0.0000	0.0000	0.0000	0.0000	0.0000	0.0000	0.0000	0.0000	0.0000	0.0000
3	0.9841	0.8670	0.6477	0.5665	0.4114	0.2252	0.1071	0.0604	0.0444	0.0160	0.0049	0.0013	0.0003	0.0000	0.0000	0.0000	0.0000	0.0000	0.0000	0.0000	0.0000	0.0000	0.0000
4	0.9974	0.9568	0.8298	0.7687	0.6296	0.4148	0.2375	0.1515	0.1182	0.0510	0.0189	0.0059	0.0015	0.0003	0.0000	0.0000	0.0000	0.0000	0.0000	0.0000	0.0000	0.0000	0.0000
5	0.9997	0.9887	0.9327	0.8982	0.8042	0.6172	0.4164	0.2972	0.2454	0.1256	0.0553	0.0207	0.0064	0.0016	0.0003	0.0002	0.0000	0.0000	0.0000	0.0000	0.0000	0.0000	0.0000
6	1.0000	0.9976	0.9781	0.9629	0.9133	0.7858	0.6080	0.4793	0.4166	0.2500	0.1299	0.0577	0.0214	0.0065	0.0015	0.0009	0.0003	0.0000	0.0000	0.0000	0.0000	0.0000	0.0000
7	1.0000	0.9996	0.9941	0.9887	0.9679	0.8982	0.7723	0.6615	0.6010	0.4159	0.2520	0.1316	0.0580	0.0210	0.0060	0.0037	0.0013	0.0002	0.0000	0.0000	0.0000	0.0000	0.0000
8	1.0000	0.9999	0.9987	0.9972	0.9900	0.9591	0.8867	0.8095	0.7624	0.5956	0.4143	0.2517	0.1308	0.0565	0.0196	0.0130	0.0051	0.0009	0.0001	0.0000	0.0000	0.0000	0.0000
9	1.0000	1.0000	0.9998	0.9994	0.9974	0.9861	0.9520	0.9081	0.8782	0.7553	0.5914	0.4119	0.2493	0.1275	0.0532	0.0376	0.0171	0.0039	0.0006	0.0001	0.0000	0.0000	0.0000
10	1.0000	1.0000	1.0000	0.9999	0.9994	0.9961	0.9829	0.9624	0.9468	0.8725	0.7507	0.5881	0.4086	0.2447	0.1218	0.0919	0.0480	0.0139	0.0026	0.0006	0.0002	0.0000	0.0000
11	1.0000	1.0000	1.0000	1.0000	0.9999	0.9991	0.9949	0.9870	0.9804	0.9435	0.8692	0.7483	0.5857	0.4044	0.2376	0.1905	0.1133	0.0409	0.0100	0.0028	0.0013	0.0001	0.0000
12	1.0000	1.0000	1.0000	1.0000	1.0000	0.9998	0.9987	0.9963	0.9940	0.9790	0.9420	0.8684	0.7480	0.5841	0.3990	0.3385	0.2277	0.1018	0.0321	0.0113	0.0059	0.0004	0.0000
13	1.0000	1.0000	1.0000	1.0000	1.0000	1.0000	0.9997	0.9991	0.9985	0.9935	0.9786	0.9423	0.8701	0.7500	0.5834	0.5207	0.3920	0.2142	0.0867	0.0371	0.0219	0.0024	0.0000
14	1.0000	1.0000	1.0000	1.0000	1.0000	1.0000	1.0000	0.9998	0.9997	0.9984	0.9936	0.9793	0.9447	0.8744	0.7546	0.7028	0.5836	0.3828	0.1958	0.1018	0.0673	0.0113	0.0003
15	1.0000	1.0000	1.0000	1.0000	1.0000	1.0000	1.0000	1.0000	1.0000	0.9997	0.9985	0.9941	0.9811	0.9490	0.8818	0.8485	0.7625	0.5852	0.3704	0.2313	0.1702	0.0432	0.0026
16	1.0000	1.0000	1.0000	1.0000	1.0000	1.0000	1.0000	1.0000	1.0000	1.0000	0.9997	0.9987	0.9951	0.9840	0.9556	0.9396	0.8929	0.7748	0.5886	0.4335	0.3523	0.1330	0.0159
17	1.0000	1.0000	1.0000	1.0000	1.0000	1.0000	1.0000	1.0000	1.0000	1.0000	1.0000	0.9998	0.9991	0.9964	0.9879	0.9824	0.9645	0.9087	0.7939	0.6713	0.5951	0.3231	0.0755
18	1.0000	1.0000	1.0000	1.0000	1.0000	1.0000	1.0000	1.0000	1.0000	1.0000	1.0000	1.0000	0.9999	0.9995	0.9979	0.9967	0.9924	0.9757	0.9308	0.8696	0.8244	0.6083	0.2642
19	1.0000	1.0000	1.0000	1.0000	1.0000	1.0000	1.0000	1.0000	1.0000	1.0000	1.0000	1.0000	1.0000	1.0000	0.9998	0.9997	0.9992	0.9968	0.9885	0.9739	0.9612	0.8784	0.6415
20	1.0000	1.0000	1.0000	1.0000	1.0000	1.0000	1.0000	1.0000	1.0000	1.0000	1.0000	1.0000	1.0000	1.0000	1.0000	1.0000	1.0000	1.0000	1.0000	1.0000	1.0000	1.0000	1.0000

Cumulative binomial probabilities   The tables give the value of $P(X \leq x)$, where $X \sim B(n, p)$.

$n = 25$

p	0.05	0.10	0.15	1/6	0.20	0.25	0.30	1/3	0.35	0.40	0.45	0.50	0.55	0.60	0.65	2/3	0.70	0.75	0.80	5/6	0.85	0.90	0.95
x = 0	0.2774	0.0718	0.0172	0.0105	0.0038	0.0008	0.0001	0.0000	0.0000	0.0000	0.0000	0.0000	0.0000	0.0000	0.0000	0.0000	0.0000	0.0000	0.0000	0.0000	0.0000	0.0000	0.0000
1	0.6424	0.2712	0.0931	0.0629	0.0274	0.0070	0.0016	0.0005	0.0003	0.0001	0.0000	0.0000	0.0000	0.0000	0.0000	0.0000	0.0000	0.0000	0.0000	0.0000	0.0000	0.0000	0.0000
2	0.8729	0.5371	0.2537	0.1887	0.0982	0.0321	0.0090	0.0035	0.0021	0.0004	0.0001	0.0000	0.0000	0.0000	0.0000	0.0000	0.0000	0.0000	0.0000	0.0000	0.0000	0.0000	0.0000
3	0.9659	0.7636	0.4711	0.3816	0.2340	0.0962	0.0332	0.0149	0.0097	0.0024	0.0005	0.0001	0.0000	0.0000	0.0000	0.0000	0.0000	0.0000	0.0000	0.0000	0.0000	0.0000	0.0000
4	0.9928	0.9020	0.6821	0.5937	0.4207	0.2137	0.0905	0.0462	0.0320	0.0095	0.0023	0.0005	0.0001	0.0000	0.0000	0.0000	0.0000	0.0000	0.0000	0.0000	0.0000	0.0000	0.0000
5	0.9988	0.9666	0.8385	0.7720	0.6167	0.3783	0.1935	0.1120	0.0826	0.0294	0.0086	0.0020	0.0004	0.0001	0.0000	0.0000	0.0000	0.0000	0.0000	0.0000	0.0000	0.0000	0.0000
6	0.9998	0.9905	0.9305	0.8908	0.7800	0.5611	0.3407	0.2215	0.1734	0.0736	0.0258	0.0073	0.0016	0.0003	0.0000	0.0000	0.0000	0.0000	0.0000	0.0000	0.0000	0.0000	0.0000
7	1.0000	0.9977	0.9745	0.9553	0.8909	0.7265	0.5118	0.3703	0.3061	0.1536	0.0639	0.0216	0.0058	0.0012	0.0002	0.0001	0.0000	0.0000	0.0000	0.0000	0.0000	0.0000	0.0000
8	1.0000	0.9995	0.9920	0.9843	0.9532	0.8506	0.6769	0.5376	0.4668	0.2735	0.1340	0.0539	0.0174	0.0043	0.0008	0.0004	0.0001	0.0000	0.0000	0.0000	0.0000	0.0000	0.0000
9	1.0000	0.9999	0.9979	0.9953	0.9827	0.9287	0.8106	0.6956	0.6303	0.4246	0.2424	0.1148	0.0440	0.0132	0.0029	0.0016	0.0005	0.0000	0.0000	0.0000	0.0000	0.0000	0.0000
10	1.0000	1.0000	0.9995	0.9988	0.9944	0.9703	0.9022	0.8220	0.7712	0.5858	0.3843	0.2122	0.0960	0.0344	0.0093	0.0056	0.0018	0.0002	0.0000	0.0000	0.0000	0.0000	0.0000
11	1.0000	1.0000	0.9999	0.9997	0.9985	0.9893	0.9558	0.9082	0.8746	0.7323	0.5426	0.3450	0.1827	0.0778	0.0255	0.0164	0.0060	0.0009	0.0001	0.0000	0.0000	0.0000	0.0000
12	1.0000	1.0000	1.0000	0.9999	0.9996	0.9966	0.9825	0.9585	0.9396	0.8462	0.6937	0.5000	0.3063	0.1538	0.0604	0.0415	0.0175	0.0034	0.0004	0.0001	0.0000	0.0000	0.0000
13	1.0000	1.0000	1.0000	1.0000	0.9999	0.9991	0.9940	0.9836	0.9745	0.9222	0.8173	0.6550	0.4574	0.2677	0.1254	0.0918	0.0442	0.0107	0.0015	0.0003	0.0001	0.0000	0.0000
14	1.0000	1.0000	1.0000	1.0000	1.0000	0.9998	0.9982	0.9944	0.9907	0.9656	0.9040	0.7878	0.6157	0.4142	0.2288	0.1780	0.0978	0.0297	0.0056	0.0012	0.0005	0.0000	0.0000
15	1.0000	1.0000	1.0000	1.0000	1.0000	1.0000	0.9995	0.9984	0.9971	0.9868	0.9560	0.8852	0.7576	0.5754	0.3697	0.3044	0.1894	0.0713	0.0173	0.0047	0.0021	0.0001	0.0000
16	1.0000	1.0000	1.0000	1.0000	1.0000	1.0000	0.9999	0.9996	0.9992	0.9957	0.9826	0.9461	0.8660	0.7265	0.5332	0.4624	0.3231	0.1494	0.0468	0.0157	0.0080	0.0005	0.0000
17	1.0000	1.0000	1.0000	1.0000	1.0000	1.0000	1.0000	0.9999	0.9998	0.9988	0.9942	0.9784	0.9361	0.8464	0.6939	0.6297	0.4882	0.2735	0.1091	0.0447	0.0255	0.0023	0.0000
18	1.0000	1.0000	1.0000	1.0000	1.0000	1.0000	1.0000	1.0000	1.0000	0.9997	0.9984	0.9927	0.9742	0.9264	0.8266	0.7785	0.6593	0.4389	0.2200	0.1092	0.0695	0.0095	0.0002
19	1.0000	1.0000	1.0000	1.0000	1.0000	1.0000	1.0000	1.0000	1.0000	0.9999	0.9996	0.9980	0.9914	0.9706	0.9174	0.8880	0.8065	0.6217	0.3833	0.2280	0.1615	0.0334	0.0012
20	1.0000	1.0000	1.0000	1.0000	1.0000	1.0000	1.0000	1.0000	1.0000	1.0000	0.9999	0.9995	0.9977	0.9905	0.9680	0.9538	0.9095	0.7863	0.5793	0.4063	0.3179	0.0980	0.0072
21	1.0000	1.0000	1.0000	1.0000	1.0000	1.0000	1.0000	1.0000	1.0000	1.0000	1.0000	0.9999	0.9995	0.9976	0.9903	0.9851	0.9668	0.9038	0.7660	0.6184	0.5289	0.2364	0.0341
22	1.0000	1.0000	1.0000	1.0000	1.0000	1.0000	1.0000	1.0000	1.0000	1.0000	1.0000	1.0000	0.9999	0.9996	0.9979	0.9965	0.9910	0.9679	0.9018	0.8113	0.7463	0.4629	0.1271
23	1.0000	1.0000	1.0000	1.0000	1.0000	1.0000	1.0000	1.0000	1.0000	1.0000	1.0000	1.0000	1.0000	1.0000	0.9997	0.9995	0.9984	0.9930	0.9726	0.9371	0.9069	0.7288	0.3576
24	1.0000	1.0000	1.0000	1.0000	1.0000	1.0000	1.0000	1.0000	1.0000	1.0000	1.0000	1.0000	1.0000	1.0000	1.0000	1.0000	0.9999	0.9992	0.9962	0.9895	0.9828	0.9282	0.7226
25	1.0000	1.0000	1.0000	1.0000	1.0000	1.0000	1.0000	1.0000	1.0000	1.0000	1.0000	1.0000	1.0000	1.0000	1.0000	1.0000	1.0000	1.0000	1.0000	1.0000	1.0000	1.0000	1.0000

$n = 30$

p	0.05	0.10	0.15	1/6	0.20	0.25	0.30	1/3	0.35	0.40	0.45	0.50	0.55	0.60	0.65	2/3	0.70	0.75	0.80	5/6	0.85	0.90	0.95
$x = 0$	0.2146	0.0424	0.0076	0.0042	0.0012	0.0002	0.0000	0.0000	0.0000	0.0000	0.0000	0.0000	0.0000	0.0000	0.0000	0.0000	0.0000	0.0000	0.0000	0.0000	0.0000	0.0000	0.0000
1	0.5535	0.1837	0.0480	0.0295	0.0105	0.0020	0.0003	0.0001	0.0000	0.0000	0.0000	0.0000	0.0000	0.0000	0.0000	0.0000	0.0000	0.0000	0.0000	0.0000	0.0000	0.0000	0.0000
2	0.8122	0.4114	0.1514	0.1028	0.0442	0.0106	0.0021	0.0007	0.0003	0.0000	0.0000	0.0000	0.0000	0.0000	0.0000	0.0000	0.0000	0.0000	0.0000	0.0000	0.0000	0.0000	0.0000
3	0.9392	0.6474	0.3217	0.2396	0.1227	0.0374	0.0093	0.0033	0.0019	0.0003	0.0000	0.0000	0.0000	0.0000	0.0000	0.0000	0.0000	0.0000	0.0000	0.0000	0.0000	0.0000	0.0000
4	0.9844	0.8245	0.5245	0.4243	0.2552	0.0979	0.0302	0.0122	0.0075	0.0015	0.0002	0.0000	0.0000	0.0000	0.0000	0.0000	0.0000	0.0000	0.0000	0.0000	0.0000	0.0000	0.0000
5	0.9967	0.9268	0.7106	0.6164	0.4275	0.2026	0.0766	0.0355	0.0233	0.0057	0.0011	0.0002	0.0000	0.0000	0.0000	0.0000	0.0000	0.0000	0.0000	0.0000	0.0000	0.0000	0.0000
6	0.9994	0.9742	0.8474	0.7765	0.6070	0.3481	0.1595	0.0838	0.0586	0.0172	0.0040	0.0007	0.0001	0.0000	0.0000	0.0000	0.0000	0.0000	0.0000	0.0000	0.0000	0.0000	0.0000
7	0.9999	0.9922	0.9302	0.8863	0.7608	0.5143	0.2814	0.1668	0.1238	0.0435	0.0121	0.0026	0.0004	0.0000	0.0000	0.0000	0.0000	0.0000	0.0000	0.0000	0.0000	0.0000	0.0000
8	1.0000	0.9980	0.9722	0.9494	0.8713	0.6736	0.4315	0.2860	0.2247	0.0940	0.0312	0.0081	0.0016	0.0002	0.0000	0.0000	0.0000	0.0000	0.0000	0.0000	0.0000	0.0000	0.0000
9	1.0000	0.9995	0.9903	0.9803	0.9389	0.8034	0.5888	0.4317	0.3575	0.1763	0.0694	0.0214	0.0050	0.0009	0.0001	0.0000	0.0000	0.0000	0.0000	0.0000	0.0000	0.0000	0.0000
10	1.0000	0.9999	0.9971	0.9933	0.9744	0.8943	0.7304	0.5848	0.5078	0.2915	0.1350	0.0494	0.0138	0.0029	0.0004	0.0002	0.0000	0.0000	0.0000	0.0000	0.0000	0.0000	0.0000
11	1.0000	1.0000	0.9992	0.9980	0.9905	0.9493	0.8407	0.7239	0.6548	0.4311	0.2327	0.1002	0.0334	0.0083	0.0014	0.0007	0.0002	0.0000	0.0000	0.0000	0.0000	0.0000	0.0000
12	1.0000	1.0000	0.9998	0.9995	0.9969	0.9784	0.9155	0.8340	0.7802	0.5785	0.3592	0.1808	0.0714	0.0212	0.0045	0.0025	0.0006	0.0001	0.0000	0.0000	0.0000	0.0000	0.0000
13	1.0000	1.0000	1.0000	0.9999	0.9991	0.9918	0.9599	0.9102	0.8737	0.7145	0.5025	0.2923	0.1356	0.0481	0.0124	0.0072	0.0021	0.0002	0.0000	0.0000	0.0000	0.0000	0.0000
14	1.0000	1.0000	1.0000	1.0000	0.9998	0.9973	0.9831	0.9565	0.9348	0.8246	0.6448	0.4278	0.2309	0.0971	0.0301	0.0188	0.0064	0.0008	0.0001	0.0000	0.0000	0.0000	0.0000
15	1.0000	1.0000	1.0000	1.0000	0.9999	0.9992	0.9936	0.9812	0.9699	0.9029	0.7691	0.5722	0.3552	0.1754	0.0652	0.0435	0.0169	0.0027	0.0002	0.0000	0.0000	0.0000	0.0000
16	1.0000	1.0000	1.0000	1.0000	1.0000	0.9998	0.9979	0.9928	0.9876	0.9519	0.8644	0.7077	0.4975	0.2855	0.1263	0.0898	0.0401	0.0082	0.0009	0.0001	0.0000	0.0000	0.0000
17	1.0000	1.0000	1.0000	1.0000	1.0000	0.9999	0.9994	0.9975	0.9955	0.9788	0.9286	0.8192	0.6408	0.4215	0.2198	0.1660	0.0845	0.0216	0.0031	0.0005	0.0002	0.0000	0.0000
18	1.0000	1.0000	1.0000	1.0000	1.0000	1.0000	0.9998	0.9993	0.9986	0.9917	0.9666	0.8998	0.7673	0.5689	0.3452	0.2761	0.1593	0.0507	0.0095	0.0020	0.0008	0.0000	0.0000
19	1.0000	1.0000	1.0000	1.0000	1.0000	1.0000	1.0000	0.9998	0.9996	0.9971	0.9862	0.9506	0.8650	0.7085	0.4922	0.4152	0.2696	0.1057	0.0256	0.0067	0.0029	0.0001	0.0000
20	1.0000	1.0000	1.0000	1.0000	1.0000	1.0000	1.0000	1.0000	0.9999	0.9991	0.9950	0.9786	0.9306	0.8237	0.6425	0.5683	0.4112	0.1966	0.0611	0.0197	0.0097	0.0005	0.0000
21	1.0000	1.0000	1.0000	1.0000	1.0000	1.0000	1.0000	1.0000	1.0000	0.9998	0.9984	0.9919	0.9688	0.9060	0.7753	0.7140	0.5685	0.3264	0.1287	0.0506	0.0278	0.0020	0.0000
22	1.0000	1.0000	1.0000	1.0000	1.0000	1.0000	1.0000	1.0000	1.0000	1.0000	0.9996	0.9974	0.9879	0.9565	0.8762	0.8332	0.7186	0.4857	0.2392	0.1137	0.0698	0.0078	0.0001
23	1.0000	1.0000	1.0000	1.0000	1.0000	1.0000	1.0000	1.0000	1.0000	1.0000	0.9999	0.9993	0.9960	0.9828	0.9414	0.9162	0.8405	0.6519	0.3930	0.2235	0.1526	0.0258	0.0006
24	1.0000	1.0000	1.0000	1.0000	1.0000	1.0000	1.0000	1.0000	1.0000	1.0000	1.0000	0.9998	0.9989	0.9943	0.9767	0.9645	0.9234	0.7974	0.5725	0.3836	0.2894	0.0732	0.0033
25	1.0000	1.0000	1.0000	1.0000	1.0000	1.0000	1.0000	1.0000	1.0000	1.0000	1.0000	1.0000	0.9998	0.9985	0.9925	0.9878	0.9698	0.9021	0.7448	0.5757	0.4755	0.1755	0.0156
26	1.0000	1.0000	1.0000	1.0000	1.0000	1.0000	1.0000	1.0000	1.0000	1.0000	1.0000	1.0000	1.0000	0.9997	0.9981	0.9967	0.9907	0.9626	0.8773	0.7604	0.6783	0.3526	0.0608
27	1.0000	1.0000	1.0000	1.0000	1.0000	1.0000	1.0000	1.0000	1.0000	1.0000	1.0000	1.0000	1.0000	1.0000	0.9997	0.9993	0.9979	0.9894	0.9558	0.8972	0.8486	0.5886	0.1878
28	1.0000	1.0000	1.0000	1.0000	1.0000	1.0000	1.0000	1.0000	1.0000	1.0000	1.0000	1.0000	1.0000	1.0000	1.0000	0.9999	0.9997	0.9980	0.9895	0.9705	0.9520	0.8163	0.4465
29	1.0000	1.0000	1.0000	1.0000	1.0000	1.0000	1.0000	1.0000	1.0000	1.0000	1.0000	1.0000	1.0000	1.0000	1.0000	1.0000	1.0000	0.9998	0.9988	0.9958	0.9924	0.9576	0.7854
30	1.0000	1.0000	1.0000	1.0000	1.0000	1.0000	1.0000	1.0000	1.0000	1.0000	1.0000	1.0000	1.0000	1.0000	1.0000	1.0000	1.0000	1.0000	1.0000	1.0000	1.0000	1.0000	1.0000

Cumulative Poisson probabilities

The tables give the value of P $(X \leqslant x)$, where $X \sim$ Po(λ).

λ		0.01	0.02	0.03	0.04	0.05	0.06	0.07	0.08	0.09
$x = 0$		0.9900	0.9802	0.9704	0.9608	0.9512	0.9418	0.9324	0.9231	0.9139
1		1.0000	0.9998	0.9996	0.9992	0.9988	0.9983	0.9977	0.9970	0.9962
2		1.0000	1.0000	1.0000	1.0000	1.0000	1.0000	0.9999	0.9999	0.9999
3		1.0000	1.0000	1.0000	1.0000	1.0000	1.0000	1.0000	1.0000	1.0000

λ		0.10	0.20	0.30	0.40	0.50	0.60	0.70	0.80	0.90
$x = 0$		0.9048	0.8187	0.7408	0.6703	0.6065	0.5488	0.4966	0.4493	0.4066
1		0.9953	0.9825	0.9631	0.9384	0.9098	0.8781	0.8442	0.8088	0.7725
2		0.9998	0.9989	0.9964	0.9921	0.9856	0.9769	0.9659	0.9526	0.9371
3		1.0000	0.9999	0.9997	0.9992	0.9982	0.9966	0.9942	0.9909	0.9865
4		1.0000	1.0000	1.0000	0.9999	0.9998	0.9996	0.9992	0.9986	0.9977
5		1.0000	1.0000	1.0000	1.0000	1.0000	1.0000	0.9999	0.9998	0.9997
6		1.0000	1.0000	1.0000	1.0000	1.0000	1.0000	1.0000	1.0000	1.0000

λ	1.00	1.10	1.20	1.30	1.40	1.50	1.60	1.70	1.80	1.90
$x = 0$	0.3679	0.3329	0.3012	0.2725	0.2466	0.2231	0.2019	0.1827	0.1653	0.1496
1	0.7358	0.6990	0.6626	0.6268	0.5918	0.5578	0.5249	0.4932	0.4628	0.4337
2	0.9197	0.9004	0.8795	0.8571	0.8335	0.8088	0.7834	0.7572	0.7306	0.7037
3	0.9810	0.9743	0.9662	0.9569	0.9463	0.9344	0.9212	0.9068	0.8913	0.8747
4	0.9963	0.9946	0.9923	0.9893	0.9857	0.9814	0.9763	0.9704	0.9636	0.9559
5	0.9994	0.9990	0.9985	0.9978	0.9968	0.9955	0.9940	0.9920	0.9896	0.9868
6	0.9999	0.9999	0.9997	0.9996	0.9994	0.9991	0.9987	0.9981	0.9974	0.9966
7	1.0000	1.0000	1.0000	0.9999	0.9999	0.9998	0.9997	0.9996	0.9994	0.9992
8	1.0000	1.0000	1.0000	1.0000	1.0000	1.0000	1.0000	0.9999	0.9999	0.9998
9	1.0000	1.0000	1.0000	1.0000	1.0000	1.0000	1.0000	1.0000	1.0000	1.0000

λ	2.00	2.10	2.20	2.30	2.40	2.50	2.60	2.70	2.80	2.90
$x = 0$	0.1353	0.1225	0.1108	0.1003	0.0907	0.0821	0.0743	0.0672	0.0608	0.0550
1	0.4060	0.3796	0.3546	0.3309	0.3084	0.2873	0.2674	0.2487	0.2311	0.2146
2	0.6767	0.6496	0.6227	0.5960	0.5697	0.5438	0.5184	0.4936	0.4695	0.4460
3	0.8571	0.8386	0.8194	0.7993	0.7787	0.7576	0.7360	0.7141	0.6919	0.6696
4	0.9473	0.9379	0.9275	0.9162	0.9041	0.8912	0.8774	0.8629	0.8477	0.8318
5	0.9834	0.9796	0.9751	0.9700	0.9643	0.9580	0.9510	0.9433	0.9349	0.9258
6	0.9955	0.9941	0.9925	0.9906	0.9884	0.9858	0.9828	0.9794	0.9756	0.9713
7	0.9989	0.9985	0.9980	0.9974	0.9967	0.9958	0.9947	0.9934	0.9919	0.9901
8	0.9998	0.9997	0.9995	0.9994	0.9991	0.9989	0.9985	0.9981	0.9976	0.9969
9	1.0000	0.9999	0.9999	0.9999	0.9998	0.9997	0.9996	0.9995	0.9993	0.9991
10	1.0000	1.0000	1.0000	1.0000	1.0000	0.9999	0.9999	0.9999	0.9998	0.9998
11	1.0000	1.0000	1.0000	1.0000	1.0000	1.0000	1.0000	1.0000	1.0000	0.9999
12	1.0000	1.0000	1.0000	1.0000	1.0000	1.0000	1.0000	1.0000	1.0000	1.0000

The tables give the value of P $(X \leqslant x)$, where $X \sim$ Po(λ).

λ	3.00	3.10	3.20	3.30	3.40	3.50	3.60	3.70	3.80	3.90
$x = 0$	0.0498	0.0450	0.0408	0.0369	0.0334	0.0302	0.0273	0.0247	0.0224	0.0202
1	0.1991	0.1847	0.1712	0.1586	0.1468	0.1359	0.1257	0.1162	0.1074	0.0992
2	0.4232	0.4012	0.3799	0.3594	0.3397	0.3208	0.3027	0.2854	0.2689	0.2531
3	0.6472	0.6248	0.6025	0.5803	0.5584	0.5366	0.5152	0.4942	0.4735	0.4532
4	0.8153	0.7982	0.7806	0.7626	0.7442	0.7254	0.7064	0.6872	0.6678	0.6484
5	0.9161	0.9057	0.8946	0.8829	0.8705	0.8576	0.8441	0.8301	0.8156	0.8006
6	0.9665	0.9612	0.9554	0.9490	0.9421	0.9347	0.9267	0.9182	0.9091	0.8995
7	0.9881	0.9858	0.9832	0.9802	0.9769	0.9733	0.9692	0.9648	0.9599	0.9546
8	0.9962	0.9953	0.9943	0.9931	0.9917	0.9901	0.9883	0.9863	0.9840	0.9815
9	0.9989	0.9986	0.9982	0.9978	0.9973	0.9967	0.9960	0.9952	0.9942	0.9931
10	0.9997	0.9996	0.9995	0.9994	0.9992	0.9990	0.9987	0.9984	0.9981	0.9977
11	0.9999	0.9999	0.9999	0.9998	0.9998	0.9997	0.9996	0.9995	0.9994	0.9993
12	1.0000	1.0000	1.0000	1.0000	0.9999	0.9999	0.9999	0.9999	0.9998	0.9998
13	1.0000	1.0000	1.0000	1.0000	1.0000	1.0000	1.0000	1.0000	1.0000	0.9999
14	1.0000	1.0000	1.0000	1.0000	1.0000	1.0000	1.0000	1.0000	1.0000	1.0000

λ	4.00	4.10	4.20	4.30	4.40	4.50	4.60	4.70	4.80	4.90
$x = 0$	0.0183	0.0166	0.0150	0.0136	0.0123	0.0111	0.0101	0.0091	0.0082	0.0074
1	0.0916	0.0845	0.0780	0.0719	0.0663	0.0611	0.0563	0.0518	0.0477	0.0439
2	0.2381	0.2238	0.2102	0.1974	0.1851	0.1736	0.1626	0.1523	0.1425	0.1333
3	0.4335	0.4142	0.3954	0.3772	0.3594	0.3423	0.3257	0.3097	0.2942	0.2793
4	0.6288	0.6093	0.5898	0.5704	0.5512	0.5321	0.5132	0.4946	0.4763	0.4582
5	0.7851	0.7693	0.7531	0.7367	0.7199	0.7029	0.6858	0.6684	0.6510	0.6335
6	0.8893	0.8786	0.8675	0.8558	0.8436	0.8311	0.8180	0.8046	0.7908	0.7767
7	0.9489	0.9427	0.9361	0.9290	0.9214	0.9134	0.9049	0.8960	0.8867	0.8769
8	0.9786	0.9755	0.9721	0.9683	0.9642	0.9597	0.9549	0.9497	0.9442	0.9382
9	0.9919	0.9905	0.9889	0.9871	0.9851	0.9829	0.9805	0.9778	0.9749	0.9717
10	0.9972	0.9966	0.9959	0.9952	0.9943	0.9933	0.9922	0.9910	0.9896	0.9880
11	0.9991	0.9989	0.9986	0.9983	0.9980	0.9976	0.9971	0.9966	0.9960	0.9953
12	0.9997	0.9997	0.9996	0.9995	0.9993	0.9992	0.9990	0.9988	0.9986	0.9983
13	0.9999	0.9999	0.9999	0.9998	0.9998	0.9997	0.9997	0.9996	0.9995	0.9994
14	1.0000	1.0000	1.0000	1.0000	0.9999	0.9999	0.9999	0.9999	0.9999	0.9998
15	1.0000	1.0000	1.0000	1.0000	1.0000	1.0000	1.0000	1.0000	1.0000	0.9999
16	1.0000	1.0000	1.0000	1.0000	1.0000	1.0000	1.0000	1.0000	1.0000	1.0000

The table gives the value of P $(X \leqslant x)$, where $X \sim$ Po(λ).

λ	5.00	5.50	6.00	6.50	7.00	7.50	8.00	8.50	9.00	9.50
$x = 0$	0.0067	0.0041	0.0025	0.0015	0.0009	0.0006	0.0003	0.0002	0.0001	0.0001
1	0.0404	0.0266	0.0174	0.0113	0.0073	0.0047	0.0030	0.0019	0.0012	0.0008
2	0.1247	0.0884	0.0620	0.0430	0.0296	0.0203	0.0138	0.0093	0.0062	0.0042
3	0.2650	0.2017	0.1512	0.1118	0.0818	0.0591	0.0424	0.0301	0.0212	0.0149
4	0.4405	0.3575	0.2851	0.2237	0.1730	0.1321	0.0996	0.0744	0.0550	0.0403
5	0.6160	0.5289	0.4457	0.3690	0.3007	0.2414	0.1912	0.1496	0.1157	0.0885
6	0.7622	0.6860	0.6063	0.5265	0.4497	0.3782	0.3134	0.2562	0.2068	0.1649
7	0.8666	0.8095	0.7440	0.6728	0.5987	0.5246	0.4530	0.3856	0.3239	0.2687
8	0.9319	0.8944	0.8472	0.7916	0.7291	0.6620	0.5925	0.5231	0.4557	0.3918
9	0.9682	0.9462	0.9161	0.8774	0.8305	0.7764	0.7166	0.6530	0.5874	0.5218
10	0.9863	0.9747	0.9574	0.9332	0.9015	0.8622	0.8159	0.7634	0.7060	0.6453
11	0.9945	0.9890	0.9799	0.9661	0.9467	0.9208	0.8881	0.8487	0.8030	0.7520
12	0.9980	0.9955	0.9912	0.9840	0.9730	0.9573	0.9362	0.9091	0.8758	0.8364
13	0.9993	0.9983	0.9964	0.9929	0.9872	0.9784	0.9658	0.9486	0.9261	0.8981
14	0.9998	0.9994	0.9986	0.9970	0.9943	0.9897	0.9827	0.9726	0.9585	0.9400
15	0.9999	0.9998	0.9995	0.9988	0.9976	0.9954	0.9918	0.9862	0.9780	0.9665
16	1.0000	0.9999	0.9998	0.9996	0.9990	0.9980	0.9963	0.9934	0.9889	0.9823
17	1.0000	1.0000	0.9999	0.9998	0.9996	0.9992	0.9984	0.9970	0.9947	0.9911
18	1.0000	1.0000	1.0000	0.9999	0.9999	0.9997	0.9993	0.9987	0.9976	0.9957
19	1.0000	1.0000	1.0000	1.0000	1.0000	0.9999	0.9997	0.9995	0.9989	0.9980
20	1.0000	1.0000	1.0000	1.0000	1.0000	1.0000	0.9999	0.9998	0.9996	0.9991
21	1.0000	1.0000	1.0000	1.0000	1.0000	1.0000	1.0000	0.9999	0.9998	0.9996
22	1.0000	1.0000	1.0000	1.0000	1.0000	1.0000	1.0000	1.0000	0.9999	0.9999
23	1.0000	1.0000	1.0000	1.0000	1.0000	1.0000	1.0000	1.0000	1.0000	0.9999
24	1.0000	1.0000	1.0000	1.0000	1.0000	1.0000	1.0000	1.0000	1.0000	1.0000

The table gives the value of P ($X \leqslant x$), where $X \sim$ Po(λ).

λ	10.00	11.00	12.00	13.00	14.00	15.00	16.00	17.00	18.00	19.00
$x = 0$	0.0000	0.0000	0.0000	0.0000	0.0000	0.0000	0.0000	0.0000	0.0000	0.0000
1	0.0005	0.0002	0.0001	0.0000	0.0000	0.0000	0.0000	0.0000	0.0000	0.0000
2	0.0028	0.0012	0.0005	0.0002	0.0001	0.0000	0.0000	0.0000	0.0000	0.0000
3	0.0103	0.0049	0.0023	0.0011	0.0005	0.0002	0.0001	0.0000	0.0000	0.0000
4	0.0293	0.0151	0.0076	0.0037	0.0018	0.0009	0.0004	0.0002	0.0001	0.0000
5	0.0671	0.0375	0.0203	0.0107	0.0055	0.0028	0.0014	0.0007	0.0003	0.0002
6	0.1301	0.0786	0.0458	0.0259	0.0142	0.0076	0.0040	0.0021	0.0010	0.0005
7	0.2202	0.1432	0.0895	0.0540	0.0316	0.0180	0.0100	0.0054	0.0029	0.0015
8	0.3328	0.2320	0.1550	0.0998	0.0621	0.0374	0.0220	0.0126	0.0071	0.0039
9	0.4579	0.3405	0.2424	0.1658	0.1094	0.0699	0.0433	0.0261	0.0154	0.0089
10	0.5830	0.4599	0.3472	0.2517	0.1757	0.1185	0.0774	0.0491	0.0304	0.0183
11	0.6968	0.5793	0.4616	0.3532	0.2600	0.1848	0.1270	0.0847	0.0549	0.0347
12	0.7916	0.6887	0.5760	0.4631	0.3585	0.2676	0.1931	0.1350	0.0917	0.0606
13	0.8645	0.7813	0.6815	0.5730	0.4644	0.3632	0.2745	0.2009	0.1426	0.0984
14	0.9165	0.8540	0.7720	0.6751	0.5704	0.4657	0.3675	0.2808	0.2081	0.1497
15	0.9513	0.9074	0.8444	0.7636	0.6694	0.5681	0.4667	0.3715	0.2867	0.2148
16	0.9730	0.9441	0.8987	0.8355	0.7559	0.6641	0.5660	0.4677	0.3751	0.292
17	0.9857	0.9678	0.9370	0.8905	0.8272	0.7489	0.6593	0.5640	0.4686	0.3784
18	0.9928	0.9823	0.9626	0.9302	0.8826	0.8195	0.7423	0.6550	0.5622	0.4695
19	0.9965	0.9907	0.9787	0.9573	0.9235	0.8752	0.8122	0.7363	0.6509	0.5606
20	0.9984	0.9953	0.9884	0.9750	0.9521	0.9170	0.8682	0.8055	0.7307	0.6472
21	0.9993	0.9977	0.9939	0.9859	0.9712	0.9469	0.9108	0.8615	0.7991	0.7255
22	0.9997	0.9990	0.9970	0.9924	0.9833	0.9673	0.9418	0.9047	0.8551	0.7931
23	0.9999	0.9995	0.9985	0.9960	0.9907	0.9805	0.9633	0.9367	0.8989	0.8490
24	1.0000	0.9998	0.9993	0.9980	0.9950	0.9888	0.9777	0.9594	0.9317	0.8933
25	1.0000	0.9999	0.9997	0.9990	0.9974	0.9938	0.9869	0.9748	0.9554	0.9269
26	1.0000	1.0000	0.9999	0.9995	0.9987	0.9967	0.9925	0.9848	0.9718	0.9514
27	1.0000	1.0000	0.9999	0.9998	0.9994	0.9983	0.9959	0.9912	0.9827	0.9687
28	1.0000	1.0000	1.0000	0.9999	0.9997	0.9991	0.9978	0.9950	0.9897	0.9805
29	1.0000	1.0000	1.0000	1.0000	0.9999	0.9996	0.9989	0.9973	0.9941	0.9882
30	1.0000	1.0000	1.0000	1.0000	0.9999	0.9998	0.9994	0.9986	0.9967	0.9930
31	1.0000	1.0000	1.0000	1.0000	1.0000	0.9999	0.9997	0.9993	0.9982	0.9960
32	1.0000	1.0000	1.0000	1.0000	1.0000	1.0000	0.9999	0.9996	0.9990	0.9978
33	1.0000	1.0000	1.0000	1.0000	1.0000	1.0000	0.9999	0.9998	0.9995	0.9988
34	1.0000	1.0000	1.0000	1.0000	1.0000	1.0000	1.0000	0.9999	0.9998	0.9994
35	1.0000	1.0000	1.0000	1.0000	1.0000	1.0000	1.0000	1.0000	0.9999	0.9997
36	1.0000	1.0000	1.0000	1.0000	1.0000	1.0000	1.0000	1.0000	0.9999	0.9998
37	1.0000	1.0000	1.0000	1.0000	1.0000	1.0000	1.0000	1.0000	1.0000	0.9999
38	1.0000	1.0000	1.0000	1.0000	1.0000	1.0000	1.0000	1.0000	1.0000	1.0000

The normal distribution function

If Z has a normal distribution with mean 0 and variance 1 then, for each value of z, the table gives the value of $\Phi(z)$, where

$$\Phi(z) = P(Z \leqslant z).$$

For negative values of z use $\Phi(-z) = 1 - \Phi(z)$.

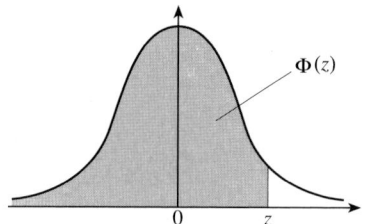

z	0	1	2	3	4	5	6	7	8	9	1	2	3	4	5	6	7	8	9
															ADD				
0.0	0.5000	0.5040	0.5080	0.5120	0.5160	0.5199	0.5239	0.5279	0.5319	0.5359	4	8	12	16	20	24	28	32	36
0.1	0.5398	0.5438	0.5478	0.5517	0.5557	0.5596	0.5636	0.5675	0.5714	0.5753	4	8	12	16	20	24	28	32	36
0.2	0.5793	0.5832	0.5871	0.5910	0.5948	0.5987	0.6026	0.6064	0.6103	0.6141	4	8	12	15	19	23	27	31	35
0.3	0.6179	0.6217	0.6255	0.6293	0.6331	0.6368	0.6406	0.6443	0.6480	0.6517	4	7	11	14	18	22	25	29	32
0.4	0.6554	0.6591	0.6628	0.6664	0.6700	0.6736	0.6772	0.6808	0.6844	0.6879	4	7	11	14	18	22	25	29	32
0.5	0.6915	0.6950	0.6985	0.7019	0.7054	0.7088	0.7123	0.7157	0.7190	0.7224	3	7	10	14	17	20	24	27	31
0.6	0.7257	0.7291	0.7324	0.7357	0.7389	0.7422	0.7454	0.7486	0.7517	0.7549	3	7	10	13	16	19	23	26	29
0.7	0.7580	0.7611	0.7642	0.7673	0.7704	0.7734	0.7764	0.7794	0.7823	0.7852	3	6	9	12	15	18	21	24	27
0.8	0.7881	0.7910	0.7939	0.7967	0.7995	0.8023	0.8051	0.8078	0.8106	0.8133	3	5	8	11	14	16	19	22	25
0.9	0.8159	0.8186	0.8212	0.8238	0.8264	0.8289	0.8315	0.8340	0.8365	0.8389	3	5	8	10	13	15	18	20	23
1.0	0.8413	0.8438	0.8461	0.8485	0.8508	0.8531	0.8554	0.8577	0.8599	0.8621	2	5	7	9	12	14	16	19	21
1.1	0.8643	0.8665	0.8686	0.8708	0.8729	0.8749	0.8770	0.8790	0.8810	0.8830	2	4	6	8	10	12	14	16	18
1.2	0.8849	0.8869	0.8888	0.8907	0.8925	0.8944	0.8962	0.8980	0.8997	0.9015	2	4	6	7	9	11	13	15	17
1.3	0.9032	0.9049	0.9066	0.9082	0.9099	0.9115	0.9131	0.9147	0.9162	0.9177	2	3	5	6	8	10	11	13	14
1.4	0.9192	0.9207	0.9222	0.9236	0.9251	0.9265	0.9279	0.9292	0.9306	0.9319	1	3	4	6	7	8	10	11	13
1.5	0.9332	0.9345	0.9357	0.9370	0.9382	0.9394	0.9406	0.9418	0.9429	0.9441	1	2	4	5	6	7	8	10	11
1.6	0.9452	0.9463	0.9474	0.9484	0.9495	0.9505	0.9515	0.9525	0.9535	0.9545	1	2	3	4	5	6	7	8	9
1.7	0.9554	0.9564	0.9573	0.9582	0.9591	0.9599	0.9608	0.9616	0.9625	0.9633	1	2	3	4	4	5	6	7	8
1.8	0.9641	0.9649	0.9656	0.9664	0.9671	0.9678	0.9686	0.9693	0.9699	0.9706	1	1	2	3	4	4	5	6	6
1.9	0.9713	0.9719	0.9726	0.9732	0.9738	0.9744	0.9750	0.9756	0.9761	0.9767	1	1	2	2	3	4	4	5	5
2.0	0.9772	0.9778	0.9783	0.9788	0.9793	0.9798	0.9803	0.9808	0.9812	0.9817	0	1	1	2	2	3	3	4	4
2.1	0.9821	0.9826	0.9830	0.9834	0.9838	0.9842	0.9846	0.9850	0.9854	0.9857	0	1	1	2	2	2	3	3	4
2.2	0.9861	0.9864	0.9868	0.9871	0.9875	0.9878	0.9881	0.9884	0.9887	0.9890	0	1	1	1	2	2	2	3	3
2.3	0.9893	0.9896	0.9898	0.9901	0.9904	0.9906	0.9909	0.9911	0.9913	0.9916	0	1	1	1	1	2	2	2	2
2.4	0.9918	0.9920	0.9922	0.9925	0.9927	0.9929	0.9931	0.9932	0.9934	0.9936	0	0	1	1	1	1	1	2	2
2.5	0.9938	0.9940	0.9941	0.9943	0.9945	0.9946	0.9948	0.9949	0.9951	0.9952	0	0	0	1	1	1	1	1	1
2.6	0.9953	0.9955	0.9956	0.9957	0.9959	0.9960	0.9961	0.9962	0.9963	0.9964	0	0	0	0	1	1	1	1	1
2.7	0.9965	0.9966	0.9967	0.9968	0.9969	0.9970	0.9971	0.9972	0.9973	0.9974	0	0	0	0	0	1	1	1	1
2.8	0.9974	0.9975	0.9976	0.9977	0.9977	0.9978	0.9979	0.9979	0.9980	0.9981	0	0	0	0	0	0	0	1	1
2.9	0.9981	0.9982	0.9982	0.9983	0.9984	0.9984	0.9985	0.9985	0.9986	0.9986	0	0	0	0	0	0	0	0	0

Critical values for the normal distribution

If Z has a normal distribution with mean 0 and variance 1 then, for each value of p, the table gives the value of z such that $P(Z \leq z) = p$.

p	0.75	0.90	0.95	0.975	0.99	0.995	0.9975	0.999	0.9995
z	0.674	1.282	1.645	1.960	2.326	2.576	2.807	3.090	3.291

Answers

Most non-exact numerical answers are given correct to 3 significant figures.

1 Continuous random variables

Exercise 1A (page 9)

1 (a) $\frac{1}{4}$ (b) $\frac{1}{16}$ (c) $\frac{3}{16}$

2 (a) $\frac{1}{9}$ (b) $\frac{8}{27}$ (c) 0.454 (d) 1.75

3 (a) $\frac{1}{15}$ (b) $\frac{11}{40}$

4 (a) $\frac{3}{32}$ (b) $\frac{1}{2}$ (c) $\frac{5}{32}$ (d) $\frac{5}{16}$ (e) $\frac{47}{128}$

5 (a) 2 (b) 0.135 (c) 0.632

6 (a) 400 (b) $\frac{4}{5}$ (c) $\frac{1}{3}$ (d) $\frac{1}{9}$ (e) $\frac{8}{27}$

7 (a) 3, $\frac{1}{9}$ (b) $\frac{1}{8}$

Exercise 1B (page 13)

1 2.38, 2.73, 1.89

2 800

3 (b) $2 + \frac{1}{2}\sqrt{2}$ (c) $\frac{1}{2}\left(1 + \sqrt{3}\right)$

4 (b) 347

5 (b) $5 - \frac{5}{2}\sqrt{2}$

Exercise 1C (page 18)

1 $\frac{9}{4}, \frac{27}{80}$

2 $\frac{8}{3}, \frac{1}{18}$

3 (b) $\frac{8}{3}, \frac{32}{9}$

4 (b) 2, $\frac{4}{5}$

5 (b) 15, 75

6 (c) 584, 19 100

Miscellaneous exercise 1 (page 18)

1 (a) $\frac{1}{4}$ (b) $\frac{8}{3}$

2 (a) 2.5 (b) 2.08

3 (a) $\frac{1}{50}$ (b) $\frac{10}{3}$ (c) $\frac{50}{9}$

4 (b) $\frac{1}{8}$ (c) 0.141 (d) $\frac{4}{3}$

5 (a) $\sqrt{2}$, 1, $\sqrt{3}$ (b) $\frac{4}{3}$ (c) $\frac{2}{9}$

6 (a) f$(u) = \frac{1}{2}$, for $0.5 \leqslant u \leqslant 2.5$, and 0 otherwise
  (b) $\frac{3}{2}$ (c) $\frac{1}{3}$

7 (a) 0.6 (b) 0.5 (c) 0.03 (d) $\frac{2}{9}$

8 (a) $\frac{1}{4}$ (b) 1.6 (c) 0.107
  (d) 1.68 (e) 0.697 (f) 0.351

9 (a) $\frac{1}{64}$ (b) $\frac{16}{5}$ (c) 0.427 (d) $\frac{15}{256}$

10 (a) $\dfrac{1}{\ln 2}$ (b) $\dfrac{1}{\ln 2}$ (c) 0.083 (d) $\sqrt{2}$

11 (b) 0.330 (c) 0.368

12 (a) $\dfrac{\ln 2}{a}$ (b) 6 (to the nearest integer)

13 (b) $\frac{3}{2}a$

14 (b) 3 years (c) 0.315

2 The normal distribution

Exercise 2A (page 30)

1 (a) 0.8907 (b) 0.9933 (c) 0.5624
  (d) 0.1082 (e) 0.0087 (f) 0.2783
  (g) 0.9664 (h) 0.9801 (i) 0.5267
  (j) 0.0336 (k) 0.0030 (l) 0.4184
  (m) 0.95 (n) 0.05 (o) 0.95
  (p) 0.05

2 (a) 0.0366 (b) 0.1202 (c) 0.3417
  (d) 0.4394 (e) 0.9555 (f) 0.7804
  (g) 0.8559 (h) 0.2088 (i) 0.0320
  (j) 0.1187 (k) 0.4459 (l) 0.95
  (m) 0.98 (n) 0.8064 (o) 0.0164

3 (a) 0.44 (b) 1.165 (c) 2.15
  (d) 1.017 (e) 0.24 (f) 1.178
  (g) 2.452 (h) 0.758 (i) −2.834
  (j) −1.955 (k) −1.035 (l) 0
  (m) −2.74 (n) −2.192 (o) −1.677
  (p) −0.056 (q) 1.645 (r) 1.282
  (s) 2.576 (t) 0.674

Exercise 2B (page 33)

1 (a) 0.9332 (b) 0.0062
  (c) 0.7734 (d) 0.0401

2 (a) 0.9522 (b) 0.0098
  (c) 0.7475 (d) 0.0038

3 (a) 0.1359 (b) 0.0606 (c) 0.7333
  (d) 0.7704 (e) 0.8664

4 0.0668

5 (a) 0.1587 (b) 0.0228

6 (a) 54.35 (b) 40.30 (c) 52.25 (d) 41.85

7 (a) 17.73 (b) 14.62 (c) 17.51 (d) 14.45
  (e) 3.29

8 (a) 41.6 (b) 29.9 (c) 37.3 (d) 31.7

Exercise 2C (page 36)

1 (a) 0.0370   (b) 0.0062   (c) 0.8209

2 (a) 0.2094   (b) 0.0086
  (c) 0.1788   (d) 0.6405
  105, 4, 89, 320

3 (a) 13   (b) 84   (c) 121

4 (a) 0.0048   (b) 0.1944   (c) 80, 100

5 1970; 0.109

6 (a) 0.614   (b) 20.9, 16.3   (c) 17

Exercise 2D (page 39)

1 10.03

2 65

3 42.0, 8.47

4 9.51, 0.303

5 336 ml

6 0.041 kg

7 47

8 49.1, 13.4

Exercise 2E (page 46)

1 (a) $np = 10$, $nq = 40$, yes
  (b) $np = 6$, $nq = 54$, yes
  (c) $np = 0.7$, no
  (d) $np = 21$, $nq = 9$, yes
  (e) $np = 36$, $nq = 4$, no

2 (a) 0.0288   (b) 0.114
  (c) 0.0805   (d) 0.375

  $np = 12$, $nq = 28$, valid normal
  approximation

3 (a) 0.0121 (b) 0.117

  $np = 15$, $nq = 285$, valid normal
  approximation

4 (a) 0.0117 (b) 0.0122, 0.0169

  $np = 9$, $nq = 9$, valid normal
  approximation

5 (a) 0.0083 (b) 0.9110

  $np = 6$, $nq = 44$, valid normal approximation

6 0.083, $np = 32$, $np = 8$, valid normal
  approximation

7 (a) 0.300   (b) 0.301

8 0.0168, 34

9 0.0264, 26

10 (a) 0.189, binomial, $np = 1$
   (b) 0.642, binomial, $np = 1$
   (c) 0.223, normal, $np = 32.1$, $nq = 17.9$

Miscellaneous exercise 2 (page 48)

1 0.0913

2 0.9213

3 10.3

4 (a) 25   (b) 0.6730

5 0.1977

6 0.960

7 0.933

8 0.957

9 0.525

10 0.367

11 0.7734

12 10.2

13 53.18

14 0.936, 0.928, Luxibrite

15 (a) 0.886   (b) probably not symmetric

16 (a) 20.2% (b) 81.0 g

17 (a) 70   (b) 45   (c) 0.0299

18 6.82, 0.443

19 18.9

20 (a) 9.68% (b) 28.5% (c) 40

21 (b) 0.069

22 47, 15

23 (a) 0.488   (b) 281, 5.00

24 $np > 5$ and $n(1 - p) > 5$

   (a) 0.1853   (b) 0.1838   (c) 0.816%

25 0.0608
   n is fixed; acceptable corks occur
   independently of each other.

   (a) 0.354   (b) 0.288

26 (a) 0.590   (b) 0.081;

   The model assumes that defective syringes
   occur independently of each other, but this
   may not be realistic in a manufacturing
   process. It is convenient to use the normal
   approximation because less calculation is
   involved; 0.0668.

27 (a) Late trains occur independently of each
       other. The probability that a train is late
       is constant.
   (b) 0.0184   (c) 0.744; 0.803

28 (a) (i) 0.236   (ii) 0.206
   (b) 0.672   (c) H, p is closer to $\frac{1}{2}$

29 0.397

30 (a) 46.49% (b) 0.532 m (c) 1.00 m

3   The Poisson distribution

Exercise 3A (page 56)

1 (a) 0.2240   (b) 0.1991   (c) 0.5768
2 (a) 0.2218   (b) 0.3696   (c) 0.8352
3 (a) 0.7787   (b) 0.6916   (c) 0.2090
4 (a) 0.1353   (b) 0.2707   (c) 0.2381
5 (a) 0.0821   (b) 0.5162   (c) 19
6 (a) 0.6065   (b) 0.4634
7 (a) 0.00674   (b) 49.9 s
8 (a) 0.0916   (b) 0.206 particle s^{-1}

Exercise 3B (page 62)

1 (a) Yes   (b) No   (c) Yes
   (d) Yes, provided claims are not caused by, say,
       freak weather conditions.
2 (a) 8, 8; yes, as mean = variance
   (b) 0.6866   (c) 2.8
3 (a) 0.29, 0.39, 0.16, 0.13, 0.03
   (b) 1.23, 1.21; Poisson is a suitable model.
   (c) 0.29, 0.36, 0.22, 0.09, 0.03
   (d) Supports comment in part (b).
4 1.71, 1.97;
   0.12, 0.45, 0.21, 0.12, 0.05, 0.02, 0, 0.02
   0.18, 0.31, 0.26, 0.15, 0.06, 0.02, 0.01, 0.002
   Poisson is not suitable.
5 $\mu = 0.79$, $\sigma^2 = 0.87$
   Theoretical probabilities 0.45, 0.36, 0.14, 0.04,
   0.01, 0.001. Yes.

Exercise 3C (page 66)

1 (a) (i) 0.222   (ii) 0.221
   (b) (i) 0.0966   (ii) 0.0965
2 (a) 0.8795   (b) 0.0077
3 (a) 0.108   (b) 0.0273
4 0.0190
5 (a) 0.953   (b) 0.434
6 (a) 0.171   (b) 1 473 574

Exercise 3D (page 69)

1 (a) 0.608   (b) 0.178   (c) 0.212
2 (a) 0.265   (b) 0.0497
3 0.209
4 0.0442
5 (a) 0.689   (b) 0.0446

6 (a) 0.759   (b) 0.0599
7 62
8 123

Miscellaneous exercise 3 (page 70)

1 0.191
2 Because n is large (> 50) and p is small
   ($np < 5$); 0.1953
3 The calls occur randomly, independently,
   singly and at a constant rate; 0.790
4 (a) 0.268   (b) 0.160
5 2; 0.188; 0.929
6 Y because $np = 4.2 < 5$; 0.210
7 The injuries occur randomly, independently,
   singly and at a constant rate.
   0.5, 0.481; possibly Poisson since the mean
   and variance are approximately equal.
   32, 16, 4, 1, 0; note that the frequencies do
   not add up to 52 because of rounding errors.
8 (a) 0.067   (b) 0.286   (c) 1   (d) 0.465
   (e) Po(29.7); 0.442, using N(29.7, 29.7)
9 $Y \sim B(100, \frac{1}{36})$. This may be approximated by
   $Y \sim Po(100 \times \frac{1}{36})$ since $n > 50$ and $np < 5$.
   $\frac{25}{9}$; 0.240; 0.303
10 (a) (i) 0.741   (ii) 0.037   (c) 100
11 3; 18.5%
12 0.647; 0.185

4   Sampling

Exercise 4A (page 87)

1 A sample of 200 chosen in such a way that
   each possible sample of 200 is equally likely
   to be picked. Method will not produce a
   random sample because people from large
   households have a lower probability of
   being chosen than those from small
   households.
2 (a) Number the hours 01, 02, 03, ..., 24.
       Taking pairs of digits starting from the
       beginning of given table would give the
       sample 09 and 03.
   (b) Number the students 001, 002, 003, ...,
       400. Taking groups of 3 digits starting
       from the beginning of given table would
       give students with numbers 285, 287 and
       357.

3 Some relevant points are:

  (a) All adults on electoral register equally likely to be chosen. People not on register omitted. Very time consuming and labour intensive.

  (b) Only people entering supermarket can be chosen but sample should be representative of these people.

  (c) People from large households have a lower probability of being chosen than those from small households. Time consuming – people may be out.

  (d) Only people whose names are in the phone book will be chosen. Quick and cheap provided that interviewees will respond over the phone.

4 N(50, 25)

  (a) 0.8413   (b) 0.9772   (c) 0.8185

5 (a) 2.8   (b) 0.76   (c) 0.0524   (d) 0.8952

6 $P(X = x) = \frac{1}{6}$, $x = 1, 2, 3, 4, 5, 6$

  (a) 0.155   (b) 0.0662

7 (a) 0.968   (b) 0.955

8 (a) 0.0084   (b) 82

9 94.8%

10 0.010

11 0.996

12 0.9615 > 95%

13 (a) $p = 0.8$, $n = 80$ (b) 0.037

Exercise 4B (page 90)

1 (a) 0.4602

  (b) (i) 0.3821   (ii) 0.1587

2 (a) False. $\overline{X}(n)$ has an *approximate* normal distribution for *large values* of n if X is not normally distributed.

  (b) True   (c) False. See part (a).

  (d) False. True for any n.

3 (a) N(2.4, 0.0432)   (b) 0.3152

  Neither of them depends on the central limit theorem.

4 (a) 0.271   (b) 0.0021

  The second, because n is larger; the larger n, the closer the distribution of the mean is to a normal distribution.

5 24.9; no, since X has a normal distribution.

6 2.11 hours

7 0.0434

8 (a) 0.981   (b) $1 - \Phi(-3.338) \approx 1$

Exercise 4C (page 100)

1 £1.83, 0.119 £^{2}

2 (a) 48, 0.24   (b) 48, 0.245

3 (a) 0.013 775 cm^2 (b) 0.0145 cm^2

4 (a) 2.49, 1.61

  (b) 0.182, month may give a biased sample; for example, April may have Easter holiday traffic.

5 (a) 50.633, 147.365   (b) 0.37

6 5.6, 2.569, 0.0248; variance approximate and normal approximation used.

Miscellaneous exercise 4 (page 101)

1 (a) Biased; people are likely to approve.

  (b) All ages are represented, but not necessarily in proportion to age distribution.

  (c) Satisfactory if chosen at a suitable time.

2 Each selection is independent and has an equal probability of being chosen.

  (a) Biased; not all people have a telephone.

  (b) Biased; only one area chosen and at only one time.

  (c) Should be satisfactory.

3 (a) Biased; does not include people who have a home delivery or buy the paper, say, from a street vendor.

  (b) Biased; respondents are only those who care enough to complete the form.

4 The number of words starting with the same initial letter is different for each letter. For example, number the letters from 1 to 26 and use some form of random number generator.

5 30

6 101.1 g, 1.369 g^2, $\Phi(2.973) \approx 1$; it assumes that sample parameters are good approximations to population parameters.

7 (a) 16   (b) 0.6554

8 (a) Sample restricted by length of throw. Satisfactory if researcher moves to different parts of the field before throwing.

  (b) Sample points restricted to centres of grid squares, also to points greater than 0.5 m from the boundary. However, sample should be satisfactory.

9 (a) $\frac{9}{7}$, $\frac{3}{49}$

(b) 0.0299; distribution of T is very skewed so answer not very accurate.

10 (a) 0.0594   (b) 0.0023

11 (a) 2.7, $\frac{2.7}{n}$ (b) 0.0192

12 (a) $N\left(50, \frac{64}{n}\right)$ (b) 0.0062   (c) 22

Approximately normal if n is large, but nothing if n is small.

13 (8.49, 9.51), $k = 5$, (7.75,10.25); interval wider, probability greater than 0.96.

5 Hypothesis testing: continuous variables

Exercise 5A (page 106)

1 $H_0 : \mu = 102.5$, $H_1 : \mu < 102.5$

2 $H_0 : \mu = 84$, $H_1 : \mu \neq 84$

3 $H_0 : \mu = 53$, $H_1 : \mu > 53$

4 $H_0 : \mu = 30$, $H_1 : \mu < 30$. A one-tail test is more appropriate for the customer.

5 $H_0 : \mu = 5$, $H_1 : \mu < 5$. A one-tail test for a decrease is appropriate since the only cause for concern is μ falling below 5.

Exercise 5B (page 110)

The end-points of the critical regions are given correct to 2 decimal places.

1 (a) Reject H_0 and accept that $\mu > 10$.
(b) Accept $H_0 : \mu = 10$.

2 (a) Accept $H_0 : \mu = 15$.
(b) Reject H_0 and accept that $\mu < 15$.

3 (a) Accept $H_0 : \mu = 20$.
(b), (c) Reject H_0 and accept that $\mu \neq 20$.

4 $H_0 : \mu = 102.5$, $H_1 : \mu < 102.5$; $\overline{X} \leqslant 101.69$; accept $\mu < 102.5$.

5 $H_0 : \mu = 84.0$, $H_1 : \mu \neq 84.0$; $\overline{X} \leqslant 82.11$ or $\overline{X} \geqslant 85.89$; reject H_0 and accept that mean time differs from 84.0 s.

6 $\overline{x} = 4.87$; $H_0 : \mu = 5$, $H_1 : \mu < 5$; $\overline{X} \leqslant 4.71$; accept H_0, mean is at least 5 microfarads.

7 $H_0 : \mu = 85.6$, $H_1 : \mu < 85.6$; $\overline{X} \leqslant 78.39$; reject H_0 and accept that the mean is less than 85.6.

8 $H_0 : \mu = 6.8$, $H_1 : \mu \neq 6.8$; $\overline{X} \leqslant 6.69$, $\overline{X} \geqslant 6.91$; reject H_0, and accept that the mean is greater than 6.8.

9 $H_0 : \mu = 30$, $H_1 : \mu < 30$; $\overline{X} \leqslant 28.94$; accept H_1, there is cause for complaint.

10 $H_0 : \mu = 3.21$, $H_1 : \mu \neq 3.21$; $\overline{X} \leqslant 2.92$, $\overline{X} \geqslant 3.50$; accept H_0; the sample does not differ significantly from a random sample drawn from the population of all of the hospital births that year.

Exercise 5C (page 114)

1 $H_0 : \mu = 330$, $H_1 : \mu > 330$; $z = 2.504 > 1.96$; accept H_1, manager's suspicion is correct.

2 $H_0 : \mu = 508$, $H_1 : \mu \neq 508$; $z = -1.622$. This lies between -1.645 and 1.645, so accept H_0 and the process is under control.

3 $H_0 : \mu = 45.1$, $H_1 : \mu \neq 45.1$; $z = -2.758$. This is outside -2.054 to 2.054, so accept H_1, the mean has changed.

4 $H_0 : \mu = 160$, $H_1 : \mu > 160$; $z = 2.546 > 2.326$, so accept H_1, that the mean is greater than 160.

5 $H_0 : \mu = 276.4$, $H_1 : \mu > 276.4$; $z = 1.328 < 1.645$, so accept H_0, the campaign was not successful. This assumes that the sample can be treated as random; normal distribution of daily sales; the standard deviation remains unchanged.

6 $H_0 : \mu = 4.3$; $H_1 : \mu < 4.3$; $z = -1.581 < -1.282$, so accept H_1 that the mean waiting time has decreased.

7 $H_0 : \mu = 42.3$, $H_1 : \mu > 42.3$; $z = 2.594 > 2.326$, so accept H_1, the results are unusually good.

Exercise 5D (page 117)

1 $H_0 : \mu = 23$, $H_1 : \mu \neq 23$; $z = -2.359$. This is outside the acceptance region -2.326 to 2.326, so reject H_0 and accept $H_1 : \mu \neq 23$.

2 $H_0 : \mu = 11.90$, $H_1 : \mu > 11.90$; $z = 2.5 > 2.326$, so reject H_0 and accept that the mean diameter is greater than 11.90 cm.

3 $H_0 : \mu = 5\frac{1}{4}$, $H_1 : \mu \neq 5\frac{1}{4}$; $s = 1.582$, $z = 0.554$. This lies between -1.645 and 1.645, so accept H_0, the results were not unusual that April.

4 $H_0 : \mu = 375$, $H_1 : \mu < 375$;
$\bar{x} = 373.85$, $s = 3.800$, $z = -1.914 < -1.645$,
so reject H_0 and accept that the mean is less
than 375 g.

5 $H_0 : \mu = 0.584$, $H_1 : \mu > 0.584$;
$\bar{x} = 0.6052$, $s = 0.1452$, $z = 1.264 < 1.282$, so
accept H_0, melons grown organically are not
heavier on average.

6 $\bar{x} = 6.815$, $s = 0.06058$; $z = 1.918$;
$H_0 : \mu = 6.8$

(a) $H_1 : \mu \neq 6.8$, z lies between -2.24 and
2.24, so accept that $\mu = 6.8$.

(b) $H_1 : \mu > 6.8$, $z < 1.96$, so accept
$H_0 : \mu = 6.8$.

(c) $H_1 : \mu < 6.8$, $z > -1.96$, so accept
$H_0 : \mu = 6.8$

Note that in part (c) where the alternative
hypothesis suggests that the population mean
is less than 6.8 but the sample mean is greater
than 6.8, there is no need to calculate the
value of Z. In this situation H_1 cannot be
accepted at any significance level.

Exercise 5E (page 120)

1 (a) 0.076

(b) (i) no   (ii) yes

2 $\bar{x} = 8.768$, $s = 2.075$;
$H_0 : \mu = 8.54$, $H_1 : \mu \neq 8.54$;
$z = 0.777$, $P(\bar{X} > 8.768) = 0.2185 = 21.85\% >$
$2\frac{1}{2}\%$. Mean not different from £8.54.

3 $H_0 : \mu = 8.42$, $H_1 : \mu > 8.42$;
$z = 1.703$, $P(\bar{X} > 8.63) = 0.044 = 4.4\%$.
(a) Mean greater than 8.42,
(b) mean not greater than 8.42.

4 $s = 0.3084$; $H_0 : \mu = 7$, $H_1 : \mu < 7$;
$z = -1.421$, $P(\bar{X} < 6.92) = 0.078 = 7.8\%$
$< 10\%$. Accept that mean is less than 7 hours.

5 $H_0 : \mu = 31$, $H_1 : \mu > 31$; $z = 2.085$,
$P(\bar{X} > 31.18) = 0.019 = 1.9\% < 5\%$. Accept
that the mean is greater than 31%.

6 $z = 2.856$; approximately 0.44%.

Miscellaneous exercise 5 (page 121)

1 (a) $H_0 : \mu = 2.855$, $H_1 : \mu \neq 2.855$;
$Z \leq -1.96$, $Z \geq 1.96$.

(b) $z = -1.540$, so accept $H_0 : \mu = 2.855$, the
batch is from the specified population.

2 (a) $\mu < 25$ (b) $z = -2.326$, 1%
(c) $z < -2.326$, significance level $< 1\%$

3 (a) $\mu_0 = 210$ (b) 3.9%

4 (a) $z = 2.630 > 1.96$, so accept $\mu > 6.0$, Sarah's
average blood glucose level is higher than
6.0.

(b) $\mu_0 < 6.420$

(c) (i) Valid; sample size large enough for
central limit theorem and to replace σ
by a value estimated from the sample.

(ii) Readings at weekend may be biased
by different life style, so results not
valid.

5 $\hat{\mu} = 4.741$, $\hat{\sigma}^2 = 2.820$. $z = -1.236 > -1.282$,
so accept H_0, the mean crop weight per plant
is 5 kg. Smallest significance level is 10.8%.

6 $\bar{x} = 98$, $H_0 : \mu = 100$, $H_1 : \mu < 100$;
$z = -2.108 < -1.645$, so accept $\mu < 100$,
athlete's performance has improved. The total
maximum time is 964.4 s.

7 (a) (i) 10.46   (ii) 15.64
Expected (average) value of estimates of
the parameter is equal to the parameter.

(b) (i) 1.0 approximately

(ii) Since $10.46 < 10.65$, H_0 is accepted:
the mean distance of the houses from
the station is not more than 10 miles.

(c) Part (a) answers only require randomness
of sample, so they are still valid. Part (b)
has a large enough sample for the central
limit theorem to hold, so the results are
valid.

6 Hypothesis testing: discrete variables

Exercise 6A (page 126)

1 $P(X \leq 1) = 0.0017 < 0.10$, so accept
$H_1 : p < 0.6$.

2 $P(Y \geq 15) = 1 - P(Y \leq 14) = 0.0207 < 0.025$, so
accept $H_1 : p \neq 0.5$.

3 $H_0 : p = \frac{1}{2}$, $H_1 : p \neq \frac{1}{2}$, p is proportion of boys;
$X \sim B(18, \frac{1}{2})$; $P(X \geq 12) = 0.1189 > 0.05$, so
accept H_0, the numbers of boys and girls are
equal.

4 $H_0 : p = 0.95$, $H_1 : p < 0.95$; $X \sim B(25, 0.95)$;
$P(X \leq 22) = 0.1271 > 0.05$, so accept H_0, there
are at least 95% satisfied customers.

5 $H_0 : p = \frac{1}{2}$, $H_1 : p > \frac{1}{2}$ (or $\mu = 2.5$ and $\mu > 2.5$); p is the proportion of nails with length greater than 2.5 cm; $X \sim B(16, \frac{1}{2})$; $P(X \geq 13) = 0.0106 < 0.025$, so accept H_1, $p > \frac{1}{2}$ and $\mu > 2.5$.
The symmetry of the normal distribution about its mean is used in the statement $H_0 : p = \frac{1}{2}$.

6 (a) $H_0 : p = \frac{1}{4}$, $H_1 : p > \frac{1}{4}$; $X \sim B(20, \frac{1}{4})$; $P(X \geq 8) = 0.1018 > 0.05$, so accept H_0, the results are no better than those obtained by chance.
(b) 11

7 $H_0 : p = \frac{1}{6}$, $H_1 : p > \frac{1}{6}$; $X \sim B(30, \frac{1}{6})$; $P(X \geq 10) = 0.0197 < 0.05$, so the suspicion that the dice is loaded is confirmed.

8 (a) $H_0 : p = 0.8$, $H_1 : p \neq 0.8$; $X \sim B(12, 0.8)$; $P(X \leq 6) = 0.0194 < 0.05$, so reject H_0 and accept that the true figure is not 80%.
(b) Lisa's friends do not comprise a random sample, so test is unreliable.

Exercise 6B (page 129)

1 $H_0 : p = 0.3$, $H_1 : p \neq 0.3$; $X \sim B(80, 0.3) \approx N(24, 16.8)$; $P(X \leq 19) = \Phi(-1.098)$, since $-1.098 > -1.645$ (or since $0.136 > 0.05$), accept H_0, 30% of the beads are red.

2 $H_0 : p = 0.75$, $H_1 : p > 0.75$; $X \sim B(150, 0.75) \approx N(112.5, 28.125)$; $P(X \geq 124) = 1 - \Phi(2.074)$, since $2.074 > 1.96$ (or since $0.0194 < 0.025$), reject H_0 and accept that more than 75% get relief.

3 $H_0 : p = 0.4$, $H_1 : p > 0.4$; $X \sim B(50, 0.4) \approx N(20, 12)$; $P(X \geq 29) = 1 - \Phi(2.454)$; since $2.454 > 2.326$ (or since $0.0074 < 0.01$), reject H_0, the company should adopt the price.

4 $H_0 : p = 0.8$, $H_1 : p < 0.8$; $X \sim B(200, 0.8) \approx N(160, 32)$; $P(X \leq 152) = \Phi(-1.326)$; since $-1.326 > -1.645$ (or since $0.0924 > 0.05$), accept H_0, the deliveries are as stated.

5 $H_0 : p = 0.08$, $H_1 : p \neq 0.08$; $X \sim B(500, 0.08) \approx N(40, 36.8)$; $P(X \geq 53) = 1 - \Phi(2.061) = 0.0197 = 1.97\%$.
(a) Reject H_0.
(b) Accept H_0.

6 $H_0 : p = 0.132$, $H_1 : p > 0.132$; $X \sim B(95, 0.132) \approx N(12.54, 10.884\,72)$;

$P(X \geq 20) = 1 - \Phi(2.110)$; since $2.110 > 2.054$ (or since $0.0174 < 0.02$), reject H_0 and accept that the drop-out rate is greater for science students.

Exercise 6C (page 132)

1 $P(Y \leq 3) = 0.1512 > 0.10$, so accept $H_0 : \lambda = 6$.

2 $X \sim Po(3.40)$; $P(X \geq 8) = 0.0231 < 0.05$, so accept H_1 that $\lambda > 3.4$.

3 $H_0 : \mu = 4$, $H_1 : \mu < 4$, where μ is mean number of accidents per week. $X \sim Po(8)$; $P(X \leq 3) = 0.0424 < 0.05$, so accept that the mean has reduced. $X \sim Po(12)$ including third week, $P(X \leq 7) = 0.0895 > 0.05$, so the conclusion changes.

4 (a) $n = 60 > 50$ and $np = 4.2 < 5$, so Poisson approximation to binomial distribution applies.
(b) $H_0 : \mu = 4.2$ or $p = 0.07$, $H_1 : \mu \neq 4.2$ or $P \neq 0.07$; $X \sim Po(4.2)$; $P(X \geq 9) = 0.0279 > 0.025$, so accept H_0, the proportion is 7%.

5 $H_0 : \mu = 1.4$, $H_1 : \mu \neq 1.4$; $X \sim Po(1.4)$; $P(X \geq 4) = 0.0537 > 0.05$, so accept H_0, secretary is probably responsible.

6 $H_0 : \mu = 6$, $H_1 : \mu < 6$; $X \sim Po(18)$; $P(X \leq 9) = 0.0154 < 0.05$, so accept that the mean is lower.

Miscellaneous exercise 6 (page 132)

1 (a) $H_0 : p = \frac{2}{3}$, $H_1 : p > \frac{2}{3}$; $X \sim B(20, \frac{2}{3})$; $P(X \geq 17) = 0.0604 < 0.1$, so reject H_0 and accept that the proportion is greater than $\frac{2}{3}$.
(b) Statistical tests are not proofs: they indicate the likelihood of a hypothesis being correct.

2 (a) $X \sim B(25, 0.4)$; $P(X \leq 5) = 0.0294 > 0.025$, so accept that $p = 0.4$.
(b) Greater than about 0.5.

3 $H_0 : p = \frac{1}{3}$, $H_1 : p \neq \frac{1}{3}$; $X \sim B(174, \frac{1}{3}) \approx N(58, 38.67)$; $P(X \leq 51) = \Phi(-1.045)$; since $-1.96 < -1.045 < 1.96$ (or since $0.148 > 0.025$), accept H_0, the proportion of left-handed mathematicians is $\frac{1}{3}$.

4 (a) $H_0 : p = \frac{1}{2}$, $H_1 : p > \frac{1}{2}$ (p is proportion preferring Doggo); $X \sim B(40, \frac{1}{2}) \approx N(20, 10)$; $n = 26$.
(b) 4.1%

5 $H_0 : p = 0.07$, $H_1 : p > 0.07$;
$X \sim B(125, 0.07) \approx N(8.75, 8.1375)$;
$P(X \geqslant 14) = 1 - \Phi(1.665)$; since
$1.665 < 1.881$ (or since $0.048 > 0.03$), accept
H_0 and retain the batch.

6 (a) Computers must be lost randomly
throughout the period at a uniform rate.
(b) $H_0 : \mu = 17$, $H_1 : \mu < 17$; 8

7 (a) Flaws must occur randomly at a uniform
rate per metre length.
(b) $H_0 : \mu = 1.8$, $H_1 : \mu < 1.8$; $X \sim Po(5.4)$;
$P(X \leqslant 2) = 0.0948 > 0.05$, so accept H_0,
the rate has not decreased.
(c) $X \sim Po(7.2)$; $P(X \leqslant 2)$ between 0.0203 and
0.0296, so accept H_1, the conclusion
changes.

8 (a) $X \sim Po(1.9)$
(b) $H_0 : \mu = 1.9$, $H_1 : \mu \neq 1.9$;
$P(X = 0) = 0.1496 > 0.05$, so accept H_0,
there is no decrease.
(c) $H_0 : p = 0.1496$, $H_1 : p > 0.1496$;
$X \sim B(50, 0.1496) \approx N(7.48, 6.361)$;
$P(X \geqslant 13) = 1 - \Phi(1.990)$; since
$1.990 > 1.645$, reject H_0 and accept that
the numbers have decreased.

9 $z = -2.069$; either $-2.069 < -2.054$ or
$0.0193 < 0.02$, so reject H_0 and accept that
$\mu < 5.00$.

10 $H_0 : p = 0.036$, $H_1 : p > 0.036$;
$X \sim B(500, 0.036) \approx N(18, 17.352)$;
$P(X \geqslant 28) = 1 - \Phi(2.281)$; since $2.281 >$
1.645 (or since $0.0113 < 0.05$), accept that
0.036 is an underestimate.

11 $H_0 : \mu = 2.04$, $H_1 : \mu > 2.04$; since
$z = 2.361 > 1.881$ (or since $0.0088 < 0.03$),
accept $\mu > 2.04$.
Replace the last 8 words of the sentence by
' ... states that the sample mean is
approximately normally distributed for large
samples even when the population is not
normal.'

12 $H_0 : p = 0.2$, $H_1 : p < 0.2$. Since
$P(X \leqslant 2) = 0.098 < 0.1$ accept that the
percentage of defective vases has been
reduced.

13 (a) 28.9, 83.41
(b) $z = -1.319 > -1645$, so accept H_0.
(c) $106\ 610.5$

14 (a) $H_0 : p = 0.8$, $H_1 : p > 0.8$; $X \sim B(20, 0.8)$;
$P(X \geqslant 19) = 0.0692 > 0.05$, so accept
$H_0 : p = 0.8$.
(b) 6.92%
(c) Less than 0.75 from the table; a more
accurate value is 0.7860.

15 (a) $z = 0.9474$; the rejection region is in the
negative tail and z is positive.
(b) 0.172; accept $H_0 : \mu = 15\frac{1}{2}$.

16 (a) $Po(5)$; calls occur randomly, at a uniform
rate over 2 days.
(b) $H_0 : \mu = 5$, $H_1 : \mu > 5$, where μ is the
mean number of calls per 2-day interval.
$P(X \geqslant 9) = 0.0681 > 0.05$ so accept H_0,
the daily average has not increased.

17 $H_0 : \mu = 0.5$; $H_1 : \mu > 0.5$; $X \sim Po(0.5)$;
$P(X \geqslant 3) = 0.0144$; any level ≥ 0.0144.

18 $H_0 : p = 0.25$, $H_1 : p < 0.25$; $X \sim B(12, 0.25)$;
$P(X \leqslant 2) = 0.3907 > 0.10$, so accept H_0, the
student did no worse than by guessing.
However, the result is less than expected by
guesswork.

19 $n > 50$ and $np = 3 < 5$, so the Poisson
approximation to binomial distribution is
applicable. $X \sim Po(3)$;
$P(X = 0) = 0.0498 \approx 0.05$.
$H_0 : p = 0.05$, $H_1 : p > 0.05$; $X \sim B(10, 0.05)$;
$P(X \geqslant 2) = 0.0861 < 0.10$, so reject H_0 and
accept that $p > 0.05$.

20 $H_0 : \mu = 1.005$, $H_1 : \mu > 1.005$;
$z = 0.977 < 1.645$, so accept $H_0 : \mu = 1.005$.
$H_0 : p = 0.65$, $H_1 : p < 0.65$;
$X \sim B(100, 0.65) \approx N(65, 22.75)$;
$P(X \leqslant 53) = \Phi(-2.411)$; since $0.0080 < 0.05$,
reject H_0 and accept that $p < 0.65$.

21 (a) $n > 50$ and $np = 2.4 < 5$, so the Poisson
approximation to binomial distribution is
applicable.
(b) $H_0 : \mu = 2.4$, $H_1 : \mu > 2.4$; $X \sim Po(2.4)$;
$P(X \geqslant 6) = 0.0357 < 0.05$, reject H_0 and
accept that mean has increased.

22 $H_0 : \mu = 3000$, $H_1 : \mu > 3000$; $z = 2.036$;
since $2.036 > 1.96$ (or since $0.0209 < 0.025$),
reject H_0 and accept that the mean is greater
than 3000. $H_0 : p = 0.4$, $H_1 : p \neq 0.4$;
$X \sim B(150, 0.4) \approx N(60, 36)$;
$P(X \leqslant 51) = \Phi(-1.417)$; since $-1.417 < -1.96$
(or since $0.0783 > 0.025$), accept H_0, the
proportion agreeing with the manufacturer is
40%.

7 Errors in hypothesis testing

Exercise 7A (page 143)

1 (a) $\overline{X} \geqslant 6.316$ (b) 0.1963

2 (a) $\overline{X} \leqslant 9.7419$ (b) Type I error
  (c) 0.1404

3 (a) 9.78   (b) 0.2039
  (c) It will be smaller.

4 (a) $H_0 : \mu = 1.94$, $H_1 : \mu < 1.94$; rejection
     region: $\overline{X} \leqslant 1.883$; $\overline{x} = 1.7$, reject H_0 and
     accept that new system had the desired
     effect.
  (b) 0.0087
  (c) Accepting that the mean absence rate is
     1.94 when it is actually less than 1.94.

5 (a) $\overline{T} \leqslant 3.3065$ (b) 0.0877
  (c) 0.0647, which is less than 0.0877

6 (a) $H_0 : \mu = 30$, $H_1 : \mu < 30$; $\overline{X} > 29.7782$
  (b) $0 < \mu < 29.530$

Exercise 7B (page 149)

1 (a) $N \leqslant 10$, $N \geqslant 23$ (b) 0.0259
  (c) Accept H_0: $p = 0.55$ (d) 0.9536

2 (a) $R \geqslant 18$, Mrs Robinson should be elected.
  (b) 2.16%   (c) 0.6939

3 (a) 0.0635   (b) 0.8593
  α is bigger and β is smaller.

4 (a) $H_0 : p = 0.1$, $H_1 : p < 0.1$
  (b) $P(X = 0) = 0.0798 < 0.10$, so reject H_0 and
     accept that the modified toaster is more
     reliable.
  (c) 0.0798   (d) $p < 0.0119$

5 (a) $S \geqslant 95$ (b) 0.018   (c) $p_0 = 0.79$

6 (a) $X \leqslant 51$, $X \geqslant 69$ (b) 0.083
  (c) Accept that 60% is correct.   (d) 0.0094

7 (a) 0.0066   (b) 0.2121   (c) 0.0024
  The probability of a Type II error is decreased
  by increasing the sample size.

Exercise 7C (page 153)

1 (a) $X \leqslant 2$ (b) 0.0430
  (c) 0.9116; accept that the mean is 6.5; Type II
     error if the mean is actually 5.5.

2 $X \sim Po(12)$, $P(X \leqslant 6) = 0.0458 < 0.05$ and
  accept that mean has reduced; Type I error.

3 (a) $X \leqslant 5$, $X \geqslant 20$ (b) 4.16%
  (c) The mean has not changed.   (d) 0.5543

4 Sales must occur randomly over time and at a
  uniform rate.
  (a) $T \sim Po(16)$, $T \geqslant 23$ (b) 5.82%
  (c) 0.8551, a large value

5 (a) Sample size n is greater than 50 and
     $np = 4.5 < 5$.
  (b) One-tail since it would not be concerned if
     the rate were smaller than 5%.
  (c) Using $Po(4.5)$, one-tail test, $N \geqslant 8$
  (d) (i) Type II   (ii) Type I   (e) 0.324

6 (a) $R \leqslant 18$ (b) 0.0374   (c) 0.4695

Miscellaneous exercise 7 (page 155)

1 (a) 0.1
  (b) Not possible since Type I error made when
     H_0 is rejected and Type II when H_0 is
     accepted.
  (c) Type I

2 (a) The number of misprints $X \leqslant 1$.
  (b) Accept that mean has reduced.
  (c) 0.0902

3 (a) $B(200, 0.9) \approx N(180, 18)$ since
     $np = 180 > 5$ and $nq = 20 > 5$; $k \leqslant 171$
  (b) The variable is discrete and only
     approximated by a normal distribution.
     2.3%
  (c) Type II, 0.383

4 (a) $H_0 : p = 0.1$, $H_1 : p > 0.1$
  (b) $r > 4$, do not reject H_0 (c) 0.4207

5 (a) 2%
  (b) Geometric distribution with $p = 0.02$.
     Expectation = 50.
  (c) Reject H_0 ($\mu = 100$) when $\mu = 101$.
     $P(X > 98.9) + P(X \geqslant 101.1) = 0.4164$.
     This is $1 - P(\text{Type II error})$.

6 (a) $200 > 50$ and $np = 4 < 5$, parameter 4.
  (b) $H_0 : p = 0.02$, $H_1 : p > 0.02$, where p is the
     proportion of all cups that are defective.
     Using $X \sim Po(4)$, $P(X \geqslant 8) = 0.0511 > 0.05$
     and accept that $p = 0.02$.
  (c) 2.14%
  (d) Acceptance region $X \leqslant 8$, $X \sim N(6, 5.82)$,
     0.8499

7 (a) 0.4218 mm^2
  (b) Expectation of the estimate of the
     parameter is equal to the parameter.
  (c) $\overline{X} \geqslant 7.4755$ (d) 0.297
  (e) The variance is an estimate.

8 (a) $H_0 : p = 0.2$, $H_1 : p > 0.2$, where p is the probability of Emma choosing the correct colour.

(b) $X \sim B(20, 0.2)$, $P(X \geqslant 7) = 0.0867 > 0.05$, so accept that Emma is not telepathic.

(c) Type II, when the null hypothesis was true.

9 (a) $H_0 : \mu = 75$, $H_1 : \mu > 75$

(b) Type I, accept that the regulations are not met when they are; Type II, accept that the regulations are met when they are not.

(c) Type I since ecosystem not affected.

(d) $Z \leqslant 2.425 > 1.282$, so accept H_1, regulations are not met.

10 (a) $H_0 : \mu = 12.4$, $H_1 : \mu < 12.4$; 0.58%

(b) Approximately 0   (c) $n = 7$, 0.0931

11 (a) $X \leqslant 20 - \dfrac{6.41}{\sqrt{n}}$ (c) 0.0429

(d) Decreases   (e) 325

Revision exercise (page 159)

1 0.0161

2 The Poisson distribution is appropriate when counting the number of occurrences in a fixed interval of independent, random events occurring at a constant rate. 0.0181; one-tail test, $H_0 : \mu = 5$, $H_1 : \mu > 5$; $P(X \geqslant 10) = 0.0318 > 0.02$, so accept H_0, there is no evidence of increase. $P(X \geqslant 10) < 0.05$, so H_1 would have been accepted in this case. The larger significance level gives a greater chance of rejecting H_0 when it is true.

3 The binomial distribution is appropriate when counting the number of successes in a fixed number of trials which are independent of one another and have a constant probability of success.

(a) $H_0 : p = \frac{1}{2}$, $H_1 : p > \frac{1}{2}$; $P(X \geqslant 6) = 0.145 > 0.05$, so accept H_0, there is no favoured colour.

(b) Test statistic, $z = 3.019 > 1.645$, so there is significant evidence that blue is not the people's favourite.

(c) There is a 5% chance of wrongly rejecting H_0.

4 (a) 8.01, 0.000 175

(b) Test statistic, $z = 2 > 1.96$, so there is significant evidence, just, at the 5% level to accept H_1 that $\mu \neq 8.00$.

5 A measure obtained from the sample where the expected value is equal to the population variance.

(a) $\mu = 2$, $\sigma^2 = \frac{2}{3}$

(b) Possible samples

(1,1), (1,2), (1,3), (2,2), (2,3), (3,3);
Mean   1,   1.5,   2,   2,   2.5,   3

Distribution of sample mean

Value	1	1.5	2	2.5	3
Probability	$\frac{1}{9}$	$\frac{2}{9}$	$\frac{3}{9}$	$\frac{2}{9}$	$\frac{1}{9}$

E(sample mean) = 2; hence sample mean is an unbiased estimator of population mean in this case.

(c) Distribution of sample variance

Value	0	$\frac{1}{4}$	1
Probability	$\frac{3}{9}$	$\frac{4}{9}$	$\frac{2}{9}$

E(sample variance) = $\frac{1}{3} \neq \sigma^2$.
$E\left(\dfrac{n}{n-1}(\text{sample variance})\right) = \frac{2}{1} \times \frac{1}{3} = \frac{2}{3} = \sigma^2$ so $\dfrac{n}{n-1}(\text{sample variance})$ is an unbiased estimator of σ^2.

6 The binomial distribution is appropriate when counting the number of successes in a fixed number of trials which are independent of one another, and have a constant probability of success.
Either n large and p close to 0.5 or $np > 5$, $nq > 5$.

(a) (i) 0.196   (ii) 0.598

(b) 0.933; N(250, 125) is the approximation.

7 (a) 0.0618   (b) 0.9069   (c) 0.0079

(d) 0.195

8 (a) 0.0765   (b) 9.12   (c) 0.000 161

9 (a) $a = \frac{2}{3}$ (b) E(X) = 1   (c) Var(X) = $\frac{11}{45}$

10 Po(4n), this can be approximated by N(4n, 4n) when n is large; $n = 30$.

11 (a) Test statistic, $z = -1.66 < -1.645$, so there is significant evidence, just, at the 5% level that there has been a reduction in service time.

(b) P(Type II error) = 0.786

12 (a) N$\left(15, \frac{9}{5}\right)$ (b) 0.932   (c) 7, $\frac{1}{5}$

(d) N$\left(7, \frac{1}{5}\right)$; central limit theorem

(e) 0.178

Practice examinations

Practice examination 1 (page 163)

1 0.897

2 (i) In a random sample of size n, every possible set of n items from the population has an equal chance of being chosen. Random samples are used to avoid bias, so that inferences about the population from which they are drawn may be made.

   (ii) Number the students from 001 to 763, and use 3-digit random numbers (ignoring any repetitions and any numbers from 764 to 999) to make the selection. The students chosen will be numbers 220, 058, 173, 381 and 003.

3 (ii) $\frac{8}{27}$

   (iii) Median is less than 1, since probability in part (ii) is less than $\frac{1}{2}$.

   (iv) $\frac{3}{4}$

4 (i) 0.660   (ii) $\mu = 16.1$, $\sigma = 1.66$

5 (i) 3.045, 3.439

   (ii) $H_0 : \mu = 2.82$, $H_1 : \mu \neq 2.82$; $z = 1.750 < 2.576$ so conclude that there is no difference in the means for shells from exposed and sheltered shores.

6 (i) $H_0 : p = \frac{1}{2}$, $H_1 : p > \frac{1}{2}$, where p is the probability of a baby being a boy.

   (ii) $X \geqslant 18$

   (iii) Accepting that more boys are born when in fact numbers of boys and girls are equal; 0.0216.

   (iv) 0.936

7 (i) Defects occur independently and at random, at a constant average rate.

   (ii) 0.740   (iii) 0.915   (iv) 2.77

8 (i) $B\left(600, \frac{1}{6}\right)$, $N\left(100, 83\frac{1}{3}\right)$

   (ii) 0.0163

   (iii) $n - 5.201\sqrt{n} - 297 > 0$, 402

Practice examination 2 (page 166)

1 $H_0 : p = \frac{1}{3}$, $H_1 : p < \frac{1}{3}$, where p is the proportion of viewers watching the match; $X \sim B(200, \frac{1}{3}) \approx N\left(\frac{200}{3}, \frac{400}{9}\right)$; $P(X \leqslant 56) = \Phi(-1.525)$; since $-1.525 > -1.645$ (or since $0.0637 > 0.5$) there is insufficient evidence to reject H_0, so accept the claim that the proportion watching is one third.

2 $25 < n < 48$

3 (i) A *population* is a complete set of items sharing some property or being investigated; a *sample* is a subset of a population.

   (ii) For reasons of cost, convenience or practicability, e.g. when a testing process might result in items being destroyed; samples that are *random* are not biased and allow inferences about the population to be made.

   (iii) Number everyone on an appropriate electoral roll, from 1 to N, and then use random integers in the range 1 to N (ignoring repetitions) to identify individuals until the required size of sample has been selected.

   (iv) Many adults will not be buyers of baby foods so the sampling method is inefficient, with many of the sample not likely to contribute anything to the investigation.

4 (i) 0.876   (ii) 34.7

5 (i) 0.933   (ii) 0.986

6 (i) Po(3)   (ii) 0.101
   (iii) 0.765   (iv) 25

7 (i) $H_0 : \mu = 2$, $H_1 : \mu \neq 2$; $z = 1.878 < 1.96$, insufficient evidence to reject H_0, so accept that the setting is accurate.

   (ii) 0.391

8 (i) $\frac{1}{4}$ (ii) 0.2601
   (iii) 10 700 litres, 4420 litres
   (iv) 10 800 litres

Index

The page numbers refer to the first mention of each term, or the shaded box if there is one.